Chronicles of Matthew Paris

*Monastic Life
in the Thirteenth Century*

Chronicles of Matthew Paris

*Monastic Life
in the Thirteenth Century*

Edited, translated and with an
introduction by Richard Vaughan

ALAN SUTTON · Gloucester
ST. MARTIN'S PRESS · New York
1984

First published in Great Britain in 1984
Alan Sutton Publishing Limited
17a Brunswick Road
Gloucester GL1 1HG

British Library Cataloguing in Publication Data

Paris, Matthew
　　[Chronica majora. *English. Selections*]
　　Monastic life in the thirteenth century.
　　1. Monastic and religious life—History—Middle Ages, 600–1500
　　I. Title　　II. Vaughan, Richard, *1927–*
　　III. Monastic life in the thirteenth century　　271'.0094　　　BX2590

　　ISBN 0-904387-98-4

First published in the United States of America in 1984
St. Martin's Press, Inc.
175 Fifth Avenue
New York, NY 10010

Library of Congress Cataloging in Publication Data

Paris, Matthew, 1200–1259
　　The chronicles of Matthew Paris.

　　Translated from Latin.
　　Includes index.
　　Contents: The deeds of the abbots of St. Albans, 1195–1255 – The Chronica majora, 1247–1250.
　　1. Monastic and religious life – Addresses, essays, lectures.　I. Vaughan, Richard, 1927–　.　II. Title.　BX2435.P2542 1984　　　940.1'84　　　83–40602
　　ISBN 0-312-13452-5

Typesetting and origination by
Alan Sutton Publishing Limited.
Printed in Great Britain.

Contents

Introduction

You have to be something more than an ordinary tourist to penetrate into the library of Corpus Christi College, Cambridge. It is open only for a few hours a week at different times on different days. But a glimpse of its treasures, in priceless medieval manuscripts and early printed books, is an unforgettable experience. Among the parchment volumes displayed in the showcases, taking its place beside the sixty-century Gospels of St. Augustine and the earliest surviving version of the Anglo-Saxon chronicle, is the autograph manuscript of the chronicle of the medieval English monk Matthew Paris.

There are actually two autograph volumes of Matthew Paris's chronicle, or *Chronica majora* as he called it, in the library at Corpus; a third, continuing the chronicle up to the point when the author's death cut short his work in 1259, is in the British Library in London. Curiously, Manuscript No. 26 in Corpus library is Matthew Paris's first volume, covering all history from the Creation to 1188, and MS. 16 is the second, containing Matthew's chronicle from 1189 to 1253. The explanation of this separation and apparent inversion of the two volumes is simple. The thousand-odd medieval manuscripts in the college library were not at all numbered in terms of their subject matter, but strictly in terms of size, beginning with the largest, which is thus MS. No. 1.

The autograph chronicles of Matthew Paris, one or other volume of which is always on show in Corpus library, are thick folio-sized books. The text, written with a goose quill on parchment, is in somewhat crabbed, angular, gothic letters more or less typical of the thirteenth century. There are two closely written columns of text on each page, and the uniformity of the dark brown or black ink of this text is relieved by chapter headings in bright red – rubrics. Furthermore, here and there are decorated capital letters in blue and red, more or less elaborate drawings in the margin, and many marginal corrections and additions. These last are often surrounded by a red line, and the place where they belong in the text is pointed out. Across the top of each page up to the end of the annal, or year entry, for 1250, where Matthew Paris at first intended to draw his work to a close (see pp. 277–8 below), are head-lines with bright blue coil and line ornamentation. After the 1250 annal these page headings or running titles continue without the blue decoration and arranged in a different manner. They simply tell the reader which king's reign is being described on that page.

If the visitor to Corpus library were to make an appointment with the librarian so that he could look through the whole of MS. 16, he would find a Latin inscription in Matthew Paris's handwriting on the first page in which he presents the book to the monastery of St. Albans, namely to his own abbey where he had been a monk since his youth. Here it must have remained until the dissolution of the monasteries by King Henry VIII in 1539. Thereafter for a time the history of these two Matthew Paris autograph manuscripts is obscure. The incalculable riches of the English monasteries, above all in land, building stones, and manuscript books, were looted on a large scale by the English aristocracy. Among those to profit from this situation was the scholar, book collector and Protestant churchman Matthew Parker, who became Master of Corpus Christi College and, in 1559, archbishop of Canterbury. Armed with an order of the Privy Council commanding people to help him, he borrowed, purchased or purloined the priceless books which had been transferred by fair means or foul from the monastic libraries to private individuals. He thus put together a splendid library which he later bequeathed to his college. Among these books were the two Matthew Paris volumes: MS. 26 belonged to an Edward Aglionby of Balsall Temple, who was foolish enough to lend it to Matthew Parker; MS. 16 was in the possession of a Norwich ecclesiastic, Robert Talbot, when Parker laid his hands on it (see James 1912:50-8).

Matthew Paris was probably born about 1200. He became a monk in the Benedictine monastery of St. Albans on 21 January 1217 and died there in June 1259. His name probably has nothing to do with Paris and, though he wrote in Latin and at times also in French, English seems to have been his native language. No evidence whatever of the events of Matthew Paris's life has survived outside his own mention of himself in his own writings. Fortunately he was by no means reticent, and so we know that he was at the royal court at Westminster in 1247, and with the king at Winchester in July 1251, and that he probably made other similar visits. We also know from his own account of the affair (below pp. 158–61) that in the summer of 1248 he travelled as far as Bergen in Norway, and that he had been sent to that country by the pope to advise and reform the monks of a Norwegian Benedictine monastery. Two contemporary fellow monks of his at St. Albans mention Matthew Paris. The infirmarer, John of Wallingford, who wrote a short chronicle of his own based on Matthew's materials, refers the reader at one point to "the chronicle of Matthew Paris of St. Albans" (Vaughan 1958a: 68), and elsewhere he mentions the "*Book of additamenta* of St. Albans" (Ellis 1859: 197/217), a book which we know was written by Matthew Paris. The monk who took up the pen to write Matthew's chronicle for him at the end of his life, and who continued it after his death, has this to say about him: "Thus far wrote the venerable man, Brother Matthew Paris. . . . What has been added and continued from this point onwards may be ascribed to another brother, who, presuming to approach the works of so great a predecessor, and unworthy to continue them, as he is unworthy to undo the latchet of his shoe, has not deserved to have even his name mentioned on the page" (Vaughan 1958b: 7). One other early mention shows that Matthew Paris's fame quickly extended beyond St. Albans: an anonymous monk of Ramsey Abbey, writing before 1267, advises the reader to consult, for Henry III's reign, "the chronicle of Master Matthew, a monk of St. Albans" (Vaughan 1958b: 20).

What was Europe like in the first half of the thirteenth century, seven hundred and fifty years ago? The student wishing to gain a first hand impression could hardly do better than read Matthew Paris. It was of course not yet a Europe of states but already a Europe of recognisable peoples: the English, the French, the Germans. It was a Europe of kings, princes, dukes, earls and barons, of feudal lords and of villains, some of the better-off of whom were exchanging irksome labour services owed to the lord for money rents. The developing money economy was reflected in increasing trade and in a rapid growth of towns, some of which, by conquering the surrounding countryside, were on their way to becoming veritable city-states. All this is apparent in the pages of Matthew Paris but, as a monk, it is only natural that *his* Europe was in the first place an ecclesiastical Europe. A Europe which accepted the pope as spiritual and even sometimes temporal, overlord, though the pope's practical power and spiritual influence was perhaps already waning; at any rate in this respect Brother Matthew lived in a period of change. In his boyhood, the renowned Innocent III had been pope; through the greater part of Matthew's lifetime, the pope's pretensions to universal rule were being challenged by his traditional rival the Holy Roman Emperor, in the shape of that most famous and remarkable of all medieval rulers, Frederick II of Hohenstaufen.

In the world of monks and churchmen a vital and to Matthew Paris unwelcome change took place in his lifetime. His own Benedictine monks, following the rule of St. Benedict and for a long time the only significant order of monks, were being challenged by newcomers in the form of the friars — Franciscans, Grey Friars or Friars Minor, and Dominicans or Friars Preacher. These new-fangled religious orders seemed a threat to Matthew Paris and his Benedictines. Many of them were devoting themselves to the study of theology and indeed were busy creating scholastic philosophy, but these elevated intellectual endeavours passed our humble Benedictine monk by; he was more of the man in the street.

Europe in the thirteenth century was an expanding, outward-looking Europe, still living in the world of the crusades, and these naturally figure largely in the pages of the *Chronica majora*. The first and only successful crusade had ended with the Christians' triumphant entry into Jerusalem in July 1099. But the Latin kingdom of Jerusalem had been short lived; the city had been reconquered for Islam in 1187 just before Matthew's time. Still, right through the thirteenth century until 1291, the city of Acre remained in Christian hands. Matthew drew a plan of it on one of his maps of the Holy Land and he reports very fully on the crusading expeditions of his own lifetime. Eastwards in Asia the rise of Mongol (or Tartar, to use Matthew Paris's word) power in the early thirteenth century, which was accompanied by Mongol incursions into Christendom and soon followed by Europe's first contacts with eastern Asia and China, roused Matthew's interest. It was in the year after his death, namely 1260, that the two brothers Niccolo and Maffeo Polo made their remarkable journey to Peking.

As a Benedictine monk Matthew Paris lived in a monastery, an institution with which the average modern English-speaking person may not be very familiar. A medieval Benedictine abbey was by no means cut off from the world, but was at the very centre of everyday life. It was a hive of economic activity, being often the greatest single landowner in the district and a major employer of labour of every sort. It was of course a spiritual and religious centre, but it was also a cultural and often artistic and intellectual centre. It occupied the most complex and imposing range of stone buildings in the neighbourhood, comprising a large and fine abbey church, kitchens, refectory, dormitories, a cloister, an infirmary, abbot's lodgings, guest houses and so forth. It represented a considerable concentration of wealth and its occupants, numbering around anything from fifty to two hundred monks, not surprisingly came from the better-off element of society.

St. Albans was even more in the centre of affairs than most abbeys. It was one day's journey north of London – the first halting place on the Great North Road. The stabling facilities for guests could take care of 300 horses. In Matthew's own time, King Henry III visited the abbey at least nine times and he and other guests were an important source of information for the assiduous monk-chronicler. These guests included papal emissaries, bishops, counts and earls, priors and officials of other monasteries, royal officials and councillors, on one occasion a party of Armenians and on another a deputation of M.A.s of the University of Oxford.

In the middle ages there were no historians in the modern sense of the word. Nobody set out to study and describe some period or series of events in the past. In an earlier age, scholars like the Anglo-Saxon monk Bede had written a history of their own people, but the object was to elucidate the present rather than the past. By the thirteenth century most historians or chroniclers no longer limited themselves to a particular area, and almost all followed the convention of the day and began their histories at the beginning, namely the Creation. The past was seen as a linear projection of events, unfolding themselves through time and through a succession of ages from Creation at the start to the second coming of Christ, the final judgement, and the end of the world. Most medieval chroniclers seem to have thought that they were not far from that end. The medieval chronicler need have no special theme, no specific subject-matter, he could just describe what happened. Up to his own times, he merely copied out the histories of his predecessors, and the early part of most medieval chronicles is thus mainly derivative. What the medieval chronicler concentrated on was the describing of the events of his own lifetime; he was more of a reporter, a journalist, than a historian. Matthew Paris was no exception to this.

Extremely popular among medieval chroniclers, most of whom were in any case monks, were histories of individual monasteries. A famous and very readable example of this genre is Jocelin of Brakelond's chronicle of the monastery of Bury St. Edmunds, popularised by Thomas Carlyle in *Past and present*. Matthew Paris, in the history of his own monastery of St. Albans, does not lag behind Jocelin in interest or readability, though he lived a half-century later. His *Deeds of the abbots of St. Albans* follows tradition in the way it really only forms a continuation to an existing work. In this case two successive later monks continued the work of Matthew Paris and his anonymous predecessor, so that the history of St. Albans, like those of other monasteries and, for example, many towns, was kept up to date and continued century after century through the middle ages.

Matthew Paris is one of Europe's outstanding medieval chroniclers. As a mirror of his age, he is second to none. He excels alike in his colourful style, in the variety of his interests, in the warmth of his feelings and prejudices. He is unique in the sheer quantity and contemporaneity of his information; unique too in the amount of autograph material that has survived, some of it illustrated by himself. Unfortunately, Matthew Paris's artistic works, whether marginal illustrations in his chronicle or illustrations of saints' lives, are beyond the scope of this book. So too are his several hundred correctly drawn and coloured shields of arms, his remarkable maps of Britain, the Holy Land and the world, which are a landmark in the history of European cartography, and his contribution to hagiography in the shape of Latin lives of Stephen Langton and Edmund Rich and lives in French (Anglo-Norman) verse of SS. Alban (see now McCulloch 1981), Edward the Confessor, Thomas Becket and Edmund Rich. Also beyond the scope of the present work are Matthew Paris's minor historical works, all of which are dependent in some sense on his greater chronicle or *Chronica majora*. These are the *Historia Anglorum*, or *History of the English*, which is abridged from the larger work; the *Book of additamenta*, which is an appendix of documents to it, and two shorter works, the *Flores historiarum* and the *Abbreviatio chronicorum*. Lastly, we have had to omit here any excerpt from Matthew Paris's *Lives of the two Offas*, which is a contribution to the history of the foundation of his own monastery by King Offa of Mercia.

The aim of this book is to introduce this most colourful and informative of European medieval chroniclers to the interested student and general reader by means of an extended excerpt from each of his most important works, namely the *Chronica majora* or, literally, greater chronicle, and the *Gesta abbatum*, or deeds of the abbots of St. Albans. The reader will find here something like one-sixth of Matthew Paris's own part of the *Chronica majora*, which extends from 1236 to 1259, namely four complete annals out of twenty-three, and what probably amounts to nearly the whole of his own contribution to the *Gesta abbatum*. There is no intention here of providing a summary or replacement of my *Matthew Paris*, originally published in 1958, reissued in 1979, and currently in print; this book, rather, is designed as a companion volume to that work. Hopefully, it will provide the beginner with a meaningful introduction to the middle ages, and both him and the more knowledgeable reader with a first-hand acquaintance with Matthew Paris.

Owing to the fortunate survival of the autograph manuscripts we can gain important insights into Matthew Paris's working methods as a historian. Some knowledge of these is necessary for the understanding of the texts translated here. Not that the *Deeds of the abbots* presents many problems in this respect. We have omitted here the early part of the work, describing the doings of the Anglo-Saxon and immediately post-Conquest abbots, which Matthew probably took over from an earlier monk of St. Albans, Adam the Cellarer, who died in about 1170. We include his account of Abbot John de Cella, who died three years before Matthew took the habit at St. Albans, and the much fuller description of William of Trumpington's abbacy; thus, Matthew's history of his own abbey from 1195 to 1235. It seems likely that Matthew wrote this part of the *Deeds of the abbots* before, but probably not very long before, or in, 1250; while the account of the abbacy of Abbot John of Hertford, also included here, was apparently written in 1255.

Not only did Matthew Paris complete the *Deeds of the abbots* in the first place up to the year 1250, but, as we have already noticed, he at first proposed to finish off his *Chronica majora* at the same time. Internal evidence shows that in the 1240s Matthew was writing each annal or year entry in the *Chronica majora* not long, certainly not more than a year or two, after the events described occurred. Moreover, the insertion of the reports of Frederick II's death in December 1250 over an erasure in, or in the margin of, the 1250 annal, shows that that annal was completed by February 1251, when the news of the emperor Frederick's death reached him (below p. 272 and Vaughan 1958b: 60–1). In the years before 1250, Matthew's chronicle was becoming unmanageably long, and from 1247 onwards he began to omit some texts of documents, inserting them instead into his *Book of additamenta* and referring to them only in the main chronicle. He used a system of signs to facilitate reference between the two books. As soon as he had brought the chronicle up to date at the close of 1250, where he intended to stop, a scribe, probably another monk, made a fair copy of the whole chronicle from 1189 onwards up to that point, which is known as MS. C and is in fact British Library Cotton MS. Nero D v, Part II.

The reader will find frequent reference, in the four annals from the *Chronica majora* translated here, to this fair copy (C) of Matthew's autograph manuscript. The autograph itself, namely Corpus Christi College, Cambridge, MS. 16, from which C was copied, is known as B. Now it is a curious fact, frequently made apparent in what follows, that Matthew went through his autograph manuscript of the *Chronica majora* altering, erasing and rewriting, but this expurgation was not extended to the fair copy C. Because of this, we have been able to recover from the copy C what he originally wrote in his autograph manuscript B. This expurgation was apparently carried out right at the end of Matthew's life, in 1258-1259, and its purpose seems to have been to remove or tone down the more offensive passages, whether against the king, the pope or the archbishop. Perhaps the thought of approaching death encouraged Brother Matthew to give way to qualms of conscience and to eradicate or soften the many aspersions he had cast on leading members of the medieval establishment. His very hostile and disrespectful account of the archbishop's bad behaviour towards the monks when on visitation, that is, on an official tour of inspection, he tore out altogether. We know this because we can see how he thereafter made good the text of B in his own handwriting (below pp. 218–24). It is fortunate that Matthew was unsystematic and incomplete in this work of, as it were, death-bed expurgation and contrition, or he might altogether have failed to merit his reputation for outspokenness, or never left some of his most colourful prejudices on record.

Some idea of the way Matthew expurgated his chronicle may be obtained from the excerpt translated here. Some idea, too, of the way he put it together and of his working methods is afforded by the frequent repetition, the passages added in the margin after the original text had been written, and the references from one part of the work to another, all of which occur in the annals printed here. Sometimes the way he uses his sources is revealed, but it must be admitted, and deplored, that space has made it impossible here to show how he treated his earlier sources, in particular how he revised and tried to improve on the text of his predecessor Roger Wendover, upon whose chronicle up to 1234 or 1235 Matthew based his own *Chronica majora*. Nor have we been able here to demonstrate Matthew's use and treatment of the texts of contemporary documents (see now Hilpert 1981).

The excerpt from the *Deeds of the abbots* which follows is more or less typical, in its content, of the chronicles of other religious houses in the middle ages. The abbey of St. Albans was, however, one of the largest and best endowed in Britain; it was the mother house of a group of dependent priories called cells, of which the most important were Tynemouth, Belvoir, Binham, Wymondham and Wallingford. Bulking large in Matthew's narrative, the reader will find a detailed record of the elections of abbots, of gifts of land and valuables, or litigation in which the abbey was involved, of the building works of successive abbots and of injuries done to the convent or its interests. Particularly notable is Matthew Paris's constant upholding of the rights of the convent monks even against their own abbot or prior.

The subject matter of Matthew Paris's *Chronica majora* is not untypical of that of other chronicles of his age, but it is more various and wide-ranging and much more demonstrative of the author's personality. In the annals translated here the reader will come across frequent mention of the increasingly strained relations between the king of England and his barons, Matthew often taking the part of the barons and being highly critical of the king, even though he knew him personally. Matthew resents the way in which King Henry III's foreign relatives, in particular the queen's uncle Boniface of Savoy and the king's uterine brother Aethelmar of Lusignan, were favoured and promoted by the king, the former to be archbishop of Canterbury, the latter to be bishop of Winchester. Partly because of his prejudice against foreigners and his innate constitutionalism, Matthew is often critical of the pope and his officials in England and, doubtless keeping in mind the material interests of his own wealthy landowning abbey, invariably critical of taxation, whether the twentieth, or whatever proportion of valuables in question, was being levied for the benefit of king or pope. Births and deaths of important people, the elections and appointments of prelates, wars and battles, miracles and freaks, scandals, the 'translations' or removals of the relics of saints, crusades and the assumption of the sign of the cross by would-be crusaders, all attract notice in the *Chronica majora*; so do tourneys, the coinage, the 'crossing over' or going abroad of important people and their return, the weather and other natural phenomena. The dispute between Empire and papacy is seen by Matthew as a central element in European events. The way in which Matthew refers to Frederick II merely as "Frederick" without title, in line with his deposition by the Council of Lyons in 1245 at the pope's instigation, shows where his deepest loyalty lies. This use of "Frederick" by itself contrasts conspicuously with the habitual "the lord pope" or "the lord king" used for other dignitaries.

In the translation printed here notes have been kept to a minimum. Instead, where possible or necessary, persons and places have been identified in square brackets in the text. Cross-references to the author's numerous repetitions have for the most part not been made, but care has been taken to note all passages which are added in the margin in the manuscript. The Latin text has been followed as closely as possible. Thus phrases like "the lord king" and "the lord pope" have usually been retained in the English version and not simplified to "the king" or "the pope". Similarly the Latin original's *rex Francorum* has been rendered "king of the French" and its *rex Franciae* "king of France". Matthew seems to have meant the same thing by these two phrases, just as with "king of the English/England". He seems to have preferred "of the French" or "of the English" and to have used "of France" or "of England" more occasionally, perhaps just to ring the stylistic changes, or because this phrase was something of a novelty. The word *peregrinatio*, which Matthew often used for 'crusade', has been translated "pilgrimage", and the word *frater* in reference to Dominicans and Franciscans has been translated "brother" not "friar". The principle here has been to follow the Latin original as closely as possible and avoid unnecessary and perhaps confusing modernisation. Wherever possible, which is very often, the Latin word has been translated into its nearest English equivalent. Thus *vehementer* is rendered "vehemently" and *extorsit* "he extorted". Names, too have been given in the nearest acceptable form to Matthew's own, thus the king's uterine brother is called Aethelmar and not Aymer because Matthew calls him Aethelmar.

All Matthew Paris's main historical works were edited in the nineteenth century for the Rolls Series. The two relevant here are the *Chronica majora* edited by H.R. Luard between 1872 and 1883 in seven volumes, and the *Gesta abbatum* edited in 1867 by H.T. Riley, though in the later version of Thomas Walsingham. The *Chronica majora* was translated into French in 1840-1841 and, as will be mentioned below, into English in 1852-1854, but unfortunately these versions were, inevitably, based on the very faulty sixteenth- and seventeenth-century editions by Matthew Parker and William Wats. The *Gesta abbatum* albeit a part of it only, is translated here for the first time.

In spite of its many blunders and inadequacies, I found the Rev. J.A. Giles's translation of Matthew Paris, published in 1852-4 in Bohn's Antiquarian Library, quite invaluable in making my own translation of the *Chronica majora*. Time and again, he helped me out of a difficulty. I also willingly, but sadly because he died in 1981, pay tribute to Dr. Frederick W. Brooks, sometime colleague of mine at the University of Hull. He helped me a great deal in the often not too easy task of translating the *Gesta abbatum*. I also thank Professor Fritz Levy of the University of Washington, Seattle, for substantial help and useful advice with this same text, and Miss Susan Appleton for typing it for me. Finally, I must thank Gerda Huisman and Fred Bosman and other members of the staff of the University Library here in Groningen, for their cheerful assistance on numerous occasions during the book's final stages.

Richard Vaughan
Groningen, The Netherlands, Autumn 1983.

Bibliography

Ellis, H. (ed.) 1859. *Chronica Johannis de Oxenedes.* Rolls Series. London.

Giles, J.A. (Transl.) 1852–4. *Matthew Paris's English history.* 3 vols. London.

Hilpert, H.-E. 1981. *Kaiser-und Papstbriefs in den Chronica majora des Matthaeus Paris.* German Historical Institute, London. Stuttgart.

James M.R. (ed.) 1926. *The drawings of Matthew Paris.* Walpole Society 14: 1–26.

Liebermann, F. (ed) 1879. *Ungedruckte anglo-normannische Geschichts-quellen.* Strasbourg.

Luard, H.R. (ed.) 1872, 1874, 1876, 1877, 1880, 1882, 1883. *Mathaei Parisiensis. . . Chronica majora.* 7 vols. Rolls Series. London.

Mansi, J. (ed.) 1778. *Sacrorum conciliorum nova et amplissima collectio,* 22. Venezia.

McCulloch, F. 1981. Saints Alban and Amphibalus in the works of Matthew Paris: Dublin, Trinity College MS. 177. *Speculum* 56: 761–85.

Powicke, F.M. and E.B. Fryde. 1961. *Handbook of British chronology.* Second edition. Royal Historical Society. London.

Riley, H.T. (ed.) 1867. *Gesta abbatum monasterii Sancti Albani.* 3 vols. Rolls Series. London.

Vaughan, R. 1958a. The chronicle of John of Wallingford. *English historical review* 73: 66–77.

Vaughan, R. 1958b. *Matthew Paris.* Reissued 1979. Cambridge.

The deeds of the abbots of St. Albans [1195-1255]

Here are recorded the names of the abbots of the church of St. Alban, many of whom made by their own efforts numerous gains in possessions, dignities, sacred vessels and ornaments and constructed many buildings. Accordingly we have taken the trouble to put accurately into writing not only their names, but the gains, or indeed losses, which they conferred or inflicted on this church, in so far as these have indubitably come to our notice through the statements of truthful and trustworthy people or by inspection of the writers of their deeds. In this way neither their good works nor indeed their bad ones will perish in future times through oblivion and by this means not only will people now and in the future be incited to do good, but evil people will be deterred from doing harm by fear of scandal. Furthermore, if any secular or ecclesiastical person has piously conferred benefits on this church, not only his name, but the benefit itself and in which abbot's time it was conferred, will be perpetuated without a thread of falsity.[1]

---

1. The text of the *Deeds of the abbots* omitted here continues with Willegod the first abbot through till Warin, the twentieth abbot, who died on 29 April 1195.

Concerning Abbot John I,
the twenty-first abbot

After him succeeded John, called Master John de Cella, who came from a modest family originating not far from a place called Studham, a man of uncommon piety, who was an enthusiast for order and for firm monastic discipline. In his youth an assiduous frequenter of the schools at Paris, he was found worthy of joining the company of elect masters, so that he could when of mature age be considered a Priscian in grammar, an Ovid in versifying and a Galen in medicine. This man, having become a monk, improved so much from day to day that, mounting from virtue to virtue, he was called on to rule the priory of Wallingford,[1] and at last was happily promoted because of his notable merits to be abbot of the church of St.Alban. Ignorant of everyday affairs after the fashion of scholars, he engaged in study, contemplation and continual prayer, preferring the better part of Mary and shunning the solicitude of Martha.[2] Encouraged, as was proper, by this precedent, to make himself freer for contemplation and prayer by sharing his responsibilities with others, he committed the reins of government in internal and claustral affairs to Dom Reimund his prior, who was of great prudence and religion and experienced in counsel, and in external affairs to Dom Roger de Parco his cellarer, a man provident and circumspect in secular affairs. Being thus contemplative rather than active, as was fitting, he prudently limited himself only to weighing on the scales of reason important matters which specially concerned him.

Relying, therefore, on the counsels and strengthened by the support of these two brothers, and prompted by his conscience, for as has been mentioned above, he had received from his predecessor Abbot Warin 100 marks to be kept and used for the church buildings, Abbot John demolished down to the ground the wall of the west front of our church, with its old bricks, which was solidly built with mortar. But, he paid too little attention to that gibe mentioned in the gospel, namely

14

that unless the builder estimates the sums necessary for finishing the work so that after laying the foundations he can complete it, everyone will begin to taunt him "saying, this man began to build and was not able to finish."[3] For he began to drag up timbers and to collect a good many stones together including pillars and capitals. Then, having brought together a number of picked masons and placed them under Master Hugh de Goldclif, a deceitful man and a liar but a preeminent craftsman, and having laid out and dug a trench, he spent in a short time the above-mentioned 100 marks with a good many more, not counting the considerable daily wages, yet the foundation of the wall was not up to ground level. And it happened that, as a result of this Hugh's treacherous advice to add unnecessary, futile and excessively expensive ornaments, before half the work had risen above the level of the first floor, the abbot grew tired and began to lose interest and got scared. The work languished and in the winter stones from the uncovered walls, since they were very soft, broke into pieces, and the wall, like a broken-down and ruined wall, fell down, with its bases, columns and capitals, destroyed merely by its own weight. The remains of sculpted images and flowers caused the laughter and derision of those looking on, and the despairing workmen withdrew, nor did they receive wages for their work. However, the abbot did not give up but appointed Brother Gilbert de Eversolt to look after the work, assigning to it one sheaf of corn from every field sown. This continued from when it began to be rendered, namely in the third year of his abbacy, throughout the seventeen years of his lifetime and for about ten years of the next abbot's time, but that ill-starred work never made real progress, nor was Abbot John's heart ever gladdened by the longed-for completion of the work in his time, which caused him inconsolable grief. He added many offerings of gold and silver which might perhaps have made the work progress, and he collected no small sum of money by means of a certain cleric called Amphibalus, whom the Lord had raised from the dead on the fourth day through the good offices of SS. Alban and Amphibalus. In order that this Amphibalus might attest the miracles of these saints as an eyewitness, he sent him to preach throughout the lands of St. Alban and in the dioceses of many bishops, taking the saints' relics with him. But that unfortunate building work absorbed everything as the sea does rivers, and still made no progress. Thus the years passed uselessly in so far as that work was concerned. After the death of Brother Gilbert de Eversolt, the custodianship of the moribund and languishing works passed into the hands of Gilbert de Sisseverne, who was in charge of them for about thirty years, but he, though appropriating for this purpose the above-mentioned revenues, scarcely doubled the extent of it in all this time.

Averting his eyes but grieving in his heart, the aforesaid Abbot John turned his attention on happier advice to other works, leaving aside, as has been said above, and not diminishing, the revenues assigned to the first work. And, having razed the dark and dilapidated old refectory to the ground, he started a most elegant new one. He deservedly completed it happily in his lifetime and feasted joyfully in it with the brethren. Thus encouraged to be more hopeful, he had the old dormitory, which was ruinous and weak through age, together with its adjunct, namely of privies for the household, demolished to the foundations and a most excellent new one constructed in its place and perfectly and blamelessly finished. [To contribute] towards the construction of these two admirable buildings the [monks of the] convent gave up their wine for fifteen years continuously, but because [the abbot] abandoned the work on the church he never deserved to see its completion in his lifetime.

1.   A cell of St. Albans.
2.   Luke 10: 41, 42.
3.   Luke 14: 28–30.

Concerning the lawsuit over the wood of Northaw between Abbot John and Robert FitzWalter

In his time a most serious dispute was started by a certain very powerful person, namely Robert FitzWalter, with whom scarcely any earl in England could compare. For he was strenuous in arms, courageous and insolent, abounding in many possessions, generous, having numerous powerful relatives, and surrounded and supported by a multitude of followers. Emboldened therefore, and thinking himself insuperable, he injuriously laid claim against the abbot to the wood of Northaw. Abbot John resisted him manfully, encouraged by the advice of the above-mentioned wise men, namely Prior Reimund and Roger de Parco the cellarer, William de Sisseverne, knight and seneschal, and Laurence de Thebrugge, a most eloquent and wise knight, because he had very little fear of the injurious attacks of this Robert. Indeed at the end of the dispute the said Robert shamefully gave way, and that litigious wood of Northaw remained in the possession of the church of St. Alban. But while the case was in progress and was being exacerbated in various ways, Abbot John suffered so many losses, so many injuries, from this Robert, and indeed he sustained in his own person in arguing the case so many anxieties, so many costly labours, that, if they were written down or recited briefly in a succinct narrative they would be tedious to those listening. Furthermore, after Robert had impudently and obstinately harassed the personnel and possessions of the church of St. Alban in various ways both in person and by means of his dependents and friends, to such an extent that, at his instigation, four of his knights, sworn together in a treacherous league, together plotted the death of the aforesaid Laurence de Thebrugge because he had conducted the lawsuit loyally and prudently, a new and unheard of crime was machinated.

There was in this church among the brothers a certain person who was indeed cowled, though by no means a monk, but rather like Lucifer among the angels or Jude among the apostles, a worthless hypocrite among monks, himself not a monk but rather a living demon. This man, who was very crafty and ingenious, noticing beforehand when the convent, through the offices of a few of their number, namely the precentor and a few specially summoned monks, were consulting the deeds about this case, intervened officiously in their aid and service. Now the seal was at that time, very incautiously, negligently, and carelessly looked after, lying among the deeds in the chest. So this man, by name William Pigun, wrote out a completely invalid document or unauthorised charter in accordance with his intentions, which were most injurious, attached thongs to it for the seal and got everything ready, including warm wax. Then, while the others were doing something else, he furtively and rapidly sealed it under his sleeve, and although [this was done] hastily, yet [the impression] was amazingly clear, elegant and exact, though the seal had been snatched away by trickery. He did this because he had been fraudulently and secretly suborned by the blandishments, gifts and promises of the aforesaid Robert our adversary. For, in order to harm us more effectively in this case, Robert had secretly and treacherously drawn up a false charter and sent it to the aforesaid William for sealing in the way described above; which was done. Also, behaving with the greatest insolence, as usual with great men, he threatened with formidable menaces and bombastic words that he had not yet drawn his bloody and versatile sword to confound his enemies; on the contrary so far he had been playing. It was then learnt and discovered by some of his associates and secretly announced to the abbot, that Robert had a novel and very effective harmful instrument, newly acquired, for damaging the church of St. Alban to destruction; it was this which made him take on such airs. The abbot therefore sagaciously enough deduced that a forger was concealed among the brothers and that a forged charter had been made fraudulently to the detriment of the church. With the help of him who said, "For there is nothing covered that shall not be revealed",[1] the trick was exposed and the deceiver was convicted, so that a deceitful person deservedly became a sorrowful one. An insufficient punishment was inflicted on him, to avoid scandal. He was sent to the cell of [St. Alban's at] Tynemouth, as if an exile and unworthy to stay any longer in his present home, which he had defiled, in order to do perpetual penance for the crime he had committed. But that miserable person, unworthy of pity, hateful to God and to men, still harboured in his obstinate heart an inveterate hatred of the abbot, conceived a long time ago; and the origin of this hatred was as follows.

William Pigun had a certain nephew Robert whom he brought up, for his advantage, in the town of St. Albans, sending him to school there, as being a youth of some talents. Afterwards, having been accepted in the monastery at Peterborough, he improved daily so much in virtues that he was deservedly made prior of the convent there. When this Robert was still a youth, William had asked Abbot John if he would accept him as a monk [at St. Albans] but he, because he was immature and not yet of a suitable and acceptable age, though not wholly refusing, deferred the matter. So William, impatient and arrogant, had immediately arranged for the said Robert his nephew to be favourably received as a monk at Peterborough. Thereafter this William had always hated Abbot John and thus more readily contrived the above-described deceit to revenge himself. Even at Tynemouth, still harbouring the long-standing poison of hatred, he swore terribly, often cursing the abbot. But all these curses rebounded on his own head, as the final conclusion of his life proved.

It happened one night, that this same William of lamentable memory was sitting on the lavatory by the dormitory, oblivious of matins, with his belly crammed, inebriated with drink and glutted with food. Nodding his head, he began to sleep and, in sleeping, to snore with an irksome noise. And so he slipped bit by bit from drunkenness into sleep and from sleep into sudden death; carried off perhaps by cold but, more likely, as one can believe, struck down by divine vengeance. For when he had ceased bellowing by exhaling through his trachea, these words were plainly heard resounding in the lavatory where the dying man was sitting; "Take him, Satan, take him, Satan". Those brothers who for some reason had at that time remained in the dormitory and were not in the choir heard this clearly. Thus, therefore, that miserable person foully voided his soul with his excrement, and when in the morning the dead body was found thus, abominable to all, it could scarcely be recommended for Christian burial. However the brothers, to avoid scandal and in reverence for the order and habit, prudently kept quiet about many things.

After this it was wisely decided at St. Albans that the seal of the church, kept, under several keys, in the custody of several senior or more reliable brothers, should be brought out in the chapter whenever any deeds were to be drawn up so that they could be produced and sealed in everyone's presence and the seal could be put back in its place, namely a strong chest, and the chest kept in the safest possible place. I have said these things and put them into writing permanently, for this reason, so that everyone can learn what great punishments, now and in the future, can strike down those contriving such troublesome damages to the well-being of the Church.

Abbot John became extremely frightened of the new and poisonous weapons of Robert, during the time when he was ill, that is to say for a year and a day while William de Sisseverne, knight and seneschal of the church as has been said above, ruled in his place. So the abbot began prudently to treat for peace, lest the efficacy of the false charters should mortally wound innocent people. Robert agreed to this, being wonderfully appeased in a short time. He was very much afraid of such an enormous breach of conscience as well as of the stern vengeance of the martyr Alban, for he had heard how his accomplice in the perpetration of the fraud, William Pigun, struck down by the Lord, had ended his miserable life horribly. Moreover he feared not a little that everything would be exposed in some way or other, to his perpetual disgrace and reproach. So the dispute was settled and brought to an amicable end and that false charter was burnt in the presence of a few persons bound to silence under the seal of confession. Robert, from being an enemy, in that moment became a friend. He did not begin to be beneficial but he stopped doing so much harm. But because he had spent a great deal of money on this case and it is necessary to guard oneself against the gaping jaws of the wolf, ten librates of land, namely most of Bishopescote, were conceded and given to the same Robert from the church's possessions in the cause of peace, concord and perpetual friendship.

1. Luke 12: 2.

Concerning the persecution of the church of Binham by Robert FitzWalter

When that most pious man William de Sisseverne, knight, departed this life, Laurence de Thebrugge, knight, an eloquent and discreet man, cautious and circumspect in civil pleas and physically handsome, was appointed seneschal of this church. Robert FitzWalter had hated this man for a long time, as has been said above, because he had vigorously opposed him in the case concerning the wood of Northaw. Now it happened at that time that Abbot John, according to the powers given him not long before by the Roman pontiff, which had [already] been exercised [on occasion], removed Prior Thomas of Binham, who was a great friend of the aforesaid Robert, against his will. Robert, who was patron of the church of Binham, took offence because the prior, whom he was in the habit of calling 'his' prior, had been removed without his being asked. He became extremely angry and threatened to deprive the abbot of his power [of deposing priors], deriving courage from a forged charter concerning the patronage of the church of Binham which contained this clause: "The abbot may not remove the prior without consulting the patron, nor against his will". William Pigun, mentioned above, who, in dying, had voided with his fetid excrement his even more fetid soul, knew of and participated in this fraud and had given [this forged charter] to him.

Thus emboldened, Robert suddenly laid hostile siege to the church of Binham with the monks in it, as if it were a castle, so that the monks, having nothing to eat or drink and being about to perish through starvation, compelled by necessity and provoked by hunger, had to take rain-water from the roof-gutters for drinking water, and get bread made of bran down their throats with a struggle. This scarcely sustained life and never satisfied them. Furthermore, those besieging them swore detestably and horribly, with all sorts of threats and outrages every day, that unless their lord Robert's orders were complied with they would speedily remove the newly-intruded prior whom the abbot of St. Albans had [appointed] in that place, in breach, as they claimed, both of justice and of the privileges of their lord the patron of these monks. Discarding their fear of and reverence for the monastic habit, they also said that they would mutilate a number of the convent's monks, up to thirteen of them. First they would castrate the said prior; then they would ignominiously submit all their opponents to this. Repeated [appeals] were made to King [John] concerning this preposterous infringement of the peace of the lord king and of the Church, and the king was moved to bitterness of heart, swearing, as was his custom, by God's feet that either he or that man would be king of England. For the king hated Robert, though secretly; and Robert hated the king, which was not unknown to the king. So the king was pleased about the manifest offence and blame of the said Robert, since revenge could follow, and he said to those standing around, crossing himself through astonishment and angrily raising his voice, with his usual oath, "Ho! By God's feet, who has heard of such things in peacetime on Christian territory?" A certain friend of Robert was there listening to this, and he, struck with astonishment and fright, sent off some fast messengers on swift horses to Robert and his accomplices while they were besieging the church of Binham. These men, even though the monks of Binham all went on their knees and prostrated themselves before them imploring mercy, kept on oppressing them mercilessly. The messengers announced that they had better flee forthwith with haste before sunrise, for they asserted that the king, having heard an extremely serious complaint about them, was not only angry but furious, and had bellowed such and such with an oath. It was night when they received this message, but they, both Robert, who was nearby, and his men, scarcely stopping to pack their things and with their horses still covered because of their hurry, disappeared at once and, eagerly encouraging their horses with spurs, fled off into the distance. Sure enough, before the third hour of the day, the king's knights with their armed servants, flying more speedily than a whirlwind, arrived at Binham and clamourously demanded where those traitors to the king and breakers of the peace of the king and the Church were hiding; making it clear that they had been sent by the king to arrest those people and having arrested them, to take them to him. But when, having searched everywhere, they could not find them, realising that they had escaped after being forewarned by a hurried message, they departed sadly. When they reported this to the king, he inveighed against their indolence and said, "Someone who eats at my table told Robert about this hurriedly and at night".

It was then the time of the interdict,[1] and some of the English nobles began, on the lord pope I[nnocent] III's instructions, to rebel against the king, who was now an open enemy of the lord pope and the Church. Their captain, or one of their captains, was this Robert. This made the king groan with regret that he had not seized him, or at least his people, in so great a crime. From this time on Robert began to fear and hate the king more and more and, the lesser matter being absorbed by the greater, he left the church of St. Alban and its cell of Binham, which clearly only differed from St. Albans as a part from the whole or a limb from the body, alone, and concealed that forged charter, on which he had relied, as if on a staff of reed, with the utmost secrecy. Nobody knew of this save Adam FitzWilliam, who afterwards made it known. He most certainly planned to make use of it later when a propitious moment favoured him, but "divine power is at work in human affairs"[2] and he was deceived in his intention. As will be related in what follows, fortune turned against him and subsequent events very much altered his situation.

Thus the monks [of Binham] were irretrievably damaged by the above-mentioned followers [of Robert FitzWalter], and had to return there on foot because of their penury. But Robert, who had been excommunicated for his deed, suffered a series of misfortunes, which neither came to an end nor were mitigated for fifteen years. What an amazing and formidable avenging judgement of God and of the holy martyr Alban! From this time on, to speak truthfully, Robert never lacked either openly hostile persecution or the misfortune of growing infirmity and old age. When the war began at that time he was made leader of the army of insurgents against the king, and so he entitled himself in his letters "Constable of the army of God".[3] But he fell into many dangers. The shifty pope Innocent III very much incited and encouraged him and all his following in this affair. Afterwards King John, to avenge himself, shamefully gave way, surrendering himself miserably to the said pope as a tributary; and the pope, changing sides, and becoming a helper and defender of his [royal] vassal, turned against Robert and all his adherents. Thus was Robert weakened, and all his possessions were confiscated. Despoiled and exasperated, a wandering unstable exile, irresolute, he conspired with those besieged in the castle of Rochester, and was discomfited at Lincoln; at London his fame was blackened. During all King John's reign he endured numerous adversities and misfortunes until, King John dead and his son King Henry succeeding, peace was restored to the Church and to the whole kingdom. This Robert, now old and consumed with infirmity and never indeed completely restored to King Henry's favour, declined from bad to worse until death mercifully released him, always infamous for his treachery and suffering insults to the end of his days. He[4] did not hand back, or dig up from the ground, or set right that above-mentioned charter, as he ought to have done. Nor indeed had he when he was dying any desire to reveal or hand over this fraudulent charter, which he had acquired some time before by means of the above-mentioned treacherous monk in order to harm the church of St. Alban. But his friend and fellow-soldier Adam FitzWilliam, who was with him at that time, grubbed up his secret and presented it to the convent when he was dead. Moreover, in expiation of that sin he gave a silver-gilt cup from the estate of the said Robert, for the altar of the blessed Alban, in which to keep the host; but it was later furtively removed.

1.   From 1208 to 1214 England was placed under interdict by Pope Innocent III.
2.   Ovid, *Epist. Pont.* iv. 3:49.
3.   See Luard 1874: 586.
4.   From here to the end of the paragraph is added in the margin of the MS.

Concerning a certain miraculous event
which happened to Abbot John
by divine providence

As a proof that truth was spoken by the prophet when he said "There is no peace for the wicked" and by the psalmist, "But the meek shall inherit the earth and shall delight themselves in the abundance of peace, turning away from the men of discord,"[1] Abbot John meekly devoted himself continually day and night to fulfilling his daily duty to God without intermission. And I think it would be unworthy and ungrateful, and offensive to God and to our souls, to pass by in silence something which can be shown to resound to the praise of God and his ministers; that is, namely, a strange thing which happened to this same Abbot John when he was keeping vigil one night until nocturns. For when the brothers, congregated in the church according to their usual custom, had accomplished the nocturnal service in the dead of night, the abbot himself, resting in his room, awoke at the proper time while his companions, that is his attendants, who were tired through keeping vigil for a long time for some good reason, were dozing. The abbot, as if gently reproving them for their somnolence, stirred them, as he thought, with a slight deliberate cough. Then he began the fifteen psalms, namely "In my distress I cried unto the Lord"[2], and so on. Behold! While the attendants were still firmly asleep, some unknown person made the responses, replying alternately verse by verse all through matins, methodically, clearly, distinctly and articulately, as it should be done; also the twelve lessons of the blessed Virgin Mary together with the responses which followed them, were read. The assistants usually went through these by heart without candles, by the tenuous light of a lamp shining through transparent glass. On that particular night, after everything was properly finished, the assistants, sufficiently refreshed by sleep, woke up. And when with a slight nod or some vocal signal, they had got the attention of the abbot, he was unwilling to utter the responses to them because he knew that everything they were supposed to sing had been correctly finished. Going up to him, fearful lest it was sickness that was keeping him silent, they asked him why he had not heard, or if he had heard, had not made, the responses to the usual office of matins; for he normally sang more eagerly and loudly than the others. He, though unwillingly, broke silence, thinking they must be drunk. "Surely everything has been properly finished? What is the point of useless repetition? Did you not respond to my singing more distinctly than usual?" And they, knowing that had not, asserted that they had been fast asleep, nor had they uttered one iota of responses. Because of his eminent sanctity they concluded that it must have been angels who responded to him so carefully and devoutly, word for word.

It should be known that no one in the church of the blessed Alban ever knew all the psalms so surely and so fluently, nor, knowing them, repeated them so often, nor treasured them in memory more tenaciously, than he. One thing, indeed, we truly remember him to have done, as if to expose ignorance, or as an experiment or an exercise. He recited first the last verse of the psalter, then the penultimate verse, afterwards the antepenultimate verse, and so on, going through the entire psalter backwards without any mistake or defect, which is true, but incredible, since no one else would trust himself to do this even with that very much used psalm, "Have mercy upon me, oh God".[3]

This Abbot John blessed nine nuns at Sopwell, according to the tenor of the blessed Alban's privileges, on the thirteenth of the kalends of June, the day of the holy Trinity [20 May 1212], in the seventeenth year of his rule; also another five on the same occasion, in order to restore the excellent privileges of St. Alban to usage and to memory.[4]

1. Isaiah 48:22 and Psalm 37:11.
2. Psalm 120:1.
3. Psalm 51.
4. This paragraph is in the margin of the MS. See Liebermann 1879:170.

Concerning the large painting in front of the high altar, and two new ornaments with paintings and carvings, executed by Brother Walter of Colchester

To the credit of Abbot John should belong whatever his monks laudably accomplished. In his time, through the industry and lawful purchase of Dom Reimund the prior and Brother Roger de Parco the cellarer, the large painting which is in front of the high altar in our church was made and most skilfully finished, part of which is of metal, part of wood. Also two ornaments, of silver-gilt, in one of which a cross with a Crucifix and Mary and John is figured; in the other extremely elegant carvings of [Christ in] Majesty with the four evangelists are sculpted by the skilful work and diligence of Brother Walter of Colchester who fortunately was attracted and persuaded by Brother Ralph Gubiun to take on the religious habit in our church. The painting in front of the altar of the blessed Virgin, together with the carved super-altar and the cross placed on it, and the painting on the wall above and to the side, is most dexterously executed by the hand of this Brother Walter[1], the above-mentioned Brother Ralph providing the things necessary; also all the paintings in front of the altars in our church, namely, those of Saints John, Stephen, Amphibalus and Benedict. By the hand of his brother and disciple Master Simon the Painter, were executed the paintings of Saints Peter and Michael; by the hand of Brother Richard, nephew of the said Master Walter[2] and the son of Master Simon, the paintings of St.Thomas both upper and lower, were executed, partly by his, partly by his father's hand. The painting of St. Benedict, and many other pictures and carvings, were executed by the above-mentioned, to the honour and adornment of the house of God, though not in Abbot John's time, but later. We have been led to commend these things to immortal writing and memory, so that our by no means ungrateful recollection of those who by their assiduous labour left adornment to our church after themselves, shall flourish with blessings. Moreover, as a result of the efforts and lawful purchase of the above-named Dom Reimund, some fine and most useful books were written and given to this church, especially the *Historia scholastica* with the *Allegories*, a most elegant book.[3] Moreover Richard de Clohale, knight, a great friend of this abbot, both for the love of God and for the love of Abbot John, as well as for the church, gave a gold chalice for the altar of St. Mary, where her office is sung daily.

1. William, MS.
2. William, MS.
3. Now British Library, Royal MS 4 D vii. The next sentence is added in the margin in the MS.

A certain most pious statute of Abbot John I

Abbot John, being the most pious of prelates and wishing to spare the labours of the brethren when on a journey and likewise their funds, with which the monks, especially the claustral monks, were not well provided, laid it down in the first year of his rule that any brother journeying towards St. Albans who was overtaken by fatigue because of the labours of the road or by sunset, so that he could not complete his day's journey without harm and trouble, might turn aside to the nearest of our farms that he knew of, and there as sufficiently and decently as necessary see to his needs, both for men and for horses.

Another statute

In the fifth year of his abbacy he laid it down that the number of brothers should not on any account exceed one hundred – unless someone was proposed for admission who had to be accepted on account of his eminence in rank and knowledge or because of the request of some powerful person, to whom it was impossible to say no without causing harmful offence.

Another statute

In his third year he ordained that, in the celebration of masses, both private and conventual, the number of collects should not exceed seven. This was on account both of the sufficiency of that number and its dignity.

He brought to a happy conclusion other works of piety and civility which the labour of the writer and the tedium of the hearer forbid us to write or expound in detail one after another to listeners.

Misericords are prohibited

This abbot also successfully brought about the prohibition of the misericords or allowances permitting detestable boozing, for which there really was no justification. This I think redounds to his praise and merit.[1]

1. The last sentence is written over an erasure, probably showing that Matthew Paris did not originally praise the abbot for this action. The paragraph is in the lower margin of the MS. The heading which follows is on an erasure above the words "He brought to a happy conclusion" . . . five lines above.

Concerning the misfortunes which happened

During the interdict this abbot suffered many troubles and tribulations, one of which we have decided to insert in this book. King John instructed him to celebrate divine service during the interdict in spite of the papal prohibition. Having taken counsel about this in the chapter, he said: "Brothers, one should obey God rather than man: we shall have to put up with the prince's anger. 'God also will put an end to these things'".[1] And thus, in obeying the lord pope, even though

Master Alexander FitzMason, then royal master-mason, advised the contrary, he was unwilling to obey the king in this matter. The king, vehemently angry at this contempt of his mandate and gladly accepting this excuse for doing injury, took the whole abbey into his hands and, ejecting our people, appointed in everything his own secular custodians; that is to say, Master Robert of London, his senior cleric, a deceitful man in every respect like his lord King John. It was he indeed who carried frequent secret messages, concerning apostasy, it is said, between the king and the emir Murmelin.[2] This Robert, having dismissed and ejected our cellarer, appointed his own, a layman and a wily and extremely avaricious man who, insofar as he could, aided and abetted Robert's avarice. Likewise, having ignominiously ejected our janitor, he appointed another, by name Robert, who became a thorn in the flesh of the convent because he searched and ill-treated people entering and leaving. Abbot John, suffering these things only with difficulty, namely that so privileged and noble a house should be so oppressed in his time by the yoke of laymen, approached the king, or tyrant rather, as a lamb approaches the leopard or a just man an unjust and gave him 600 marks to remove the custodians oppressing us and leave the whole abbey with its belongings in peace.

1. Virgil, *Aeneid* 1:99.
2. King John's embassy to the emir of Morocco is described at length in the *Chronica majora*, Luard 1874:559–64, under the year 1213. It is one of Matthew Paris's additions to the text of Roger Wendover.

Another tribulation

In the same year Richard Marsh, a man intoxicated with the poison of Satan who was elevated to the bishopric of Durham not by election but intruded by the king, was the king's chief councillor. When the king, who was extremely avaricious and needed money, bombarded the abbot with earnest requests for help and the abbot protested the very reasonable causes of his impotence, the said Richard summoned him to his presence on the king's authority. When the abbot arrived, Richard said: "Lord Abbot, as we well know, there is not a great man in England who would not help our and your needy lord in so far as he could. We know that you gave him 600 marks, but this was to free your abbey, which he had legitimately taken over. Now, however, out of mere liberality, in order to regain favour, you must give the sum of 500 marks to the king, who demands it." Since the abbot was stupefied by so great an exaction, Richard said, "Why are you silent? The decision stands. It is written thus and "what I have written I have written"[1] indelibly. And I tell you in friendship that it is better for you to give 500 marks to regain favour than 200 or 300 and remain unthanked." Then he left suddenly, as if snatched away, though he was entreated to come back. Thus was the abbot compelled, in that year, to pay out 1,000 marks to the ever-demanding ever-grasping King John, to the greatest harm of this church.

1. John 19:22.

Another trouble

This same Abbot John had a singular consolation in his tribulation, and as a councillor, helper and comforter in all affairs, even difficult ones, namely Master Adam of Linley, who was afterwards made archdeacon of Ely, a most kind and honest man, skilled in the law. When however the archbishop of Canterbury, Stephen [Langton], who had recently returned to this country after peace had been made (and the country trembled at his sight), learning of his fame, was informed about him, he sent to Abbot John to ask him if he could become his assistant, attendant, clerk and special councillor. Moreover, the same archbishop sent special letters to this Adam, entreating him not to neglect coming to him quickly for the good of his career. He felt inclined to accept the archbishop's command for he thought he would obtain richer livings through him, for it is usual for lawyers to be fond of gifts and pursue recompenses. Since therefore the abbot neither wished to nor in honesty could oppose the commands of such and so great a man, especially when he saw that Master Adam himself desired this for the sake of promotion, he said to this Master Adam, "Dearest Master, I do not wish to impede your promotion. The archbishop is greater than I; since you desire greater things you shall follow the greater man. You are taken from me; the archbishop will not permit me to enjoy the comfort of your presence, even though he is well supplied with an army of experienced people. However, take him this brief, which is brief indeed, from me." The abbot wept bitterly over Adam's departure, and Adam took the letter with him, sealed and in a cover. When the archbishop, having broken the seal, unfolded the letter, he found two verses written there: "You possess a hundred sheep with their fleeces and milk, yet you think little of taking a lamb from a poor man". When the archbishop read this, seeing himself effectively refuted, he wanted to send Adam back, but Adam, who had hoped for richer livings, would not go.

At that time, when Richard Marsh, the principal royal councillor, an inexorable exactor of money, was goading and oppressing this abbot beyond measure, to get him to pay the above-mentioned sum quickly, the abbot said of him, reproving both Richard and the king: "There will be no rest for Abimelech while Saul reigns, nor a stable peace until Doeg ceases to be."[1]

1. See I Samuel 21 and 22.

Concerning the laudable end of this same Abbot John

When indeed Abbot John had grown old, and was full of holy years, feeling and knowing that the hour for his departure from this world was approaching, he fell gravely sick. And so he came one day, supported with the aid of another person, to the threshold of the chapter house, whence he proceeded alone, as best he could in order to make a decent entry with his attendants following, to seat himself as was his custom in his place, which was high up. He had a chair brought with him which we call colloquially 'faldstool'. And when he had sat down in his usual high place, weeping profusely and with repeated sobs, having saluted the convent on one side and the other with a devout bow, he said: "Brothers and dearest sons, for a space of time I was among you, I was in charge of you, and I was useful to you, though perhaps less than I should have been. Because there is no man who does not sin and give frequent offence, if I have hurt one of you in any way, I pray you with clasped hands and bended knees, for the sake of God who ordains this, completely to forgive me all my offences and, in so far as you can, absolve me from all the misdeeds I have committed." And, with these words, as if wishing to bend his knees, he stooped down with his hands clasped. When everyone tearfully and unanimously replied "Let what you ask be done", the abbot ordered the above-mentioned chair to be brought and placed in the middle, on the carpet, in the place we call 'Judgement'. Then he sat on it, stripped himself down to his bare flesh, and asked to be given discipline individually by each monk. When the brothers saw that diminutive body, so emaciated that from a distance the structure of the bones seemed to show, they groaned with sincere compassion and much weeping and, approaching one after another, they all gave him discipline, each one as he wished. When they spared him by castigating him gently, he rebuked them for their idleness, saying to them repeatedly "I confess etc." and breaking into sobs with the words "May almighty God have mercy etc." When this was over he put on his habit with the help of his attendants, who adjusted his clothes for him and, getting up, he bowed to the convent and tearfully pronounced his last goodbye to it. Then the brothers supporting him on each side, which was necessary because of his weakness, led him, at his command, to the infirmary, where he was solemnly anointed with the holy oil of the sick on the customary stone bench and furnished with the viaticum of salvation. When these things were duly completed he said, refreshed in spirit, "It is finished" as if he were saying, as he embraced each brother: "I am leaving you, never to return; you shall commend me and I shall commend you to God. I have done what I had to do". On this he was led, or rather carried, away to his own room.

The next day he carefully examined his urine, to see what it portended, for he was, as has been said, an excellent physician, and also an incomparable judge of urine. Although he inspected it diligently he was unable, because the keeness of his eyesight had been in a large measure blunted, to observe to his liking the subtle and secret signs of death, which he knew. So he said to one of our monks, Master William the Physician, who was afterwards promoted to be prior of Worcester, "What do you see here brother?" He indicated what he saw, and the abbot said "Ah! Praise be to God! He has allowed me three days more for penance; but after the three days I shall die." Those who heard this believed it, for he was most experienced in the art of medicine and had often infallibly foretold similar things concerning others in such circumstances. When, on the next day, he had more obviously approached death, one of those most familiar with him who had gone to visit and console him at that time, said to him when all his senses had become blunted: "Oh lord, my father, how are you?" And he, looking at him almost without raising his eyes, said to him "I cannot see easily; nothing tastes; I hear with difficulty; my sense of smell has gone; I have become sluggish in everything."[1] There was much astonishment that he, though half dead, as if revived in spirit, had composed, in a spontaneous reply, so elegant, so true and so relevant a verse.

---

1. The words from "my" to "everything" are in the margin of the MS.; the abbot's words are in verse.

How a certain charter was made concerning not banishing monks

Some of our brothers went in the meantime to this abbot when he was already making the death-rattle, that is the doleful sound which those who are about to die are wont to emit in the depth of their throat because of the constriction of the arteries. They were, Brother Walter of Rheims, who afterwards became prior of this church; Brother Alexander of Langley, who was for a long time an attendant of his and of the next abbot; Brother William of Trumpington, who was likewise an attendant of this abbot and who was promoted to be abbot after him (it was from him indeed that this idea originally emanated, as he afterwards maintained); and Alexander of Appleton, bearer and guardian of the seal, and others with them. They spoke to him as follows:

"O lord, holy father, who has up to now nourished us under the wings of mercy, for the love of him who redeemed his people by his death, we pray your holy fatherhood of your great bounty to end the ancient servitude of your church and the insufferable yoke on your convent. For you know well in what an intolerable custom the convent is entrapped, namely, that anyone without a cause, at the will of the abbot, on an arbitrary impulse or as a result of the sly accusations of whisperers, can be transferred vilely to one of our most remote cells, which is equivalent to exile for us, not without much bitterness of heart and scandal. For in this way dishonour and scandal is generated in the person thus sent and the sender. The layman will say: 'This monk who has been transferred must have committed some crime; or else the abbot hates him or is envious of him because he is more distinguished than the abbot and has corrected the abbot's errors and reprehended his excesses. Therefore the abbot is giving the others a lesson in keeping quiet or in flattery, not to mention adulation'. Furthermore, holy father, it is evident that this transferring and moving around, [makes it impossible] for us to live all the days of our lives in a particular church built in honour of the holy Mary or some other saint, [in this case] our holy father Alban, [so that] we may converse, grow old and die there. Yet we have made solemn and sworn profession to continue our lives according to St. Benedict's rule in this monastery, which exists discretely, particularly and distinctly and is built in honour of St. Alban. What is to be said when we are transferred unwillingly, as if condemned and convicted of some crime, to our ignominy and yours, like exiles to the cells? As we have often heard from your own mouth, this indeed seemed absurd and oppresive to you. Lord Abbot, full of mercy and justice, see here our charter drawn up about this, stating that no monk of this church may be sent away from the others against his will to a cell; may it be [linked] with blessing to your memory in eternity."

The above-mentioned Dom Alexander, the abbot's bearer and guardian of the seal, producing the charter, wanted to read it to the abbot so that he could seal it when it had been read. But the abbot, heaving a most ponderous and profound sigh, averted his face, refusing with a shake of his head, for by this time he could not speak. And then, repeating the sign, he turned himself onto the other side, facing away. Since this Alexander had everything ready, that is, the writing and the seal, and the thong and the seal had been brought, he said angrily, "He who is silent, gives his assent." And when the others replied, "That is true," this Brother Alexander of Appleton sealed it, and this was the last impression made by that seal. The next day, which was the third after he had foretold his death to his brothers, the abbot breathed his last. When the seal had been broken, this Alexander was sent — without the prior's leave being sought, because of his indignation[1] — on his own advice and that of many others, especially the above-mentioned, to Stephen [Langton], the archbishop of Canterbury, since he was very friendly with the archbishop and had composed several eulogies of him in his praise, so that the archbishop could confirm the above-mentioned written concession with his seal. He found the archbishop willing to do this, persuaded in a friendly way by Alexander's humble prayers, especially when he saw the abbot's seal attached to the document. And when he returned, having accomplished the affair as had been hoped, each and everyone congratulated himself, except for Prior Reimund, who, subtly weighing up the thing on the scales of reason, openly foretold its outcome to certain of the brothers.

Abbot John passed from this world, from exile, that is to his country, from shipwreck to port, in the year of our Lord 1214, on [17 July] the day of the blessed Kenelm, king and martyr, as he had clearly foretold to many people, in the nineteenth year of his rule, distinguished by his holiness and religion, full of days, leaving his abbey in as good a state as the times would allow.[2]

Since the king was abroad at that time in Poitou, two of the brothers were sent to ask him for the customary licence to proceed to an election, namely Dom Robert of Britwell and Dom William of Trumpington. When they reached him and he heard their request he did not accede to it, knowing that the guardianship of the abbey was lucrative to him, but he put the matter off until his return to England, which was on the fourteenth of the kalends of November [19 October]. Meanwhile a certain William of Trumpington unknown to and without the consent of Dom William of Trumpington, did his best to see that this Dom William was created abbot through his efforts. This William, who was a knight of Trumpington and seneschal of Earl Saher [de Quincy of Winchester], claimed to be a relative of Dom William of Trumpington, and so he petitioned the king on William's part to accept him, and no one else [as abbot]. When this became known to the convent, the monks decided to try to avoid a refusal from the king lest the abbot-elect be embarrassed by being turned down and the church suffer harm and the convent be thrown into confusion. So those who had been sent to ask for the licence went to the king, whom they found at London and, more definitely informed of the king's wishes, they returned with the licence they had asked for. Without delay those who were to act as the abbot's electors were chosen, namely twelve monks who were fully instructed on all these points. Now there was at that time an outrageous custom in the church, namely that none of those twelve electors could be elected or created abbot. They therefore unwillingly arranged that this William was not one of the electors so that he could be elected without the slightest contradiction of that custom, which would remain unviolated.

Lest we proceed to the time of another abbot with Abbot John's excesses untouched upon, I think it worth while to record briefly, because indeed they were brief, the transgressions of this abbot, just as has been done with the others. He transferred the monks of this church mercilessly from here to the cells and from cell to cell, here and there, like serfs of the lowest condition, against their will and without any fault of theirs, so that many spent all their lives in the cells, especially the remote ones, in the utmost bitterness, and died there. Some indeed, forsaking the habit because of this, perished in body and soul, and it is to be feared that the abbot will be held responsible for these at the last judgement. This was done indeed at the instigation of his councillors and associates who freely removed whoever they wanted to, the abbot being more or less unaware, since he was now growing old and inclined so much towards tranquillity. These were the conspirators and flatterers who were feathering their own nests: Roger of Hertford senior, John of Shelford, Alexander of Langley; it was they who corrupted the abbot's faculties. They ended their miserable lives, which were prolonged with chagrin, most indecently, we believe as a result of [God's] vengeance for such great sin.

Furthermore, Abbot John gave his relative John de Hida 140 marks from the church's treasury so that by acquiring lands and obtaining the things necessary for his first military expedition he could become a knight. The abbot was solemnly accused of this transgression by Hubert and Almaric, monks of this church but excessively indiscreet men, along with Walter of Standon and Robert FitzBaldwin and some others who, because of their folly, do not deserve to be mentioned by name, in front of the legate Gualo at a chapter specially called for this purpose. In the opinion of many, the abbot's deposition was imminent;

but he replied modestly and circumspectly enough to this accusation. "I do not wish nor am I able to deny, that I am indebted to my church for the money for promoting one of my poor relatives. But, against this loss, I have enriched and advanced the church of my own free will with two new benefices. The church of St.Stephen, which is in this town, I am giving out of charity to the convent's kitchen, which I have always embraced with a specially heartfelt affection and which I shall continue to embrace, even if I am deposed. Certain other persons wanted this benefice, and I have not yet finally confirmed the collation of this church to my beloved convent. Furthermore I have given Hamo's land, which I bought for 120 marks, to the convent's kitchen, to its considerable improvement and enrichment. Thus, if you wish, you are in a position to know that, having salved my conscience, I have made loyal recompense for the above-mentioned loss."

To this the legate, turning to him, said, "My friend, Lord Abbot, the convent, and indeed anyone who wants to hear, should listen to this. It is quite in order for you to relieve the poverty of some poor person, especially a relative of yours, out of the wealth of the church. That is almsgiving, which I declare to be completely irreprehensible. The lord pope, father of fathers, does this; indeed I have done this. And why not? Your abbot ought not to, and cannot, be convicted of squandering, especially as this merciful almsgiving and beneficence was done with money and not with rent. For money comes and goes according to whether the giver has it or not, and this does not imply wickedness. And he added, "Oh malevolent people, who wickedly attribute evil and not good to the sword of justice". At these words all the abbot's enemies were confused and fell silent, not daring to murmur against them. But when the legate had left, the abbot, oblivious of patience and of that divine precept "Bless them that persecute you",[3] which however is a counsel of perfection, exiled his above-mentioned accusers and persecutors to remote cells. Many were by no means surprised by this since he had sent innocent monks who were of much use to the church to distant parts. It was for this reason that, at the end of his life, the monks, exasperated by such injuries, earnestly demanded the above-mentioned charter.

1.   The words from "without" to "indignation" are in the margin in the MS.
2.   This paragraph, except for the words from "leaving" to "state" is almost word for word the same as Matthew Paris's revised Wendover text in his *Chronica majora*, Luard 1874:576.
3.   Matthew 5:44.

William of Trumpington, the twenty-second abbot

Abbot William who, as has been said, was elected and installed on [20 November] the day of St. Edmund, king and martyr, succeeded him. He was solemnly consecrated at the great altar as is customary by Eustace the bishop of Ely on [30 November] St. Andrew's day, which was the first Sunday in Advent, and received benediction. Immediately after his appointment, spurning the friendly society of the cloister monks, he associated with laymen, living a worldly life, with dining and much conversation. Those who had elected him could not believe this, neither did any monk of this church: they thought that they had known him perfectly. On this matter Prior Reimund and Master Walter of Rheims, Alexander of Langley and Alexander of Appleton, the sub-prior Fabian, Amalric, Hubert Ridel, John Scot and several others conferred together: "We deserve to suffer this for our sins, in fearing the king rather than the law[1] in our election". And, when one of the electors, Master Walter of Rheims said: "When the abbot-elect, Dom William of Trumpington, was presented to the king in London, the king enquired in a low voice 'Who is your abbot-elect and what is his name?' and he was told 'Dom William of Trumpington'. 'Aha!' said the king, 'Exactly the person I wanted! it was prudent of you to elect him, to avoid being frustrated of another. He is a relative of that most distinguished knight William of Trumpington whose footsteps I believe he will follow'. And having enquired who and what sort of a person he was, he received him happily with an embrace. From these words, it is evident that this election was not proceeded with solely according to the will of God. But we must suffer this now with patience and correct his excesses first in a spirit of lenience, if indeed they can thus be corrected. If not, we must progress to severer methods."

The next day, when the abbot entered the chapter, he was severely criticised and firmly reprimanded about the above-mentioned excesses, and for infringing the charter [against banishment to cells] made under the previous abbot, in which outrageous crime he had shamelessly blemished the constancy of his words and the integrity of his faith. Giving the prior a sidelong glance with bitterness in his heart, the abbot then turned to the whole convent, concealing his anger behind a serene countenance, and said openly: "Brothers and friends, if any transgression has occurred through negligence amends will be made in full according to your wishes without any hint of dispute, for such is God's will". Then Alexander of Langley, getting to his feet among the brothers, publicly said, "You speak very well, lord, in your kindness. We all in general appeal to the liberties of the convent as set out in the recent charter, discussed by us at first, then drawn up in writing and confirmed". The abbot replied, "What is this Dom Alexander? Have you any doubts about it? Surely I played an important part, taking the utmost trouble, in the making of that charter? Far be it from me to be found against it. You may rest assured; there is no need for any further complaint about this". And so the chapter broke up peacefully that day, with an appearance of submission [on the part of the abbot].

Lo and behold! Scarcely a month later the abbot exiled a certain monk of this church to one of the cells, against his will, although he wept and lamented and with bended knees and hands clasped together mournfully implored for mercy, that is, to be allowed to remain at home. When this was not forthcoming, he lodged an appeal with the prior and senior monks. But, because the abbot was away and absent from the chapter, this monk left and went to the cell he was ordered to by the abbot, never to return; for he died there in mental anguish. After a few days another was exiled in the same way, that is without the consent of the convent. Moreover, the abbot did not deign to amend the faults which he had promised to correct. So there was a considerable uproar in the convent; but then another vexation occurred, worse and greater than the first one.

When the abbot arrived in chapter one day he was criticised much more bitterly for his many excesses as well as for his contempt of the convent and the manifest breaking of his promises, and especially for infringing the above-mentioned charter, of which he had been the principal procurer and was now the audacious violator. The abbot, gnashing his teeth as usual and with the colour of his face changed and his whole body bent and quivering, replied fast and furiously, going to the point without any beating about the bush. "It is true that I drew up the charter you are referring to and blaming me for [not observing], and I took the trouble to have it done diligently and efficiently; but I did not appreciate what I was doing. For that reason I can undo what I have done, and what has been confirmed by me can be annulled by me. The things I formerly believed in stand no longer, for I know now what I did not know before." On this Dom Amalric muttered under his breath, "That's true, for now you know you are abbot, which you didn't know before." The abbot heard this and was not pleased. When many spoke against the abbot and the uproar increased he calmed their excitement by saying "We shall take advice about this". This statement had the same effect as pouring a cup of cold water into a boiling cauldron: and so the chapter ended that day.

Shortly after this, on the prudent and secret instigation of the abbot, Nicholas, then papal legate in England, a monk of the Cistercian order, having been fully informed about all this, came to St. Albans and said that he wanted to appear in the chapter with the convent to discuss the affairs of the church. So the legate came to the chapter and, among other things, spoke as follows: "I hear that a certain new charter has been made in this monastery; I request that a copy be submitted to me for my inspection". When it was reluctantly handed to him, he inspected it and read it, exclaiming derisively when he had finished, "Oh how much and what kind of abuse is contained here! What is this, brothers? Are you insane? Do you want to renounce the obedience you have vowed to God?" With these words, bombastically pronounced, he tore the charter into pieces with his front teeth and, smashing the seal attached to it, threw it onto the floor. Then he added, "What villains you are to plot such things in a convent!" On this the satirical and vain braggings of Amalric ceased; the eloquent arguments of Alexander of Langley were silenced; the threats of Walter of Standon, who had anger in his breath, came to an end; the artful pride of John of Shelford was overthrown; and all the abbot's opponents were repelled in confusion. And so the chapter came to a close and the legate went away entreating the abbot to summon him if anyone criticised him about this, so that he could subdue the rebels more effectively. From this time on, therefore, the abbot, transformed from a king into a tyrant, though he was only a young man, behaved in all things like an old man and, although he was criticised again by some people, he made it clear, not without heat, that he had behaved correctly. In order that he could rule on his own, and lest he should experience any offence or hear any contradiction, he exiled his prior, Reimund, the most distinguished monk in the order in our times, knowing that if he subdued the greater person the rest, afraid, would be silent the more. Having deposed the prior and despoiled him by force of his books, which he had made with great care, and of other precious objects necessary to him now that he was old, and which he was entitled to enjoy during his lifetime, he sent him against his will and in a confused state of mind to the cell of Tynemouth, which was the usual place of exile for our monks. After that, all those who had opposed the abbot and confronted him remained silent in his presence, not daring to murmur against him. And the abbot prospered as much as he could desire, joyful and secure in his position. At the beginning of his abbacy he visited the cell at Tynemouth and elsewhere with much honour and magnificence and a large company, for he travelled surrounded by numerous relatives who had ignored him up to then; and he enjoyed every wordly and spiritual happiness.

1.   A play on the words *rex* and *lex*.

When the war starts the abbot's troubles increase

To avoid good fortune happening unmixed in the affairs of this world, and in order to retard the advance of prosperity, God permitted a war in England, more troublesome than any seen in the kingdom of the British, on account of the [misdeeds] of this man and others who boasted of their prosperity, so that the father strove to confound the son, the brother his brother, the citizen his co-citizen and the relative his relative, by seizing, exterminating, burning, despoiling, disinheriting, torturing and destroying. Not even the Church was strong enough to protect those fleeing to her. The religious were trodden under foot more than anyone and became a prey for the warmongers, so that the abbot and the abbey of St. Albans, lying open to the incursions of many, were attacked by many, and frequently disturbed, being irreperably affected by losses and injuries; for when one group went away another, their enemies, came back. Moreover at that time Louis, eldest son of the king of France, arrived in the kingdom,[1] which was already much disturbed. He planned to force Abbot William to do him homage, but the abbot would never do it, though many times requested and bombarded with injurious threats. So he sustained the depredations of one side when he gave satisfaction to the other, and if he supported that side he suffered the attacks of this one. Later on, when the brothers were having a private discussion among themselves, this same Abbot William swore that he had lost a hundred horses in one year in various parts of the abbey; some were draught horses, others for riding, some were sumpter horses, others were cart-horses and some were farm horses; not to mention other losses which need not be mentioned here.

1.   In May 1216.

The charter is infringed by the exile
of the leading monks

In order to be on his own, and therefore in a position to carry out more freely whatever seemed to him needed doing, the abbot exiled to the cells certain monks of the convent who saw themselves as important;[1] namely William of Colne, John of Shelford and Amalric and Walter of Standon. Alexander of Langley, however, at the instance of the earl of Arundel who was patron of the cell of Wymondham, the abbot promoted to be prior of that church but, when he arrived there, he became so crazy and out of his mind that, being quite useless, he was brought back again immediately afterwards. In the place of Prior Reimund, newly demoted, he promoted Master Walter of Rheims, in the place of Alexander, prior of Wymondham, he appointed Ralph of Whitby. This was blameless enough, since both appeared to be suitable for these offices. The above-mentioned Master Walter was a great lover of the order, and of honesty and of the scriptures, and was extraordinarily erudite in the study of literature. Ralph, surnamed de Stanham, who was appointed prior of Wymondham, was a provident and circumspect man in both spiritual and secular affairs. He was not however a monk of our profession, for he had been a monk at Whitby and prior of that house but, having suffered persecution there at some time he wisely fled to and was received by the protecting bosom of St. Alban. This same Ralph, when he was prior of the aforesaid house, had a certain cell or hermitage belonging to the house of Whitby specially assigned to him out of regard for his person, so that he could safely take refuge there when fleeing from the face of persecution. There, devoutly and blamelessly, he lived for some time before he was received in the cloister of St. Albans.

1. The words from "whatever" to "important" are on an erasure in the MS.

Called to the [Fourth Lateran] Council,
Abbot William goes to Rome

The time approached when all the prelates of Christendom were universally summoned to a council to be held under Pope Innocent III. In making his preparations for this the abbot, who was among those convoked, paid out considerable sums of money, as behoved such a great man. He set out promptly taking with him two monks whom he believed would be useful to him. One of them was Alexander of

Appleton his bearer, a man of polished education and excellent conduct who has been mentioned above; the other was Master Roger Porretanus, who knew the Roman curia. He was extremely famous in various branches of knowledge, namely grammar, dialectic, physics, and Roman and canon law, but of less good character than he should have been. The abbot therefore, without meeting any difficulties, crossed over the sea with the abbot of Westminster, traversed the Alps and successfully reached the curia. And when the plenary council was being celebrated under the presidency of the pope, with all the assembled prelates, the abbot, who had asked for an opportunity to speak during the discussions, rising to his feet, began modestly and elegantly enough in front of the pope and council to publicly put his question. "Holy Father, we who are known to have in our churches the body of some saint; could we not be permitted, in our private masses, to recite their names among those intercessors whom we invoke? We would like a ruling on this, for we know that what is decided in this holy council will remain perpetually in force." Replying to this, not indeed precipitately, but circumspectly in the hearing of everyone, the pope said, "It seems right to me and in keeping with the law that the saint with whose body some church is blessed should be devoutly named in the secret of the mass, that is to say in the first series of names, and his intercession should justly be sought for in its proper place." And the abbot, assured on this matter, was satisfied because, before his speech, there had been a most thorough discussion in the council on the mass and matters pertaining to the mass; and some things were abolished which had been done for a long time before.

Abbot William was thanked and congratulated by many people in whose churches the bodies of saints reposed, for they had learned more fully, through him, what they ought to do. This applied to the people at St. Edmunds, at Durham and others likewise. The same day, the pope privately asked who that abbot was who had publicly put this question and, when told he was the abbot of St. Albans, the pope commended such confidence in speaking and such prudence in questioning in so young a person, and the fame of this affair spread among all the prelates of our country. The abbot's above-mentioned monk, namely Roger Porretanus, a most ambitious man, advised him to resign his abbacy into the hands of the pope under the guise of sanctity, for he was convinced that he would certainly be given a more important and more lucrative dignity when the pope saw such humility and such manifest evidence of sanctity in so great a man. But the abbot, unwilling to exchange a certainty for something uncertain, in no way accepted his advice, and told him "Master, as the popular proverb says,

'Happy is he who is forewarned by the perils of others'. You did this with your rent in Bath when you surrendered it in the hopes of something better, which however you never managed to obtain." So Robert fell silent, confused and contradicted.

How the abbot was unwilling to depart, except with the pope's blessing

When this same Abbot William, after the dissolution of the council and after he had been given permission to depart, wanted to leave with the pope's blessing without giving him any sort of consideration in the form of gifts, the pope said to him, "Aren't you the abbot of St. Albans, who has so often received so many grants of privileges from our see? Surely such a man ought not to take leave of me without any consideration?" But when he offered fifty marks he was reproved in a friendly way so that, before he left the pope's chambers (which he regretted having entered), he was forced, not without a feeling of guilt, to make satisfaction by paying a hundred marks, which he had to borrow on stringent conditions from the usurers at the curia. The abbot did this the more readily and with greater equanimity because the pope treated all the other prelates in the same way. When the abbot had paid over his money, which one of his attendants humbly and devoutly offered before the pope's feet, the pope gave him leave to depart, together with his benediction, purchased in this way. And so departing, he paid his respects to Rome with a grumble. Master Roger Porretanus left him there, nor did he see him again until he arrived at Walemund, where he tarried for some time waiting for the abbot; he had been made the abbot's companion, but he did not offer companionship.

What was done when [the abbot] returned home

When Abbot William arrived home the convent went out in procession to meet him. He was joyfully embraced by each of the brothers dressed in albs, which is the customary mode of reception whenever the abbot comes from overseas. And this should be done either in the doorway of the chapter house or of the cloister, on the way to the church, reverently and joyfully, after he has accepted some small favours.

Incidentally, it occurs to me that I ought to say what happens when the abbot comes from Tynemouth. When the abbot comes from Tynemouth he should be escorted by six squires from the lands of St.

Albans who are enfeoffed on this account in a most generous and honourable way from the abbey's possessions. That is to say, one from the fief which William de Aete, knight, once held; another from the fief once held by Thomas de Wauz, knight; another from the fief which was once held by William de Wyka; another from the fief which Robert de Thebrugge once held; another from the fief once held by Nicholas Dispensator; and another from the fief which was once held by William de Ockersse.

These six ought to go and return at the abbot's expense but on their own horses, which should be powerful, and suitable for carrying, usually, one monk's clothes if this is necessary, on the squire's crupper. If, however, the horse of any one of the above-mentioned squires dies on the journey, the abbot must pay him seven shillings to make good his loss. And it should be made clear that, as often as he wishes to go to Tynemouth, the abbot must obtain permission from the king to enable him to travel to such a remote part of the kingdom bordering on the kingdom of Scotland. When he arrives there he should behave in a restrained manner, having corrected the community, not being tyrannical nor dissipating the provisions and stock of the house, as Abbot Simon did, who was laudable indeed, but not at all in this matter. For when he had snatched away everything, the oxen with the plough were led to him and he was tearfully told, "Everything has been devoured, but these our plough-oxen remain, and these we now present to you for eating." Then the abbot, deservedly perplexed, said to his people, "Saddle your horses, let's leave here". And he left the house despoiled of all that year's produce, to his eternal opprobrium.

The abbot should rather consider carefully for what purpose he has gone [to a cell]; namely to reform behaviour and the monastic order and lest there be any defect in spiritual or temporal necessities; and to visit the flock under his care in a paternal way, like a good shepherd. But it is frequently otherwise, for abbots arrive and stay far too long in order to be fed instead of supporting others; and the Lord allows us, by a just judgement, to be similarly oppressed by our superiors.

Alexander of Langley gets better, but not entirely

Meanwhile, when Alexander of Appleton, the abbot's bearer and keeper of his seal, died, Alexander of Langley, whose infirmity was now in large part mitigated, was appointed in his place, not however because he was liked, but because of his extremely perspicacious mind and because he had great literary skill. He took pleasuree, more than anything else, in the abbot's and the chamberlain's writing offices and in the methods of writing out copies. He even knew how to write, rhetorically and faultlessly, a most elegant letter to the lord pope, when this was necessary; and the seal was committed to him. But, after the fashion of those suffering from mania, he began to rave from time to time and to be amazingly haughty. Because of this the abbot rightly recalled him to the cloister where, remaining for some time, he began to go insane through too much contemplation and writing, and becoming obtuse on account of his studies, he multiplied his talents by boasting. Worried by this, the abbot summoned him to the chapter and had him flogged till he bled profusely. Even this did not humble him, so he was sent to the cell at Binham where, in solitary confinement and shackled on the abbot's instructions, he was held until he died. He was buried in his chains. In his place was substituted Richard de Brantefeld with whom, in the abbot's retinue, was associated Richard Rufus, who had been Prior Walter's bearer.

The war gets worse, and the tribulations of the monks

Meanwhile, the war got worse and, while Louis [son of the king of France] obtained the city of London, first the barons who supported him, then the royalists, extorted sums of money on every side. The soldiers so despoiled the monks who were custodians of the manors that they were left naked, refugees without breeches, not knowing where to hide. Indeed everything lay open to arson and [everyone to] slaughter, arrest, incarceration and being clapped into irons. Meanwhile, the lieutenants of Fawkes [de Breauté], who was the captain of all those abominable soldiers who were mercilessly plundering the town of St. Albans and exterminating people, killed one of the abbot's leading servants, Robert Mai by name, on the eve of St. Vincent's day in the church of St. Albans and, having thrown many other citizens into chains, they either took them away or, having devised tortures for their minds, impoverished them to a state of starvation. Among them, one person was boiled alive by these devotees of crime so that his bladder swelled to the size of a gourd. Everywhere, therefore, there was misery and lamentation; everywhere was the sound of wailing and complaint. And so this Fawkes with his accomplices withdrew to their castles nearby, dragging with them numerous prisoners and burdened with various loot. At that time all the castles and indeed the towns, in the entire area, were dens of robbers and hiding-places of booty. This provoked the holy martyr Alban to take the sternest revenge for these injuries to him, and the angry martyr reserved this revenge until the Last Judgement, which made it more to be feared. This became very clear when the whole detestable troop of the aforesaid Fawkes were hanged at Bedford in their obstinate pride. And Fawkes himself, immediately afterwards, destitute and in exile, entangled with the fetters of multiple excommunication, died of sudden poisoning when glutted after dinner without the viaticum and confession, wretched and unworthy of pity.[1] Deservedly, he who had inflicted so many injuries on priests was deprived of the presence of a priest at his death.

Thomas, bishop of Down, invited by Abbot William, conferred orders in the church of St. Alban at the high altar on the thirteenth of the kalends of January [20 December]. The same bishop dedicated the conventual cemetery at St. Albans in which the bodies of the faithful were buried during the interdict on the eleventh of the kalends of January [22 December]; he dedicated St. Peter's cemetery, in the town of St. Albans, on the seventh of the kalends of January [26 December]; he dedicated the cemetery of St. Mary des Prés on the sixth day of the kalends of January [27 December]; and he dedicated the altar of St. Leonard on the fifth of the kalends of January [28 December].[2]

1. For his death in 1226 see Luard 1876:119.
2. A paragraph in the lower margin referring to an agreement of 1219 between the abbot and Hugh of Wells, bishop of Lincoln, is omitted here.

When peace is restored Abbot William goes to [the cell of] Tynemouth to make a visitation

According to the dispositions of He who ordains everything wisely and arranges everything agreeably, serenity returned to England after the storm and, after his father John's death, King Henry III was crowned. Peace was established throughout the whole kingdom, and the servants of God could breathe again in peace. But "There is no peace saith the lord, unto the wicked,"[1] and so, by the just judgement of God, the iniquitous and impious men disappeared in various ways like smoke. And so Abbot William, strong in body, in the flower of life, alert of mind, resolved to go to Tynemouth and his other cells for a visitation, to reform whatever needed reformation. And according to the usual custom in time of war, as mentioned above, having obtained permission from the king, he made his way northwards. When he visited the cell of Belvoir he heard confidential complaints about the prior of that house, Dom Roger Wendover, to the effect that he had wasted the property of the church in careless prodigality, following in everything the footsteps of his predecessor Master Ralph the Simple, who was held guilty by everyone of manifest negligence. Having been reproved by the abbot on this matter, the prior promised to put things completely right. However, the abbot, dissembling for the time being, took note of everything and bore it in mind.

When the affairs of that cell which needed reforming, both internal and external, had been put right, the abbot moved on and came to Tynemouth. The prior of that house and the leading men of the surrounding country went to meet and to welcome him in such numbers that it seemed as if an army had been assembled. They all wished him and the newly-arrived southerners joy at table that day, although in general it is said that the southerners and northerners have no sincere liking for each other. Then after he had arrived there in good shape, he received the homage of those bound by law to do it, and, to conclude briefly, having reformed the house with prudence and moderation both internally and externally like a pious father and a discreet pastor, he politely summoned his noble compatriots and parishioners to a feast at his table, to which, neither rebelling nor excusing themselves, they came in troops. Then, when everything was settled satisfactorily, the prior of that house, Dom Ralph Gubiun of blessed memory, feeling himself to be growing old and to be debilitated by old age, work and worries, came to the abbot and prostrating himself at his feet, said in tears "Now, oh lord, dismiss me, your son, in peace, absolving me from this care and solicitude, for my death is imminent and I am already weak. From now on I need leisure to devote myself to prayer so that I can be ready with tears and remorse for the death which I know and feel to be not far away." The abbot raised him up and warmly consoled him saying, "Endure patiently a little further, until I can make provision for the future".

Leaving there, he travelled round visiting other cells discreetly and modestly, for he was very well informed about everything which concerned the monastic order, until he came to the cell of Wymondham. There, when he made diligent enquiry concerning the state of internal and external affairs, he was told that their prior, namely Dom Ralph of Whitby, to the enormous injury of the house of Wymondham, had stocked his cell of Whitby, which he came from, and to which he hoped to return some time, from the belongings of the church of Wymondham which he had secretly pilfered. Because he came from other parts, he coveted other mens' goods, like a shepherd living under canvas who moves away to other pastures on the morrow. Moreover it was said that he had to a large extent won the favour of the earl of Arundel and his people, and had occasioned considerable losses to the church; and that he loved him more than either God or the abbot or any of his brother monks. The abbot took all this to heart until the time for retribution but, dissimulating at the time, he reprimanded him for such misdeeds and let him off in peace.

Then [the abbot] came to the cell of Hatfield, and when he enquired about affairs that needed investigation, great complaints arose about the prior, Alexander de Burgo, but, dissimulating, the abbot promised those who had made these complaints about him that correction would follow shortly and, when he reached home, he thought about the punishment of these misdeeds.

At that time Dom Ralph Gubiun came to St. Albans very much vexed about certain exactions of Simon of Tynemouth which had annoyed him; for he had demanded in perpetuity two monastic corrodies which had been given to the church [of Tynemouth] by one of the abbots of this church. He brought with him a burly pugilist named William Pigun because it had been legally determined that this case should be settled by judicial combat. Which was done, but our burly pugilist was defeated and our adversary Simon won the case. The prior, covered in confusion, was unwilling ever to return to his priorate but, deposing himself of his own free will and seeking to excuse himself in the chapter, he said to the abbot, "Lord, if you remember, you said to me at Tynemouth, 'Endure a little longer my son'. I have endured, my lord, but now I have had enough. Let me resign, because I am now an old man and furthermore I need some repose." But the abbot replied: "My son, you should talk like St. Martin, who said, 'Oh lord, if I am necessary for your people, I shall not refuse to work nor shall I plead the weakness of age.' You are necessary for the people, that is the convent committed to your care, nor are you as yet enfeebled or weak-minded on account of age; endure longer." But when the prior still insisted, tearfully, that he should be absolved, the abbot dismissed him in peace with the words "I release you". And for the rest of his life the abbot had him as a special adviser and companion.

1.   Isaiah 48:22.

Some priors having been recalled, others are substituted

Immediately after this, without any fuss, the prior of Wymondham, Ralph of Whitby, who had not made amends for his former excesses, as he should have done, was recalled. Coming to St. Albans, he politely though briefly paid his respects to the abbot and convent, thanking them for the honours and benefices they had bestowed on him. Then he went to the hermitage, or little cell, which had long since been made over to him by the house of Whitby. He found it well provided with all necessaries and, after he had lived a saintly life there for some years, he went the way of all flesh in that same place. Alexander de Burgo was recalled in a similar way; a fickle and deceitful person who, like an obstinate old man, did not know how to restrain his habits. He was prudently and unexpectedly recalled to the cloister to which he was by no means accustomed. In place of Roger Wendover, prior of Belvoir, the abbot substituted the cellarer Martin de Bodekesham; in place of Ralph of Whitby, prior of Wymondham, he appointed William de Feschamp, a man who was less discreet than he ought to have been. But, when he was rightly reproved by the earl of Arundel, the patron of that house, the abbot annulled that appointment and Thomas Medicus was substituted. It was he who had gone on pilgrimage to the Holy Land with that earl's father and who brought his body back from overseas and interred it reverently at Wymondham, after he had died in the Holy Land.[1] In place of Alexander de Burgo, prior of Hatfield, Richard de Brantefeld, the abbot's bearer, was substituted; in the place of Ralph Gubiun, prior of Tynemouth, Germanus was appointed, who came from those northern parts.[2]

I think it certainly worth recording on the great roll of everlasting thanksgivings that this abbot, among all the wars which we have described, prudently calmed down every schismatic tumult, both inside and outside the cloister and, afterwards, felicitously organising everything, he reduced everyone to his beck and call so that none dared murmur against him. He then began to have many ornaments made, wishing to make continual use of the sacrist, Master Walter of Colchester, while he was alive and flourishing, for we do not remember seeing his equal in all kinds of skills, nor do we believe anyone will equal him in the future.

1. William d'Aubigny, earl of Arundel, died abroad on 1 February 1221 and was succeeded by his son and heir of the same name, who died 1224. Powicke and Fryde 1961:415. See Luard 1876:67.
2. A paragraph in the lower margin referring to an agreement of 1219 between the abbot and Hugh of Wells, bishop of Lincoln, is omitted here.

Concerning the work carried out by the abbot for the adornment of the church

First he finished the dormitory properly, together with the privies attached to it which have been mentioned above, using oak for the beds; and he handed it over to the convent. Then, in his time, both transepts of the church were strengthened in the roof with oak beams well fixed and joined together; the old beams had been letting in a great deal of rain because they were eaten away by worms and rot.

Also the top of the tower, which he extended like a huge scaffold, much higher than the old one, which was threatened by ruin, was put together, constructed and heightened with the very best materials. All these were covered with lead, not without considerable expense. This indeed was achieved by the drive and industry of Richard of Tittenhanger, one of our lay brothers, who was chamberlain, without any diminution of or defect in his obedience [to his superiors]. However, out of respect, these works are ascribed to the abbot, for the person on whose authority a thing is known to have been done, may be taken to have done it. After the death of the above-mentioned Richard of blessed memory the abbot had the roof-covering removed from the tower because it had not been properly put on and, having added no small amount of lead, he had it redone better and more carefully, adding some ornamentation, namely eight straight pilasters, extending from the wall up to the dome, so that the tower really looked like an octagon. This was done at his own expense and on the persuasion and advice of Dom Matthew, then bearer and keeper of the seal, surnamed of Cambridge, who had been appointed proctor and prosecutor of that work and its diligent custodian. He altered the roof-covering in such a way that the corners protruded and these protrusions, which are popularly known as ridges, both wonderfully strengthened the tower and embellished it, and contained the rainwater better. Before that time, the eight sides, confused together, had a rounded, unadorned and less striking appearance and did not accord so well with the walls.

Abbot William, sympathetic and compassionate, took onto his own shoulders the task of finishing the work on the west front of the church, which had become ruined because he had prolonged the irksome delay to the work. In a short time he added to the old work, now properly covered with lead, a roof of select materials, timbers and beams, and panelled ceilings and glazed windows, all finished to a nicety. Also he had stone tracery and panes of glass fitted in the windows of the large wall above the place where the great ordinal lies, where also the shorter matins are usually sung, and the hours. Moreover, with the help of the custodian of the altar of St. Amphibalus, he completed the tracery and glass panes of several other windows in the north and south aisles of the church. Thus the church, illuminated with an advantageous new light, seemed to have been renovated. In his time also Master Walter of

Colchester, then sacrist, who was an incomparable painter and sculptor, constructed the screen in the middle of the church with its great cross, also Mary and John and other sculptures and suitable stonework, at the expense of the sacristy, but by the diligence of his own labour. Abbot William solemnly translated the shrine containing relics of the blessed Amphibalus and his companions from the place where it had first been set up alongside the high altar next to the shrine of St. Alban on the north side, to a place in the middle of the church which was enclosed with an iron grating; and he constructed a very handsome altar there with a superbly painted alter-piece and superaltar. This altar he had solemnly dedicated by John, bishop of Ardfert, in honour of the Holy Cross because it had been [the altar] of the Holy Cross before, and in honour of St. Amphibalus and his companions because their bodies rested there. And he caused the great cross with its figures, which was placed above this altar, to be dedicated by the same person.

After Abbot William had finished all this nicely he gave two gilded shrines in which originally, before Abbot Warin's time, relics of the blessed martyrs Amphibalus and his companions were placed, together with their contents, to their church at Redbourn, in honour of and reverence for that place, in which those holy martyrs had undergone their last agony. And he established a vigilent and diligent monk, who really merited such responsibility, as a perpetual custodian, to be present night and day beside the treasure deposited there. Afterwards, with the abbot's permission, the monk thus assigned there obtained an assistant, while things still needed to be done. Because of the manifest miracles which God celebrated openly there in honour of the said saints we believe that this honourable translation very much pleased him.

Concerning the altar of St. Wulfstan and his rib

In praise of this abbot, it should not be forgotten that when he attended the translation of St. Wulfstan, bishop and confessor, he obtained one of his ribs for us, by asking Bishop Silvester [of Worcester] for it. Later he enclosed it in a gilt shrine. In honour of this saint he constructed an altar near the altar of St. Oswin next to the old shrine, that is towards the east.

Concerning the ornamentation round the altar of St. Alban and the great beam

Furthermore I think it ought to be recalled to mind as an addition to the roll of merits of this abbot that he put some elegant structures up round the high altar, together with a beam on which the history of St. Alban was figured, which dominated the whole of that beautifully executed feature. This work was carried out in a most splendid fashion by Master Walter of Colchester, whom we have often mentioned already, not without laborious study and studious labour, the abbot however freely helping by meeting the considerable expense.

Concerning the six candles which are round the martyr's shrine

To light all this up, and in further honour of the martyr, Abbot William set up six candles, to be lit during the feasts which are celebrated in copes, especially the more important ones. To pay for them he assigned one monk, with the convent's agreement, from the house of Binham in lieu of some herrings which we used to receive from there annually.

Concerning the candles lit daily at the mass of Our Lady which is celebrated for the abbey church without music

Moreover in the time of this Abbot William two candles, to be lit daily, were established and means made available for their upkeep, through the foresight and provision of Dom Walter of Ramsey, who also increased the maundy money paid out to individual poor people. They were to burn while the mass of Our Lady was celebrated for the church, without music. This mass is always celebrated with a chalice of gold and special vestments and with four candles lit, of[1] which [the other] two, that is those on the east side, were provided by Adam the Cellarer. Some time later Miss Alice, the daughter of Henry Cocus, bequeathed a red silk chasuble, nicely worked with gold, to this altar.

1.   The rest of this paragraph is in the margin of the MS.

How Abbot William established a daily mass to be celebrated solemnly in our church with music, which was to be sung in perpetuity

This Abbot William of happy memory realised that in all the principal churches in England a mass of Our Lady with music is solemnly celebrated every day, although in our church, but not elsewhere, a commemoration of the blessed Virgin is solemnly held every Saturday in albs throughout the day and night, unless for some good reason. So he established and with the consent and goodwill of the whole convent ordained, that a solemn mass of the blessed Virgin should be celebrated daily with music in perpetuity. For this purpose he assigned groups of six monks to serve each day without fail in rotation, first one group, then another, and had their names inscribed on a board. Besides these he appointed one monk as steward and custodian of the altar and what belonged to it and to see to the office. So that this could be carried out conveniently he chose a suitable enough place [for this custodian], namely by the altar of St. Blaise in the south aisle of our church. And since the walls were everywhere crumbling and spoilt because of their ruinous state, this abbot, at his own expense, made good all the damage. Besides this he completed the tracery of two large glazed windows so that, to consummate his good works, everything would be agreeably illuminated and the church would seem to have been to a great extent restored. To carry out these works he appointed his bearer, Dom Matthew of Cambridge, who laudably completed them in a short time. We believe that the establishment of this new altar very much pleased God and his virgin mother, for afterwards it happily and unexpectedly received gifts in the form of various ornaments, gold and silver utensils, silk vestments and lamps. When the altar had been dedicated in honour of Mary the holy mother of God by Bishop John of Ardfert, the abbot, clothed in pontificals, solemnly celebrated the first mass there and, as if for a dowry, gave the altar a fine missal, with some other things which were needed for it.

The bell of the blessed Mary

He installed a most sonorous bell, specially assigned to the office of Our Lady and consecrated by Bishop John [of Ardfert], with the name 'St. Mary', to be pealed thrice a day at the right time to convoke those assigned to administer the mass, namely the six monks and the person in charge of the altar, together with other believers and persons devoted to the blessed Mary, to support them and to pray for the prosperity of the church and their own.

Concerning the superb image of Our Lady which Abbot William had made by Master Walter of Colchester

In Abbot William's praise it should be added that he presented to our church a most elegant figure of Our Lady which the oft-mentioned

Walter of Colchester had most carefully carved, and he had it consecrated by the Bishop John above-mentioned. The figure of Mary which
was formerly in the place where he installed the new one, he moved to
the altar where the mass of Our Lady was celebrated daily with music.
He also installed a candle, which we used to decorate with flowers, to be
burned day and night before this noble figure of Mary on principal feasts
and during the procession which was made at her commemoration.

Concerning the roof of the church on the south side, which is called the ceiling

Lest the eyes of people looking should be offended by the timbers or
beams, which age had blackened, Abbot William wonderfully beautified
the church above the figure of Mary with a ceiling of what is commonly
called panelling, with which he covered the beams. For a similar reason
he whitewashed a large part of the walls of the church, which had been
disfigured for ages by the squalor of dust so that, if he had finished what
he began, he would have happily renovated the ancient church with an
agreeable transformation.

Concerning the removal of the old beam

This Abbot William, just as he moved the old statue of Mary and
installed it unharmed elsewhere in the church, so also he moved the old
beam, which Adam the Cellarer had had made, from above the high altar
to the south side of the church next to the fine image of Mary, where he
set it high up, to the considerable embellishment of the church. On this
beam were figured the Twelve Patriarchs and the Twelve Apostles and,
in the centre, a [Christ in] Majesty with the Church and the Synagogue.
Similarly with the old cross which once stood in the centre of the church,
and the previous statue of Mary which stood on the altar of St. Blaise;
having substituted new ones he had them set up in the north of the
church for the edification and worldly consolation of the lay people and
all others coming there, lest the good things he had done should seem in
any way to be spoilt.

Concerning the chapel of St. Cuthbert which he constructed

It resounds to [Abbot William's] eternal blessing and remembrance
that, having demolished the old chapel of St. Cuthbert, the roof of

which, consumed by worms and with stuff falling off it, was threatened with ruin, he constructed an elegant new one of carved stone with its glass windows and other necessities. In it he built an altar and, when it was finished, he had it and the chapel dedicated by Bishop John in honour of St. Cuthbert, John the Baptist and St. Agnes the virgin and martyr. Whence the verse: "To the confessor of God Cuthbert, John the Baptist and the Virgin Agnes, to these three this altar is consecrated." This same Bishop John granted that anyone who came, devout and repentant, on the anniversary of the dedication of this chapel or on the feast of any one of these saints, would obtain twenty days' indulgence. This chapel made good the defects and small size of the dormitory because, in the space high above its ceiling, which is commonly called the vault, [the abbot installed] a room containing about twelve beds which was adequately lit by the light from a number of glazed windows. The roof, built of selected materials, was strengthened with a lead covering.

It should be known that the aforesaid Bishop John exercised his office everywhere in our diocese, especially in dedications, and he granted indulgences to Christ's faithful according to the solemnity [of the occasion] and the competence of his office.

The church of St. Amphibalus at Redbourn is dedicated, as well as several others in our diocese

Among other works of piety [this abbot] had the church of the blessed martyr Amphibalus and his companions solemnly dedicated in the presence of the abbot himself dressed in his pontificals by Bishop John, who granted forty days' indulgence. This was in honour of and out of reverence for the place where this same saint had been martyred with his companions. Dom Gilbert de Sisseverne was prior at that time. [The bishop dedicated] several other churches or chapels in our diocese.

Concerning the house in London which [the abbot] bought

To the perpetuation of his memory with blessings, this Abbot William, having paid out no small amount of money, bought a house in London which was as large as a palace, providing for himself and his successors as well as for those monks of our convent who go there to stay. For he and all his successors, and any monks who wished, could stay there in comfort and privacy. To this house, which he acquired for us, belonged a chapel, several bedrooms, an orchard, stables, a kitchen, a courtyard, a garden and a well; also the rents from some adjoining houses bordering the street, by which the courtyard was more securely enclosed. Abbot William had prudently built these houses after he had bought the principal house, and he assigned one of them in perpetuity to someone to serve the mansion itself.

Concerning the house at Yarmouth[1]

Having purchased this house in London for 100 marks and made additions which were estimated at 50 marks, the said Abbot William bought a house at Yarmouth for 50 marks in which to store fish, especially herrings, which had been bought at an opportune time, to the inestimable benefit and honour of the house of St. Alban. To this house too he made a costly addition.

1.   This paragraph is in the lower margin of the MS., but marked to be inserted here.

Concerning some wooden cloisters which the same abbot constructed

He also constructed various cloisters, one between the chapter house and St. Cuthbert's chapel, lest those crossing from one to the other be molested by water dripping onto them. Another cloister was three-sided; one side went from the kitchen to the door of the monks' cloister, which he assigned to the care of the cooks. Another extended from the doorway of the aforesaid cloister to the entrance to the guest-house which used to be the guest-house of visiting Benedictine monks, and it was assigned to the care of the guest-master. Another side of this cloister, that is the third, extended from the above-mentioned entrance to the doorway which leads to the tailor's workroom; and it was assigned to the chamberlain's care. The way to the infirmary led through another cloister, four-sided, which he commited to the infirmarer's care. All these he constructed soundly and competently of oak, with beams and rafters, and he roofed them with oak shingles. The three-sided cloister which extended from the kitchen to the doorway leading to the tailor's workshop he strengthened with a wicker fence so that free access to the space enclosed in the middle, which was a small

shrubbery, should not be offered to all. He decided that this shrubbery
should belong to the guest-master.

Concerning the cross of Jehoshaphat

Abbot William acquired for us the cross which Dom Laurence, who
was English and a monk of St. Mary's church in the Valley of
Jehoshaphat in the Holy Land near Jerusalem and to whose reliability
the patriarch of Jerusalem, his own abbot of Jehoshaphat, besides
Bishops Peter of Winchester and William of Exeter bore witness in
their letters patent, brought to England in the following way. When the
aforesaid monk Laurence, according to his abbot's instructions, took
over unhindered the deeds which had been deposited here for a long
time unharmed, he promised that, if his plan of obtaining the manor
and the church of Britwell, where he hoped to be prior, did not
materialise and he had to return home to Jehoshaphat with his business
unfinished, he would give this cross, the authenticity and sanctity of
which is evident to us, in perpetuity to us in return for the travelling
expenses we had given him, so that he could not be accused of
ingratitude for so great a benefit. The outcome of this affair is fully set
out in a detailed narrative at the end of this book.[1]

1. It is not however to be found there.

Concerning the arm of St. Jerome

Abbot William also acquired for us from the above-mentioned monk an
arm of St. Jerome, which he enclosed in superbly-made goldsmith's
work embellished with gems. This was carried round at special
festivities, and certain other relics were added, namely part of the
clothing and staff of St. Jerome and relics of the Holy Innocents.

Concerning the cross of St. Amphibalus

Abbot William also prudently obtained for us the cross of St. Amphibalus, which had stayed hidden for a long time in London. It had been
in the possession of many people, having been passed down from father
to son. This cross, surviving in such a way, ought to be looked after all

the more carefully because, as is stated in the *History of SS. Alban and Amphibalus*, it was smeared with the blood of St. Alban when he was beheaded, and it was the first to be brought into Britain.

Concerning the sequence which is sung at the commemoration of the blessed Alban

He also had a sequence composed for St. Alban and solemnly sung, after the ringing of two small bells, at the commemoration of the blessed Alban, our patron. And in the singing of the special feasts of that martyr he added to the final verse "Commend us to the all highest, etc." the words "Praise to him, jubilation, etc."

Concerning the sequence which is sung at the feast of the relics

In the same way he decided to have a sequence sung for the saints whose relics are preserved in this church, which was specially composed for this purpose. It comprised, first, the remembrance of the Holy Cross, and then, in order, those of the saints.

In his time the monks' shoes were changed from basan to cordwain

I must not omit to mention that, in the time of this Abbot William, among the other commendable things that he did, as a result of the industry and generosity of Richard of Tittenhanger, lay brother and chamberlain, of blessed memory, he courteously changed the monks' shoes which were made of cheap leather, commonly called basan, into *aluta*, that is cordwain. From this resulted a two-fold advantage; the convent was better shod and more alms were given to the poor.

Two other statutes, concerning services

This same Abbot William laid it down, not without considerations of propriety, that the private service for All Saints, which is daily, should be said in the choir unless an important feast celebrated in copes made this difficult. In this way it would be interrupted neither by the procession usually made in the commemoration of the blessed Mary, nor by those made before the high altar or any other altar. This is what used formerly to be done, and the procession brought the monks into view of the people and in contact with a crowd of both sexes, which seemed to him improper. The same abbot also laid it down that if a nocturnal service was held for any saint, prime, tierce, sexts and nones should be sung on the day following for that saint; for he had discovered that before then only nones for that feast day had been sung.

Concerning the books dutifully collected by him

Also, he placed a superb book, namely the *Historia scholastica*, with several other books and booklets, in the ambry. Prior Reimund, as mentioned above,[1] had arranged with the utmost diligence for the writing and completion to a nicety of this historical work. Also, he gave to the church of St. Amphibalus at Redbourn a very fine psalter bound with regal splendour, together with a splendid ordinal. He gave another psalter, of no less, indeed rather of greater, value, abundantly decorated with well-contrived skill, to the church of St. Mary at Wymondham, to be attached permanently to the reading desk in front of the high altar and the statue of Our Lady which stands on it, for the constant use of the brothers praying there, and as a perpetual memorial to the donor. This Abbot William, to acquire merit through works of piety, applied himself to many similar things, mention of which in this book is unnecessary, though they will be recorded in the balance sheet of divine judgement. He laid it down, also, so that the rule of St. Benedict should be inviolably observed, that whenever the convent was in copes or indeed there was an important feast, the monks should be refreshed once in the day, unless it happened to be a Sunday, between the feast of the Exaltation of the Holy Cross [14 September] and Easter, as stated in St. Benedict's rule which we profess. Moreover he decreed that, on the completion of the Lord's prayer, which is said at each one of the hours, the Kyrie eleison should be said thrice, the Christe eleison thrice, and the Kyrie eleison thrice – and not more often as had been done in the past.

This Abbot William undoubtedly gave so many lands and rents as a result of his own most diligent acquisition that they could not be recorded without prolixity in this book – indeed they would require a separate treatise. If, however, anyone wants to know about them he should look in the oaken casket, which is kept inside the large chest of deeds, in which are contained the muniments acquired in particular by his industry, and inside the lid of which they are listed.

1. On p. 25.

Concerning the incalcuable losses which this abbot sustained for the safe state of the church

It indubitably redounds to the praise of Abbot William that, at the time of the interdict, he looked after his convent and all the lands of St. Albans in a peaceful and prosperous state, both in spiritual and temporal matters. And, leaving aside, for the sake of brevity, other hardships, which it would be difficult for us to write down or describe in detail, we can bear witness categorically to the loss he sustained in the course of a single year, for, in the time of King John – a greater tyrant than whom has never appeared among those born of women – during the interdict, on various counts [the king] truculently extorted from [the abbot] 1,000 marks in a single year. What follows are losses which he sustained during wartime, continuously, without any breathing-space, at the hands of many sons of perdition who were always prompt and ready to burn and plunder, in order that he might enjoy the protection of peace or at least of a truce at one time from these, at another from those. Nor need we keep silent the fact that Abbot William wrote out the original [description of these losses] with his own hand.

The damages which happened to the church of St. Alban during the war

During the war, not without the greatest expense and trouble, he maintained everything entrusted to his care, both spiritual and temporal, in peace and without destruction, [but only] by means of ransom payments: At Berkhamstead, £100; to Fawkes, £100 at Wancre; to the same, another £100; to Louis, at Dover, 60 marks; to the earl of Winchester and the barons, 50 marks at London; to Louis again, 50 marks in the church of St. Paul, London; to Ingelard, for Rickmansworth, 60 marks; again, to the same Ingelard, for Watford and its dependencies, £100 and a palfrey worth 10 marks; to the same again, for the town of St. Albans, 100 marks; to Louis again, by the hand of Baldwin de Turboyle, 200 marks; to the same Louis again, for respite from pillage and arson and from doing homage to him 80 marks; to Walter de Goddardvilla, 50 marks and a silver cup and to William de Goddardvilla a palfrey worth 5 marks; to Robert de la Mare, 14 marks for Sandridge; to the same again, 100 shillings over Walden; to Thomas de Blankmuster, 30 marks; for Ralph, son of Adam of Hexton, 13 marks; to Robert de la Mare, for Winslow, 14 marks at Oxford. Payments in horses and cattle, besides pigs, sheep and hens, for the manors and other things, 100 marks; not counting irretrievable damage due to the felling of trees.

Concerning the chamberlain's losses

When King John came to Redbourn this was the cost to the chamberlain: he lost three good horses and two asses and one good new cart with iron-bound wheels. These came to at least 50 shillings, besides other losses amounting to 60 shillings. Also, when Fawkes came to Langley, in the burning of three houses and 35 pigs, the cost of which came to £10. Also, the same chamberlain lost five horses and various things not easily valued, so that the total was estimated at £6 or more; also, for his plough, 10 shillings. Again, in the time of the chamberlain Richard, one mark. Also, when the marshal of France came, he lost 24 horses, and oxen, pigs and other things to the value of at least 40 marks. Again, at Winslow he lost seven horses and cows, sheep, geese, hens to the value of at least 10 marks; so that the chamberlain's total losses amounted to at least £58.

Concerning the losses of the other obedientaries, that is the sacrist, the almoner and others, because it would be tedious and difficult to relate them, we leave them to be understood through what has been said. But in his time the total of money lost and of ransoms paid during the war [to protect] Abbot William and his mens' manors, and those of Dom Martin the cellarer and Walter, was £2,555.

Concerning the kitchen

Losses at Easton, £47-2-7d; total losses of the men of Tydelnestre, £24-4s; total losses at Shephall, £48-16s; total losses of the men of Apes, £15-3s; total losses of the men of Rokemestude, £160 and £11.

A *certain laudable deed of Abbot William[1]*

It is recognised as being to Abbot William's credit that, when Master Hugo, an Italian, forcibly obtained the church of Hartburn through being intruded by the Roman curia, warned by his conscience, which he felt gravely troubled, he came in tears to Abbot William and said to him: "Lord, I have obtained possession of your church illegally, because it is in your gift. Alas! With an uneasy mind I have rashly received its produce for several years. Therefore, holy father, I resign it into your hands." The abbot, compassionate and merciful, replied, "Never have I found such conscientiousness in anyone beyond the Alps; I accept it." But after half-an-hour in silence, the abbot, relying on the advice of no one save the Holy Spirit, and recalling how blessed Thomas the Martyr resigned the archbishopric of Canterbury into the hands of the pope since he had obtained it through the imperious demands of King Henry, but deserved to be canonically instituted again, having summoned Hugo, said, "And I, out of charity, return it to you, so that your conscience may be serene". This same Hugo, accepting it with thanks, lived very devoutly for many years. When the pope heard about this, with his cardinals he very much praised the [abbot's] deed, but declined to emulate it.

1.   This paragraph and the two following are in the margin of the MS. There follows at this point in the MS. some documentary material which has been omitted here.

Concerning *lightning in the town of St. Albans*

In this Abbot William's time lightning struck the house of Simon the son of Alwin in the town of St. Albans on St. Germanus's day [31 July]. It twisted and shook the door-posts and smashed them in pieces and burned the whole house.

Concerning *lightning which struck the church of St. Alban*

In the time of this Abbot William lightning struck the church above the treasury on the upper roof. Part of the woodwork was burnt after it had penetrated and melted the lead. Fortunately a tub full of water was standing there, which had been placed there to collect the water dripping from a leak, and the fire which threatened to burn the whole church was extinguished with this water. This happened on St. Valentine's day [14 February].

Concerning the death of Abbot William

This Abbot William, whose negligences and faults we are not mentioning as we have done those of the others because they are nothing when compared to his benefactions, and are not worth considering, passed from this world in the year of Our Lord 1235 on St. Matthias's day [24 February], after he had ruled his church for twenty years and nearly three months. He was buried on the third of the kalends of March [27 February] by the abbot of Waltham. This done, three brothers were immediately sent to the king so that, having obtained from him the power to proceed to an election in the usual way, they could elect an abbot, and, so that they could keep the house in their hands without interference [during the vacancy], apart from escheats and collations to churches, they gave the king 300 marks.[1]

1. There is a break in the MS. at this point, British Library Cotton MS. Nero D 1, f. 63b. What follows, on the next leaf, was evidently written by Matthew Paris at a later date.

John, the twenty-third [abbot]

John II succeeded this man as abbot. He came from Hertford and was promoted by Abbot William first to be sacrist in the cell there, and afterward to be prior. He was a gentle and kindly man, elegant in body, sociable with his brother-monks, and amiable towards everyone else. Legitimately born, from mediocre but praiseworthy and genteel stock, and progressing from virtue to virtue, he deserved to be honoured with the gift of glittering fame and so, through his merits, he was deservedly and justly promoted to be abbot without the opposition of anyone. Because he was the first abbot created after the [Fourth] general Lateran Council celebrated by Pope Innocent III, in which it was laid down that abbots of exempt monasteries[1] should be confirmed by the pope himself, and because some twenty years had elapsed since then during which time his predecessor William had lived in prosperity, it is hardly surprising that everyone was uncertain how to proceed with and accomplish this business [of his election]. And so, having summoned the prior of Dunstable Richard de Mores, and Thomas of Tynemouth a canon of Merton, to advise the convent, both of them solemn masters who, having fully mastered logic, had lectured at Bologna and elsewhere on the decrees of Roman and canon law, together with Master Stephen de Eglefeld and Master Robert of Kingham our clerics, and the older and wiser monks of the convent, they proceeded with care and deliberation in this arduous business, and all the more cautiously in order to instruct their successors facing a similar situation. And because we had at that time some discreet men, skilled in the law, prepared to undertake difficult affairs, and loyal and friendly towards us, to whom we entrusted the conduct of our affairs and our secret deliberations, we are prompted to place the progress of affairs on permanent written record. Immediately, therefore, after the death of Abbot William and the election of the next abbot, namely John, letters were drawn up to send to the lord pope and the lord king and others.

However, in order not to pass by the ceremony of the burial of Abbot William, we shall insert an account of it here, even though it interrupts the narrative to some extent, so that the reader may be informed about the burial of the abbots as well as about the way they are elected.

The body, which lay in the abbot's chamber were he had died at about the ninth hour, was stripped and washed and, if he had not shaved the day before, his tonsure and beard would certainly have to be shaved. Then some, but by no means all, of the more senior and prudent monks and a single secular servant, namely the sacrist's assistant, who was to undertake the task of anatomist, were admitted, and the body was opened with an incision from the trachea to the lower part. Everything found in it was placed, sprinkled with salt, in a cask, which was reverently interred in the cemetery with blessings and psalms not far from the altar of St. Stephen. Here, in due process of time, a small marble tomb was put up. The body was washed and soaked inside with vinegar, a great deal of salt was sprinkled into it, and it was sewn up. This was done with care and prudence lest the body, which had to be kept for three or more days, should give off an offensive smell and occasion some unpleasantness to those handling it when it was buried. By this time, not without the admiration of many, the body was so clean and spruce, and the face so rubicund and unblemished, that to many it seemed pleasant and desirable to touch it with their hands and carry it on their shoulders like some saint. And so you would see some of the brothers grieving, wringing their hands, weeping, lamenting, and gently and tenderly kissing his vivid face while embracing him with both hands; for he looked as if he was asleep, rather than dead. While alive he had shown himself amiable to all; in death the abbot invited his monks, the father his sons, the shepherd his flock, to tender kisses and embraces.

Next the body was carried from the room which is called the abbot's chamber, where he had died, to the infirmary. There it was arrayed in pontificals; the mitre placed on the head; gloves on the hands, with the ring; the customary crosier under the right arm; the hands crossed; and sandals properly fitted to the foot. Then the cover of the shrine was taken off and the body placed on it and carefully secured with strips of cloth lest it should fall off while being carried. It was brought out from the wash-place where these things had been done, in front of the entrance to the infirmary, and put down like the bodies of other dead people. While it was in this place the usual collects were said for him, as for any other deceased brother, together with the seven penitential psalms and everything which should be said according to the usual pratice while the body was being adorned as described above.

The body was carried into the church, while a bell was solemnly peeled, and the convent followed it singing the customary psalms. There, in sight of the entire convent and anyone else who was present, the abbot's seal was broken with a hammer on a stone step in front of the high altar, so that all the embossing, that is the image and the lettering, was effaced. From then on there was no lack of solemn and assiduous psalmody, by night and by day; and solemn mass [was celebrated] daily at the high altar as is the custom for a deceased brother, in albs at prime and in copes for those in the choir, with numerous candles lit. This continued till the day of his reverent obsequies. Anyone who wished to enter the presbytery in daytime to view the corpse was allowed to do so. Nor have we ever seen a dead person appear more comely. Indeed, strange to say, we never saw this man more beautiful when he was alive and in good health. Because of this, those who inspected the beauty and cleanliness of this body were of the opinion, and truly affirmed, that this angelic person belonged to the fraternity of angels since the passage of his soul was so easy.

Meanwhile, a lengthy distribution of alms to the poor was made, while everyone groaned over the loss of such a great and good shepherd of souls and bodies, and the monks' sighs resounded on high because they had been deprived of an upholder of the monastic order and the ecclesiastical office. For he used, when he returned from a journey, to admit all the poor people at the gates, in order to feed them, and he attended every day, even on weekdays, the services held in the chapter and high mass, and by his energetic singing he incited everyone to do the same more readily. Moreover, on feast days, even minor ones of twelve lessons, he attended vespers, and compline every day. Matins, moreover, of twelve lessons, he attended unfailingly, to read his lesson and sing the responses; to begin the "We praise thee o Lord"; and to stand up at the right time with those standing so as to animate the entire choir with his enthusiastic example. He[2] also always attended, mitred, the mass which is sung in commemoration of the blessed Virgin, in the middle of the choir, and on important feasts he invariably celebrated mass at the high altar; on solemn feast-days he was in the choir, mitred; and on other days, standing in his stall, he directed the choir and sang everything eagerly. When we were in albs or copes he sang the responses of the mass at the precentor's nod and he always attended the unction of the sick, which was carried out not far from his seat, about in the centre of the choir, as well as holding obsequies in person. We never saw him receive the professions of novices elsewhere than at the high altar, because of what is said in the profession, "In this monastery, which is . . . etc"; and this has been the true and just custom of this church since its foundation, and of all other monasteries. He was present at all processions, especially on Sundays. He never anticipated the convent's normal meal-time; he applied himself effectively to the needs of the fabric of the church and its works and adornment; he studied books, preached in the chapter, and commented wisely on the scriptures, both texts and glosses. Leading the way with reason, he was the teacher and instructor of everyone, even the old, in doubtful matters both concerning the custom of the order and divine services. In the arduous affairs of the church he was always outspoken and he helped greatly with wine and other things which concerned him; as well as being an eager and devout donor, he did much to obtain gifts from others. He was revered and venerated by all the powerful people of the kingdom and by the prelates, and was on friendly terms with them.

Bearing all this in mind, the brothers sang psalms and held private devotions and daily mass for the soul of this pastor, their sighs mixed with tears, though his body was still unburied. And we invited our special old friend Henry, abbot of Waltham, so that a holy man would not omit to come in a spirit of affection and neighbourliness for the burial of the body of a holy man. He, as a holy and devout person, came willingly if not gladly to such a pious office. So this abbot [of Waltham], adorned in his pontificals, buried the body similarly adorned, but with a substitute crosier, with great solemnity in the middle of the chapter house in the presence of the entire convent, robed. The usual benefits and injunctions were established for the soul of the deceased: an annual service started by the prior, with the psalm, "I cried unto God with my voice",[3] and a daily corrody or allowance, as is customary for deceased abbots. And this anniversary was to be provided for out of the acquisitions he had abundantly made when alive. While this was being done Brother Richard, the custodian of the church of St. Mary des Prés, came and demanded the granting of a perpetual corrody or allowance on behalf of the abbot ['s soul] for the leprous women who lived there, according to the tenor of the charter of Abbot Warin who was the founder of that house. For indeed it had been laid down by him that, from the time of Abbot Geoffrey, on the death of every abbot up to the thirteenth, allowances for the redemption of their souls should be granted to these leprous women both on behalf of the abbots already dead and those who would die in the future. Since Abbots Geoffrey, Ralph, Robert, Simon, Warin and John had died and William was now deceased, the seventh corrody or allowance was due and was conceded without difficulty. Besides which it should be known that Adam the Cellarer still has a perpetual corrody or pension from this house, which is enjoyed by a female recluse of St. Michael's.

Returning however to the continuation of the matter in hand, concerning the election and the method of election, because we were unaccustomed to starting and continuing such an affair, I shall treat it more fully for the benefit of those coming afterwards.

Abbot William died, as we stated above, on the blessed apostle Matthias's day [24 February], at the ninth hour, after he had ruled St. Alban's church vigorously and firmly sustained the monastic order for twenty years and almost three months, and he was buried in the chapter house on the third of the kalends of March [27 February]. On that very same day three brothers were sent to the lord king so that, having obtained from him permission to proceed to an election freely in the usual way, they could elect an abbot, and God's flock would not suffer damage for too long. And so with the help of the blessed martyr, for whose aid the convent processed daily in bare feet in front of his shrine singing the seven penitential psalms and, kneeling down, said the collects for this devoutly and earnestly, the above-mentioned brothers obtained from the lord king, besides the licence to proceed to an election, the favour of keeping their house in their own hands, apart from escheats and collations to churches, from the day of the abbot's death for a whole year; but they had to pay 300 marks privately for this concession. Within this period St. Julian's church happened to fall vacant and Master Nicholas was appointed on the royal authority.

When these brothers, returning from court, reported this to the convent, the monks were pleased that they were not to be snared in the nets of the royal satellites. But there was a certain knight, by name Adam FitzWilliam, wealthy indeed but desiring to be wealthier, the lord of Hatfield which is not far from Sandridge, who was at that time the king's escheator. Wholly ignorant at the time of the above-mentioned royal grant, he hastened to St. Albans, dragging with him a great mob of his ruffians, whom he planned to appoint to all the offices of the house of St. Alban, after expelling the existing officers. But, when he inspected the royal letters which certified him of the truth of the above-mentioned affair, he who had arrived with a pompous bellowing departed sad and silent, as if struck by the hammer of contradiction. I have inserted this so that posterity knows how great a misery and servitude it is to be subject to the whims of such satellites, who, though they are believed to be loyally serving the king, greedily seek after their emoluments by fair means or foul. Indeed we know, from what followed, what great damage that deceiver, though a neighbour known and familiar to us, strove repeatedly to inflict on this church.

When this business was for the time being prudently completed we turned our attention to the election, and because the noble members of our church, namely the priors of the cells, who ought to take part, were remote and dispersed, we arranged for them, and all those who should be and wished to be present at the election, to be summoned. We expected to be able to discuss what was to be done more securely because of the letters we had obtained from the lord king, as mentioned above, both those permitting us to proceed to the election and those allowing us to retain the abbey in our own hands.[4]

1. That is, monasteries exempted from the jurisdiction of the local bishop by papal privilege.
2. From here to the end of the paragraph is in the margin of the MS.
3. Psalm 77.
4. The texts of a number of letters have been omitted here and below.

On the progress of the election

The brothers therefore having been assembled on the day laid down beforehand, namely the Sunday, we were unable, because of that day's solemnity, to undertake the election, for we celebrated the feast of the Annunciation on that day, putting off the Sunday services till the next day, so that we were also unable then, that is on the Monday, to tackle so difficult a business, which demanded so much careful discussion. On the Tuesday, therefore, when the priors and others who should have been and wanted to be present in the chapter house were assembled together, they solemnly elected John of Hertford, prior of Hertford, one of the monks of the convent, as pastor of their souls, a pious man and an ordained monk. Presented to the lord king on Palm Sunday, he was accepted with favour by him both because of his elegant and venerable person and because [the king] had heard that he had been civil, sociable and generous while he was prior of Hertford; all the more readily, too, because the king had always been fond of the house of St. Alban.

Immediately after this two brother monks of this church, Dom Reginald of Bocking, a physician, and Dom Nicholas of St. Albans, and one of our clerics, Master Geoffrey of Langley, were sent to the Roman curia to seek confirmation of the election, duly carried out, from the apostolic see. They set out for that place with the support of the convent's prayers, and it was resolved in chapter to institute for them certain special intercessions of masses and prayers. When they reached the Roman curia, which was then at Perugia, they offered a sum of money at the papal feet in order to obtain the lord pope's favour more promptly. This was at once gratefully accepted and the lord pope ordered a certain brother Minor, his treasurer and chamberlain, to take the money to his treasury. This friar, having added the money to other silver sterlings, would not even open the chest for them, nor did the pope, who should be polite and generous, invite them to a snack. After tipping the janitors and papal servants, which had to be done, for they gaped after gifts with open jaws, they withdrew; ready to return, as they had been advised, on the morrow. When they arrived then and showed the lord pope the royal letters, they obtained the favour of that venal court, both because of the letters and because of their gift of the previous evening. The other letters, which they had brought to friends of the lord king, also helped to some extent: they had taken care of these friends of the king with some very costly presents, for they would have thought little of letters alone, sterile and fruitless, without gifts to go with them. Once the election had been confirmed they returned joyfully with the apostolic benediction, which had cost them enough, nor ever afterwards were they able to like or commend the curia.

The form of the election and the whole prosecution of the affair was much admired by the lord pope and by all the cardinals, especially by Lord Otto, who spoke very favourably of the house of St. Alban. Everyone admired the fact that, among so many voices, there was such a rapid decision and such complete agreement. The above-mentioned Otto added in front of the pope and everyone seated round: "My lord, religion, unity and concord have always flourished in that house." Everyone said that this affair had not been accomplished without the intervention of the Holy Spirit, "For the multitude of them that believed were of one heart and of one soul."[1] And so that it should not remain unknown to those listening, here is the method of electing an abbot at St. Albans.

1.   Acts 4:32.

The procedure in the church of St. Alban for electing the abbot

Three or four confessors are strictly required, by the power of the Holy Spirit which knows the hearts and souls of individuals, to choose twelve experienced and loyal brothers, of the convent, so that they can elect as abbot a suitable person, either from among their own number or from the convent or from the cells. I say "from among their own number", though this was not the custom long ago, when it had to be someone other than one of themselves, which was illogical and absurd. On this point the old custom has been changed for the better. In order to ensure that the election, and the effort of so much deliberation in this affair, should in no way be ineffective or void, the [twelve electors] had letters from the convent, confirmed with the conventual seal, stating that the convent would willingly, unanimously and without any opposition or difficulty, accept as its pastor whoever the twelve elected as abbot. As above-mentioned, the orderly conduct of this affair was praised by the pope publicly in front of everyone, and [the election] was confirmed there after investigation by the apostolic authority. However, because the pope could not establish the [eligibility of] the abbot-elect's person, he charged the bishops of Ely [Hugh of Northwold] and London [Roger Niger] to make due enquiry into the person of the elect and then to consecrate him as abbot, instituting him fully in all his spiritual and temporal powers.

The charter of confirmation

To all the faithful in Christ seeing or hearing these letters, Hugh, by the grace of God bishop of Ely, eternal greetings in the Lord. Let it be known to you that when we and our venerable brother the bishop of London were charged by the lord pope with the examination and confirmation of the person of Brother John of Hertford, the abbot-elect of the monastery of St. Albans, the bishop of London excused himself from the affair. We therefore confirm this John as follows: in the name of the Father, the Son, and the Holy Spirit. Having examined according to the terms of the lord pope's letters the matters concerning the elect of St. Alban's person which had to be enquired about, both by sworn witnesses and by an examination of his own person, we have found him suitable for the rule of the said abbey. So we confirm his election with apostolic authority. In testimony to this we have appended our seal to these our letters patent. Done in the year of our Lord 1235, on Monday next after the feast of St. Laurence [13 August] at Royston.

The profession

On the morrow, therefore, of the nativity of the blessed Virgin [9 September], in the church of St. Alban, the same bishop consecrated the said abbot-elect at the high altar in the presence of the bishop of London and the entire convent assembled in the choir. The letters and bulls of the lord pope were opened which the elect, at the time of his consecration as abbot, had to read out in public, as follows:

> I John, abbot of the monastery of St. Albans, shall from this time on be loyal and obedient to St. Peter and to the holy and apostolic Roman church and to my lord Pope Gregory and his canonical successors. I shall neither in counsel nor in consent, nor in deed, be party to their lives being taken, or their losing a limb, or to their unlawful arrest. I shall never knowingly make known to anyone, to their damage, advice which may be entrusted to me through them or through their messengers or by letter. I shall assist them to retain and defend the Roman papacy and the possessions of St. Peter, saving my order, against all men. I shall treat the papal legates, going to and fro, honourably, and help them with their necessities. Summoned to a council, I shall go unless prevented by some canonical hindrance. Every third year I shall visit the papal curia either in person or through my deputy, unless absolved by apostolic permission. I shall neither sell the possessions of my monastery, nor shall I give them away, nor shall I mortgage them, nor alienate them in any other way, without consulting the Roman pontiff. So help me God and these holy gospels.

The contents of this statement were kept secret, closed by the seal until the abbot stood in his pontificals at the high altar, so that he could in no way escape from these obligations. When the abbot asked the bishop of London, Roger, what he should do in Rome, the bishop, being a jocular fellow, replied jokingly, and said with a smile, "Friend you should make offerings"; and there was truth in this statement.

The abbot is created

From then on the abbot, fully established, received homages and oaths and the loyalty of all the abbey's subjects and he was installed and accepted in everything. But we have been led to insert what follows so that ordinary people should not remain unaware of how he conducted himself when he was elected and how he should behave while abbot-elect.

How the abbot-elect ought to conduct himself

After the electors have named the person elected by his own name, adding something to the effect that one of the electors is speaking for all of them, and the assent of the prior and the whole convent has been expressed, the elect should get up and, accepting the dignity, ask everyone to pray on his behalf that God will allow him to undertake this responsibility and office in such a way as to redound to the honour of God and the church, and to facilitate the salvation of his soul. When the prior has finished a prayer to this effect and the convent has responded at the end with an 'Amen', the hymn "We praise thee o Lord" should be solemnly begun and the abbot-elect should be led modestly and in an orderly fashion into the church, supported by the prior on one side and the subprior on the other and with other worthy persons near him. He should be presented to God and to the holy martyr Alban at the high altar with candles burning round it and the shrine uncovered, to the peal of bells, with the clock chiming, and the sound of pipes, which we call drones. Prostrating himself completely, the elect should pray briefly but whole-heartedly that he will be worthy of such an honour. Then, at the touch of a small bell, which is called a *muta* or *scilla*, the noise and the whole tumult should cease and the "Our Father" be said by all. Then the prior says the "And lead us not" verse; also "My God, save thy servant. Send him help oh Lord from the Holy Place and from Sion protect him. The Lord be with you" and the rest, with the prayer: "Almighty and everlasting God, direct this thy servant into the way of everlasting salvation so that, by thy grace, he may both desire those things that are pleasing to thee, and perform them with all his strength, through our Lord Jesus Christ thy Son who lives with thee". And he shall respond . . . "The Lord be with thee" and "Let us bless the Lord". Then he should get up and, without any diversion or delay, be led into the prior's chamber, which ought to be called his while he is abbot-elect, until having become abbot, he withdraws to his own great chamber. Nor should any cleric, worthy or unworthy, or anyone else, be concealed so as to rush up immediately after the abbot-elect rises from his prayer demanding to become a monk or to receive the necessaries of life while he lived. This used to be done at one time as a good omen of the abbot's future liberality, but it is dishonest and an infringement of St. Benedict's rule. For it said, "Try the spirits whether they are of God",[1] as if to say, "Nothing should be done abruptly without care and deliberation. Nor should an inexperienced person be received into the congregation".

From this time onwards the elect can provide himself with companions to remain with him, whom we call bearers; he can send messengers to Rome; and he can invite whom he pleases to eat with him. But those who are invited shall come by permission of the prior; nor shall any horse go out without the prior's permission, except for the sumpter-horses of his officials, namely those of the cellarer, cook, chamberlain, infirmarer and sacrist. Even if he was one of the most recent novices, the elect shall take the highest place forthwith. If he was on the prior's side, which we call the prior's choir, he shall transfer to the abbot's choir, where he shall have the most honourable place. In the refectory he shall eat alone and supreme, with a loaf of special (wastel) bread, the prior eating at the high table, which we commonly call the dais. In processions he shall be first in the abbot's section as senior to all the other monks, not in the middle holding a crosier, where he used to be in the past, lest by chance afterwards, if his election were quashed, he had to go back, for then he would have had to "begin with shame to take the lowest place".[2] But these things have been touched on already. Let us return from this diversion to the matter in hand, which is about the deeds of the abbots.

1. 1 John 1:4.
2. Luke 14:9.

The deeds of the aforesaid abbot begin here

This second Abbot John, who came from Hertford and had been prior there, was thought by everyone to have been made abbot by God's will. He was the first who, sadly and unwillingly, suffered the yoke of servitude to the Romans for, as mentioned in that crafty profession of his, he had to visit the papal court every three years either in person or by proctor, to the great injury and damage of the church [of St. Alban] and to the arbitrary and injurious emolument of the insatiable Roman curia. He was indeed the first abbot created after the Fourth general Lateran Council held under Pope Innocent III at which that rule was promulgated, along with other matters prejudicial, and if one may say so, damaging and harmful, to the church of St. Alban, which is described as having been noble and free since its very first foundation. This abbot was troubled at first with many exactions and expenses but he was molested, above all, by the new and unheard of oppressions of the Romans for, though its ancient privileges, which cannot be infringed or disregarded without occasioning great injury and contempt of the holy fathers, stood in the way, this celebrated church was not allowed to enjoy its liberties. As a sinister presage of this thing, shortly before this abbot's creation and immediately afterwards, namely within three years, lightning struck the church of the blessed Alban twice, setting it on fire. Nobody remembered seeing this happen and nobody had heard of it happening before. And, just as it is no use relying on privileges and indulgences of the saints, so the impression of the papal seal, in which the lamb of God is figured, which is placed at the top of our tower, did not prevent the lightning, though it is said to have the virtue and power to ward off such commotions. Similarly, as a sad prognostic it happened in our time that the holy eucharist, with its precious vessels of jewelled gold and silver, was twice removed by the most infamous theft.

At the time of his creation, this Abbot John gave a cope of red satin, nicely fringed with gold, and a silver-gilt cup, extremely precious both in craftsmanship and material, which he made over to the refectory. Moreover, he built a most noble hall for the use of guests, with several bedrooms adjoining it. This was superbly decorated, with rooms and a fireplace, an entrance hall and an undercroft, so that, because it was two-storied and with an undercroft it could be called a royal palace. It had a very fine entrance hall which is called a portico or oriel, and several very fine apartments, with their bedrooms and fireplaces, for the decent maintenance of the guests. The hall which had been originally built on this spot was ugly and gloomy and had become ruinous, with old and crumbling walls. Moreover, it had been patched and covered with tiles and shingles. The new hall, of which we are speaking at the moment, together with its chapels and appurtenances, he roofed over very well with lead, and, with its adjoining room, he had it superbly painted and delightfully decorated by the hand of Dom Richard, a very fine craftsman and one of our monks. This abbot also constructed, opposite the main gateway, a fine and long stone building, with a tiled roof, containing three rooms. By its appearance and position it beautified the entire courtyard. This building had two floors: the upper was very convenient for the use of the abbot's senior servants; the lower for a store.

Moreover, in the time of this abbot, Stanmore, which is known to have been among the ancient possessions of the church but had been alienated for a long time by the idleness of his predecessors, was prudently recovered. The abbot built a manor there, with a very fine windmill. Furthermore, Abbot John fought vigorously to maintain the right of free warren which had been awarded to us at Hertford by the judges, though he had extremely powerful enemies, even to the extent of paying out 1,000 marks and more. He sustained the hostile oppressions of several powerful people, above all Ralph Cheinduit II, who by a premature death, as he himself at the end admitted, experienced the manifest punishment of the avenging St. Alban, and Geoffrey of Childwick, whose persecutions were so much harder to bear because he was obliged to the aforesaid abbot by the bond of homage. This man, in order to do more harm to the church of St. Alban, whose defender and protector he ought to have been, married the sister of John Mansel, a special councillor and clerk of the lord king, who gave strength and protection to the aforesaid knight [Geoffrey of Childwick] so that the abbot sustained so many losses and such diverse injuries [at his hands], that they would need a separate, and lengthy, tract. Here we shall draw together a great deal into a small compass.

This Geoffrey of Childwick, animated and armed with the support of the said John Mansel, attacked his lord the abbot's servants and caused them to be attacked. Riding a costly horse, armed, with his accomplices, he and they frequently plundered our warren, where he had no right to be, and the royal highways, with their hunting dogs, bows, arrows and nets, provoking people with insults and infringing the king's peace. Nor could we ever obtain justice or revenge, thanks to the friendship and counsel of the king which the aforesaid John Mansel enjoyed. Indeed fear and persuasion of this John virtually stopped the mouths of all judges and advocates of the pleas, whom we call pleaders of the bench, so that Dom William, the then cellarer, a circumspect and eloquent man, had repeatedly to put his case in person to the judges, and indeed even to the king and barons. The judges secretly protested to the said Dom William, whispering into his ear that two people dominated the kingdom at that time, Earl Richard [of Cornwall], and John Mansel, and they did not dare give sentence against them.

One day it happened that this Geoffrey of Childwick met a certain servant of the lord abbot on the road which leads to St. Albans from the archdeacon's house at Bedford. This same servant, John by name, was bringing a gift of venison from the archdeacon. The said Geoffrey impudently attacked him, maintaining that he was a robber and a traitor to the lord king, and that he had thievingly taken the venison from the royal forest. He was of the private household of the lord king and one of his marshals and could not tolerate this with patience. After insulting him in this way he threw John from his horse, and took away the gift he was carrying and his horse, adding threats to his curses. Because of this he was fully and solemnly excommunicated by the abbot himself and all the convent, by all the chaplains of the lands of St. Albans, by the above-mentioned archdeacon and by all the chaplains of the entire archdeaconry; and again by the abbot and the whole convent, at their stations, in solemn processions, with candles lit, the bell pealed, stoles on the shrine, a cross, and the monks all wearing collars, to the effect that anyone who had attempted that iniquitous deed, or any other, to the prejudice or shame of St. Alban and his church, or the abbot and convent, would be entangled with the fetters of anathema.

Because of his iniquitous deed and infringement of the royal peace, the aforesaid knight Geoffrey was accused of breaking the peace by injuring John, the servant of the abbot, and stealing his belongings and, according to the laws of the land, he was summoned by royal writ, his defender John Mansel being either unaware or overruled. But afterwards the abbot was placated by repeated prayers and Geoffrey evaded the snares of that deadly peril through the dexterity of the above-mentioned John Mansel. For the king gladly interceded for him and for almost all the great men at his court. Having taken council therefore, lest by chance we should be accused of some irregularity we withdrew our accusation. However, later on, unmindful of his fief and fealty and with the encouragement of John Mansel, Geoffrey of Childwick acquired a charter from the king which infringed our ancient charters and liberties, namely allowing him right of warren on his lands, in breach of a royal charter for which we gave this same king no small sum of money. So we, as justice demanded, went on exercising our rights as we had done in the past in the warren which this Geoffrey said had been granted him by royal charter, even though it was within the boundaries of our warren. Because of this an action was brought before the king and by judgement of the king himself, encouraged by Bishop William of Salisbury, the abbot, persecuted by iniquitous justice, was thrown on the king's mercy. For the king, dissembling his crime of avarice, said that if he had granted to someone a manor belonging to one of his magnates, even unjustly, manifestly that person ought not to seize that manor from its true lord, until the matter had been argued in court, and he ought to come to terms with the king and have his right declared so that he could enter his manor more securely. The bishop bore witness to this iniquitous judgement and wounded his conscience in this affair, because, if this were allowed to stand, the king would be able forcibly to put in any lord he pleased on any excuse, and unless the true lord was able to repel the attacks of such an invader, he would be miserably disinherited. All this was machinated by Geoffrey of Child-wick, egged on by the royal councillor John Mansel.

Besides this, the said Geoffrey, when a dispute arose over the land of Newbury and a great deal of money had been expended and much trouble taken to obtain our rights, and the land had been completely purchased from the true lord and possessor and the deeds redeemed from the Jews, this Geoffrey induced us, by means of frauds and tricks which would take too long to enumerate, to let him have the land at the original rent. Moreover, while still a young man, he retained a corrody we had granted in return for possession of the land, to the inestimable loss of this church – for there was no limiting a youth's years of life. Because the aforementioned John Mansel came to St. Albans and his presence was helpful and he could look after our interests and because we considered that we could not continue measuring our strength with him, for to continue the dispute would be daily more damaging to us in these evil times, we resolved to come to terms; so the tempest was quietened for the time being.

In a similar way Ralph Cheinduit, who has been mentioned above, made the abbot swear an oath in person, to his shame and dishonour. But, as has been said, this Ralph received the fruits of his labours in the shape of sudden death. Concerning his death, since it is not fully explained in what precedes, we are led to inform the reader of this page without any taint of falsehood. After repeatedly adding injuries to injuries, when armed and riding a valuable horse which was armoured, and supported by a numerous contingent of armed men, he wickedly struck a certain monk of ours, a bearer of the abbot named Ralph of Dunham. He also rode and chased about with his dogs and huntsmen near our court at Derefold; which indeed the abbot and convent had been able to see and hear. He was firmly taken to court over this and one day in the royal palace at Westminster, laughing, he said derisively, "The monks of St. Albans have excommunicated me so much that I have become so heavy and fat that I can hardly get into my saddle." He certainly was heavy and robust and his whole body was built like a bull's for strength. In his pride, this man had hardly reached his house, which was a short day's journey from London, when he fell gravely ill and was soon on the point of death. Having therefore summoned with the utmost haste his special friend the abbot of Missenden, who reached him breathless on a very fast horse just in time, he was appointed the executor of his will, which was made when he was not as fit as he should have been. Dying however, he devoutly sought mercy from the blessed Alban, asked for pardon to be mercifully extended to him by the brothers whom he had in any way harmed, and earnestly desired that they should be fully satisfied from his estate. When the aforesaid abbot promised to do this, this same Ralph at last gave up the ghost. We indeed more or less received satisfaction in the course of time from those appointed executors of the will. The supreme judge knows the rest, from whom no secrets are hid.

*Concerning the persecutions which [Abbot John] sustained
in defence of the church's liberties and the
punishments which happened to the persecutors*

Adding to his merits, Abbot John patiently suffered the worst possible persecutions, losses and insults of these people, which are estimated to amount to a loss of 2,000 marks. But he conserved the church's liberties unharmed and maintained the customary standards of generosity and hospitality, internally and externally.

On the church of Norton

In the time of this abbot the church of Norton was granted to us. Its rector, Laurence the Clerk, resigned it with spontaneous devotion for the improvement of our beer and to provide supplies for the guests additional to what the abbot had been used to distributing.

On the church of Eglingham

Item the church of Eglingham, which Richard Marsh, bishop of Durham, had recently made over to us, in Abbot William's time, to improve our beer, was appropriated to us for our own use in the time of this abbot John. It was worth. . . .

On the church of Hartburn

And Bishop Walter of Durham gave the church of Hartburn to us in his time, except for the vicariate, which comprised a third part of the said church. The other two parts taken together were estimated at 153 marks. It was to be used to increase hospitality and especially to provide more provisions for guests, so that no one would be refused a sufficient, even copious, portion.

On the church of Hexton

Item, this Abbot John assigned the church of Hexton, which his predecessor Abbot William had acquired for his own use, to the celebration of his own and Abbot William's anniversary, under the administration of the sacrist. He had it dedicated by the bishop of Bangor, in the year of our Lord 1254. But he retained the church of Norton, which as mentioned above was assigned for providing fodder, in his own hands. For the two churches, namely those of Eglingham and Hartburn, the prior of Tynemouth offered 200 marks and 40 marks per annum, in the presence and hearing of the person who is writing this. The said prior frequently repeated this to me, the writer of this.

On St. Michael's church

Item in this abbot's time he ceded St. Michael's church in the town of St. Albans to us for our own use and, with the agreement of the abbot and convent, it was assigned to the use of the sacristy, which was poorly provided for.

Concerning the houses in London

He acquired a messuage for us, together with certain dilapidated houses in London, next door to the houses which his predecessor Abbot William had purchased. He constructed some noble new houses there and raised the rent.

Concerning the land and house which was John Astmur's

Item, he bought for us the land and houses which had been John Astmur's. In return for them, the abbot granted the necessities of life by charter to the said John as a member of his household.

On the repair of the mills

Moreover, this Abbot John admirably repaired with oak all the abbey's mills, with the buildings belonging to them, because they had fallen into disrepair through being farmed out a long time before. And because the stream, which had deserted our water-mill next to the brewery both on account of the reed-bed which drinks up the water and because of the summer droughts, was insufficient for the needs of the entire monastery, indeed meal had to be sought over seven miles away, which was expensive and annoying, the same Abbot John constructed an excellent horse-mill by the said brewery. In this construction and repair of mills over £100 is believed to have been spent.

The improvement of the beer

Moreover the aforesaid Abbot John generously improved our beer beyond measure, which, to our loss and shame, was weak, by setting aside for its improvement about a thousand loads of corn suitable for making beer, namely of mixed oats and barley, which is called *bresia*.

[Abbot John] was not a squanderer of [the church's] goods for the sake of relatives

From the time of his creation to the twentieth year of his abbacy [1255], when this page is being written by Brother Matthew Paris, who does not presume to lay down the law about the future, Abbot John never dissipated the possessions or goods of his church for the love or friendship of relatives, kinsmen or compatriots, which can truthfully be said of none, or at least few, of his predecessors.

[*The Chronica majora 1247*]

The lord king keeps Christmas at Winchester

In the year of our lord 1247, which is the thirty-first year of the reign of the lord king Henry III, he held his court at Winchester in the presence of many of the picked nobles of the kingdom. The bishop of Winchester welcomed him joyfully on this arrival there, earnestly entreating him to dine with him on the day after Christmas day in order that, by his so doing it would be made clear to all that his lord the king had entirely forgotten all his former offences and restored him to his former friendship. To the joy of the bishop, his request was acceded to and his wishes fulfilled.

Concerning the great council convoked at London on 2 February

At this time, because of a renewed urgent papal mandate concerning an intolerable contribution to which the bishops at the general council had unfortunately bound the clergy, the king, by his royal warrant, summoned his nobles, as well as the archdeacons of England, to London. They arrived there on the appointed day but the bishops all intentionally absented themselves, lest they should appear to be opposing their own acts, for they knew that the hearts of all were wounded to bitterness, not without cause.

Concerning a conspiracy of certain French nobles against the pope

While the stream of time flowed on, the devotion of the faithful grew lukewarm, and the feelings of filial affection, which every Christian ought to entertain towards our spiritual father, that is the lord pope, died away, wounded, not without peril to our souls; nay rather they were turned into execrable hatred and secret maledictions. For each and all saw, and seeing, felt, that the said pope was insatiably intent on money and the plunder of money, to the loss and impoverishment of many. Nor did many people any longer believe that he held that power granted from heaven to St. Peter, namely of binding and loosing, since he proved himself to be entirely dissimilar to St. Peter. So the mouths of evil speakers and contradictors were everywhere opened, especially in France, where indeed many nobles conspired against the pope and the Church, which we never remember to have happened before, as can be seen from the following document, written in French, which has come to our notice.

> To all those who shall see these letters, we whose seals are attached to this present writing, make known that we, by the faith of our bodies, have pledged and bound ourselves and our heirs in perpetuity to help each other and all those of our lands and of other lands who wish to be of our association, to pursue, demand and defend our rights and theirs in good faith against the clergy. And, since it would be difficult for us all to meet on this business, we have chosen by common assent and decision of us all, the duke of Burgundy, Count Peter of Brittany, the count of Angoulême and the count of St. Pol, so that if any member of our association has to pay a contribution to the clergy, he shall only pay what these four consider ought to be paid. And, it should be known that, in order to defend, pursue and demand the above-mentioned rights, each of us will subscribe by oath a hundredth part of the annual value of his land, and every well-off member of this association shall levy this money to the best of his ability at the Purification of Our Lady [2 February] and deliver it to the place assigned by letters of these four above-named or any two of them. But if anyone is put in the wrong and is unwilling to leave the matter to the above-mentioned four, the association will not help him. If any member of this association, to the knowledge of these four, is wrongfully excommunicated by the clergy, he will not abandon his case nor his rights either because of the excommunication or because of anything else done to him, except with the agreement of these four or any two or them, but shall pursue his right. If two of these four die or leave the country the two remaining will appoint two in their place with similar powers. If it happens that three or

four of them die or leave the country, the ten or twelve principal members of the association will choose four others with the same powers as the original four. If these four, or any member of the association by order of these four, transact any business for the association, the association will take responsibility for it.

Another execrable manifesto of these same conspirators against the clergy

The superstitious clergy, disregarding the fact that, by the warfare and bloodshed of certain people, in the time of Charlemagne and others, the kingdom of France was converted from the errors of the gentiles to the catholic faith, seduced us in the first place by the appearance of humility, opposing us like foxes out of the remains of those very castles which owed their foundation to us. They arrogated to themselves the jurisdiction of secular princes so that the sons of slaves judge free men and the sons of free men according to their laws, although they ought rather to be judged by us according to the laws of their former conquerors. Nor should any detraction be made, by new decrees, from the customs of our ancestors. Otherwise they would place us in a worse condition than God wished even the gentiles to be in, when he said, "Render unto Caesar the things that are Caesar's and unto God the things that are God's."[1] Therefore all of us, chief men of the kingdom, clearly perceiving that the kingdom was neither acquired by written law nor by the arrogance of clerks, but by the sweat of war, by this present decree on the oath of all, we constitute and ordain that no cleric or layman shall henceforth drag anyone before a judge ordinary or delegate, except in a case of heresy, matrimony or usury, the loss of all their goods and the mutilation of one of their limbs awaiting any transgressors. Certain people will be deputed by us to be our agents in this matter so that, with our jurisdiction restored, we can breathe again, and those who have hitherto grown rich by our impoverishment, whose profane struggles the Lord has chosen to disclose on account of their pride, may be brought back to their condition in the early Church and by living in contemplation, may, as becomes them, show to those of us leading the active life the miracles which have long since departed from the world.

When[2] the lord pope heard of this, he groaned with a troubled mind and, hoping to soften their hearts and weaken their firmness of purpose, having first warned them, he tried to alarm them with threats; but he found that this had no effect. He therefore bestowed numerous ecclesiastical benefices on many of their relatives, with licenses for holding several together and many indulgences, and he made presents to the nobles themselves, so that he recalled many from their above-mentioned presumption. Many, however, were frightened by the contents of a letter supposed to have been issued with the consent of [the emperor] Frederick, especially as the final clause of the letter agreed with the letter Frederick sent to many of the princes, at the end of which he says: "It has always been our intention and wish to induce the clerics of every order, especially the senior ones, to continue throughout their lives in the condition they were in in the primitive Church, leading an apostolic life and imitating our Lord's humility; for such clerics used to adore the angels and shine forth in miracles . . . etc."

1. Matthew 22:21.
2. This paragraph is in the margin.

Concerning the parliament held in London, at which complaint upon complaint was made of the pope's exactions

On 3 February the lord king held a careful deliberation with his magnates and prolonged the council, as it was about urgent matters, for several days. It was greatly feared, and had been reported as a fact to the king, that the French king was preparing to subjugate Gascony. To lose it would be shameful, ignominious and damaging, for the king used to receive a thousand marks annually from Bordeaux alone.

 . At the same time, as mentioned above, the archdeacons of England had assembled there together with a large part of the clergy and the nobles, complaining in common about the intolerable and frequent exactions of the lord pope, on account of which, even the lord king, who sympathised to some extent, was saddened. For the affair concerned the entire kingdom and endangered the state, and frightful and unheard of desolation threatened both clergy and people. A grievous complaint was therefore laid before the king, whose business it was to protect the commonwealth and avert such injuries and dangers. At length it was agreed by common consent that discreet messengers should be sent to the Roman curia to explain in detail to the pope the oppressions suffered by the country, and to deliver the following letters to the lord pope and the cardinals on behalf of the community of the clergy and people of the kingdom of England.

A letter sent from the community of England to the lord pope

To the most holy father in Christ and lord Innocent, by God's providence supreme pontiff, the community of the clergy and people of the province of Canterbury, devoted kisses to his holy feet. From the time when the catholic faith was first given to it the English church has endeavoured to please, and has always adhered to and devoutly served, God and the holy Roman church, without wavering from the obligations it has accepted and always profiting from the improvement of morals. It now casts itself at the feet of your holiness and entreats that, with regard to the demand for money which is required of it in various ways by command of your holiness for the assistance of divers nations, you in your goodness will deign to be merciful to it. For what is demanded is insufferable, and impossible because we cannot afford it. For although our country from time to time produces crops for the nourishment of its people, it does not produce an abundance of money; nor could it for a long time produce as much as is demanded now. Also it has in the past been oppressed by a similar burden, though not such a heavy one, for similar reasons, and it cannot in any way accept these demands. Moreover, by command of your holiness, a subvention has been asked from the clergy for our lord the king's secular needs, whom we ought not and cannot fail in his necessities, to enable him to ward off the incursions of enemies (may God avert them from us!), to defend the rights of his patrimony and to recover more promptly what has been seized from him. We therefore send the bearers of these letters to your holiness with our supplication, to explain to you the dangers and disadvantages which would ensue from the above-mentioned exactions, and which we can on no account endure, although we are bound to you by every tie of affection, devotion and obedience. Because our community has no seal we are sending these letters to your holiness under the seal of the community of the city of London.

Another letter, concerning the same affair, sent to the cardinals

To the most reverend fathers in God and lords the cardinals of the holy Roman church, their devoted servants, etc., greetings, due reverence, and honour. We turn with humble entreaties to

your community, forming as it were the pillars supporting the
Church of God, and we earnestly beg you to take note of the
oppressions from which we suffer and to give us aid to enable the
English church to recover breath after the repeated troubles it
has met with in the past, and so that we may be bound to return
you due thanks. For, since the last Lateran Council, the English
church, by command of the apostolic see, has been harassed first
by a twentieth for three years in aid of the Holy Land, next, by a
tenth in aid of the pope, and afterwards by contributions of
various kinds for divers purposes, for which she has promptly
paid over whatever she could lay her hands on. To our king and
temporal lord, at the command of the apostolic see, it has
repeatedly granted subsidies, as far as lay in its power, and now
at your instance aid is again demanded for the said king, whom
we cannot and ought not to fail in his needs, so that he can repel
the invasion of enemies, protect the rights of his kingdom and
recover more rapidly what has been seized from him. Finally a
demand is now made from this same church which it cannot meet
because of its penury: half of their goods from some, a third
from others, and a twentieth of all they possess from the rest.
Part of this is to be used by the French, who are always
persecuting us and our nation, for the conquest of the empire of
the Greeks; part is to help the Holy Land which could, as is well
known to everyone, be recovered from the enemy with much less
trouble; and part is to be used as the apostolic see may decide. It
does indeed seem hard and absurd to us that, while others enjoy
the benefits of our goods and labour, we and our people and the
poor of our region, to whom these funds more nearly belong,
should go fasting and empty handed. Our king and the army of
the kingdom would not be able to repel the incursions and guard
against the treachery of our enemies, which God avert, nor could
any help be given to those perishing and in need, if all the money
in the kingdom is exhausted. Even if everything which the clergy
has were to be put up for sale, the sum of money now demanded
from us would not be realised. Indeed many misfortunes would
follow if, which God forbid, they were compelled to do this. We
are sending the bearers of these presents to your clemencies as
our common messengers to expound these things to you, earnestly entreating you, for the sake of God and the honour of the
apostolic see, to turn the mind of the lord pope and your hands
and counsels away from such oppression, thus ensuring, if it
please you, that you recall to the bosom and obedience of the

mother Church those about to err and disperse away from it.
Otherwise you might disperse and alienate those who were formerly gathered together in affection and devotion. And because
our community has no seal we are sending these letters to your
holinesses under the seal of the community of the city of London.

Concerning a certain shady privilege obtained by the lord king a short time before

At that time the lord king, unaware that he was being stealthily
ensared by the cunning of the Romans in the meshes of their
deceitful words, obtained through the agency of some courtiers of
his who wanted to please him a certain privilege for himself from the
Roman curia, the tenor of which was as follows. "Although the pope
has arbitrarily and to the intolerable damage of the kingdom of
England everywhere and indiscriminately made provisions of ecclesiastical benefices in England for the benefit of Italians, now by
God's grace the tempest has subsided to such an extent that
whenever the pope is providing for any of his nephews or cardinals
he or his cardinals must ask the king on bended knees if it please
him to allow the provision to be made."

By means of this shady and deceitful privilege the parasitical friends
of the lord king melted his heart and bound him more firmly to them.
Nor could the notaries and lawyers of the Roman curia, who yielded to
gifts like wax, harm their interests by sending urgent and rhetorical
petitions at the instance of the pope to the lord king, in order to enrich
themselves and pauperize him. So I consider this privilege to be
nothing but a hook with bait on it.

Foreign women are brought over to marry English nobles

Before the said council was broken up Peter of Savoy, earl of
Richmond, came to the royal court at London bringing with him some
unknown women from his distant homeland in order to marry them to
the English nobles who were royal wards. To many native and
indigenous Englishmen this seemed unpleasant and absurd, for they
felt that they were being despised.

Two English brothers of the order of Minors are sent to England by the pope to extort money

While deceitful fortune was playing such false tricks on the world two brothers of the Franciscan order, John and Alexander, both English, were sent into England by the pope with numerous papal bulls and, concealing the rapacity of the wolf under the wool of the sheep, went to the king with innocent looks, mild glances and bland speech to request permission to wander through the kingdom seeking charity on behalf of the pope. They asserted that they would not make any use of coercion. And so, with the permission of the king, who saw nothing sinister in this, the said brothers became pseudo-legates and, glorifying in the gifts of the royal clerks, they set out in secular, or rather spectacular, fashion from the king's court mounted on fine steeds with gold-ornamented saddles and wearing the most sumptuous clothes, booted and spurred in a knightly manner and wearing what is commonly called hose, to the injury and disgrace of their order and profession. Taking over the duties and the tyranny of legates, they demanded and extorted procurations, thinking twenty shillings a small price for one procuration. First they went to the more eminent English prelates boldly demanding money for the pope's use against a fearful penalty and allowing only a very short time for a reply or payment. They produced fulminating papal letters which they held out like threatening horns. When they came to the bishop of Lincoln, who had always been a special admirer and supporter of their order, so much so that he had once conceived the idea of joining it, he was utterly aghast at seeing such a monstrous transformation in the dress, behaviour and occupation of the Franciscans, for now it was not at all easy to discover what sort of people they were or to what order they belonged. When they explained the contents of their papal mandate, emphasizing especially their commission to raise money, and earnestly demanded the by no means small sum of six thousand marks from his bishopric, the bishop replied with considerable astonishment and grief, "Brother, saving the papal authority, this exaction is dishonest and unacceptable for it is impossible to implement it, nor does it concern myself alone, but rather the community of the clergy and the people and the kingdom as a whole. Indeed I think it would be rash and absurd to agree to such a difficult matter by giving you an immediate reply about it without consulting the community of the realm." On this they withdrew and went to St. Albans, decked out and transformed as described above and, not caring to stop at or stay in the Franciscans' usual hospice, which had very recently been built

inside the gate of the new court especially for the use of the Dominicans and Franciscans, they were reverently received at the grander
hospice where bishops and eminent men stay. Then, just as they had
demanded six thousand marks from the above-mentioned bishop, so
they pressingly requested four hundred from the abbot for the pope's
use, to be paid in a short time under a heavy penalty, unless they
should stipulate otherwise. The abbot replied in the same way as the
aforesaid bishop had replied, with humility, and the two brothers,
adopting secular dress and behaviour, mounted their fine steeds and
went off muttering threats.

The lord pope demands money for himself from the French prelates

At this time the lord pope sent his authentic letters by special
Franciscan and Dominican messengers to all the French prelates
individually requesting each of them to pay over whatever money he
could afford, promising that once he had recovered his breath he
would without fail repay to each one his due. When this came to the
knowledge of the king of the French, who was suspicious of the
avarice of the Roman curia, he prohibited the prelates of his kingdom,
on penalty of the confiscation of all their property, from impoverishing their lands in this way. And so the sophistical papal legates who
had been charged with this duty left the above-mentioned kingdom
empty-handed amid universal sneers and derision.

Concerning the promotion and exaltation of John Mansel

Whilst time with its unexpected events was thus elapsing, John
Mansel, chancellor of St. Paul's church in London, by the wish and
on the request of the lord king, whose demands are imperious and
coercive, undertook the custody of the royal seal, to discharge the
duties and fulfil the office of chancellor. Besides this, the provostship
of Beverley was conferred on him by the archbishop of York. The
lord king, though he was sorry that this office had not been given to
his half-brother, yet because he found the said John loyal in and
John loyal in and essential for his affairs, did not wish him to be
harmed or deprived of any honour conferred on him.

Master Marinus, chaplain of the lord pope, is sent by the pope to England

While the wheel of fortune was thus continually transforming the lowest into the highest, the lord pope, thinking that the various collectors of money already sent were not sufficient for the effective harvesting of cash, sent into England his chaplain Master Marinus, another Martin, who, in line with the meaning of his name, had prudently chosen, in the ocean of this world, to be a fisher, though not of men but of their possessions. While others were hunting them, he hoped to ensare the miserable English by hooking them at a distance or deceive them into entering his net. Though not invested with the insignia of a legate, he was fully armed with a legate's powers; thus the royal privilege was evaded.

Godfrey, son of the prefect of Rome and bishop-elect of Bethlehem, is sent as a legate into Scotland

Also at this time Godfrey, the son of the prefect of Rome and bishop-elect of Bethlehem, was sent into Scotland by the lord pope as a legate; it is not known for what purpose, because the catholic faith was flourishing uncontaminated there and a firm peace existed among both clergy and people. It was therefore believed that, in typically Roman fashion, the aforesaid Godfrey was attracted to money from the abundant and much-coveted revenues of the Scotch just as iron is attracted by a magnet.

Master John is sent to Ireland

At the same time Master John Rufus was sent to Ireland to collect money there with full legatine powers but not invested with the insignia of that office, lest the pope should appear to be offending the king of England who was delighted that he was protected, as he vainly fancied, by the privilege that no legate should enter his lands without being asked for by him. This John carried out the pope's orders and pursued his own interests and advantage so vigorously vigorously, that he extorted six thousand marks from Ireland, which he had transported to London at Michaelmas in the care of some monks, to be joyfully added to the papal treasure. All these things did not escape the notice of [the emperor] Frederick.

Concerning an earthquake in England

In this same year, on the ides of February, that is on the eve of St. Valentine's day [13 February], an earthquake was felt in various places in England, especially at London and above all on the banks of the River Thames. It shook many buildings and was extremely damaging and terrible. It was thought to be significant because earthquakes are unusual and unnatural in these western countries since the solid mass of England lacks those underground caverns and deep cavities in which, according to philosophers, they are usually generated, nor could any reason for it be discovered. It was therefore expected that the end of the ageing world was at hand according to the threats of the gospel, and it was certainly believed that this earthquake was indicative of changes in the whole world, so that the elements would be agitated and disturbed with unusual movements. Indeed as has already been mentioned, the sea, starting a few days before and continuing for about three months, ebbed and flowed but little, if at all, for a great distance along the coast of England; a thing which no one remembered seeing before. Nor had there been an earthquake in England since the year of grace 1133, namely the third year before the death of King Henry I. A long spell of bad weather followed: unseasonable, wintry, stormy, cold and wet, so that both gardeners and farmers complained that spring had been transformed into winter by a backward movement, and they very much feared that they would be deceived in their hopes of crops, plants, fruit trees and corn. This disturbed weather lasted continuously up to the feast of the translation of St. Benedict [11 July], scarcely a single fine day intervening.[1]

1. The last sentence is in the margin of B.

The death of Fulk, a knight related to the lord king

On the day after the feast of the purification of St. Mary [3 February], Fulk of Newcastle, a distinguished knight and a relative of the king, died at London. The lord king, who was present for the above mentioned parliament, had his body solemnly and honourably buried in the church at Westminster, on account of his noble birth, after a magnificent funeral.

The iniquitous[1] decree concerning persons dying intestate is revoked

Also at this time, because of the unbecoming scandal that was spread through various countries and as a result of pressure from the cardinals, the decree was revoked which the pope, motivated by manifest avarice[1], had made a short time before, stating that the belongings of persons dying intestate should be sold for the benefit of the pope. To implement it he had appointed the Franciscans his proctors, to their loss and scandal and to the damage of their order.[1] This decree redounded to the harm and loss of many nobles on account of that iniquitous additional clause, added to it against all justice and piety, which ran as follows: "If a sick man about to make his will but prevented by sudden weakness from expressing himself clearly, appoints one of his friends to make it for him and act as his executor, such a will shall not stand but shall be considered null, and such a testator shall be considered intestate." And the papal Charybdis would gulp down all his belongings.

1. The words "iniquitous", "motivated by manifest avarice" and from "to their loss" to "order", have been erased in B. They have been supplied from the fair copy, MS.C.

The reason why the lord pope was in great fear of his life

While the transient eddies in the stream of time were thus gliding past, one of Frederick's knights, by name Ralph, enraged at not receiving his pay from the emperor in due time, left his service with threats. This Ralph was astute of mind, strong in body and skilful in battle. Since he had no fixed home and wanted to do harm to his erstwhile lord Frederick, he went to Lyons to seek a lord under whom he could fight as a stipendiary to greater advantage. He stayed at the house of a certain hotelier called Reginald. A few days later Master Walter de Ocra, clerk and special councillor of the above-mentioned Frederick, happened to pass that way and put up in the same guest house, where he usually stayed. When he saw this knight Ralph there he greeted him familiarly by name as an acquaintance, enquiring what he was doing there and why he had thus left his lord, whom he had served so long. When he had ascertained the full details Master Walter asked him if he had yet acquired another lord, to which he replied, "No, because I am not known". Master Walter then said, "Friend, return to the allegiance and service of my lord, who is now much in need of such men, and I will pay everything that is owed to you and even add more." When Ralph joyfully agreed to this, Master Walter continued, "My lord would consider himself fortunate if he was not annoyed, indeed attacked, by his deadly enemy and tireless persecutor the pope. If you will and can stealthily snatch away the pope's guilty life, I will multiply your rewards. I will indubitably fulfil what I have promised you and I will add three hundred talents to the many revenues I have promised to restore to you, as well as my lord's favour, which will be a source of much gain to you. In this way the emperor's troubles, indeed the disturbance of the whole world, would be set at rest. Nor should you believe that there is any sin in this deed since the pope, who ought to be a pattern and example of all religion, has become a manifest usurer, a furnace of symony, a thirster after and plunderer of money, and his court is a market place of hawkers, or rather a brothel for prostitutes. To this Ralph replied, "If you prove your words by your deeds and recompense me, I will do what you ask". And after Master Walter had promised and bound himself on oath, the aforesaid Ralph agreed to the crime, persuaded by the presents already made and promised. In this secret plan they at length induced their host Reginald, who was known to the pope and his servants, to participate with a similar obligation. His task was to find out, by lying concealed somewhere, the time and place when and where the pope might be killed, and carefully to introduce the murderer. On this Master Walter departed. It happened however a few days afterwards that this Reginald suddenly fell ill almost to death and seeing that he was about to die, he explained all these things to his priest in confession before resigning himself to his fate. The priest at once told the pope confidentially of his imminent danger. Messengers were rapidly armed and sent off and the aforesaid knight Ralph was seized. Since he repeatedly denied everything he was put to the most excruciating tortures and, vomiting up the poison of the above-mentioned treachery, he revealed the truth of the matter to the entire papal court. This was all written up in a papal bull to the injury of

Frederick and his people, and so that he would be more gravely condemned and defamed.

Others are arrested for a similar reason

At about the same time two Italian knights were apprehended at Lyons for the same offence. After their arrest, they declared that about forty daring knights had conspired together on oath to take the pope's life. Even though Frederick were dead they would not fail for any penalty, including that of death, to cut the pope in pieces as the disturber of the whole world and the defiler of the Church. They believed most firmly that, by cutting the throat of such a person, they would do something pleasing both to God and to men. From this time on the pope stayed in his room, carefully guarded day and night by about fifty armed men. Nor did he dare to leave his room or his castle or his palace, even to go to church to celebrate mass. For it is inevitable that he who is feared by many will fear many, and he who troubles others will himself be troubled.

A great parliament is held in France

In the same year about mid-Lent, the king of the French summoned the nobles of his kingdom in general, both clerics and laymen, by a royal edict, to a parliament to consider carefully certain difficult matters concerning the state of the kingdom, for he was anxious about his own and his nobles' taking of the cross and about the unbreakable obligation of such an important vow. Also it was said that he had received a mandate from the king of the Tartars ordering him to become his subject. This king, in daring and profane words, asserted in his letter that he was immortal and that he and his followers were those of whom it was written that "the Lord gave the earth to the children of men".[1] However, leaving the things which are due and belong to God, to the divine disposition through which all adverse things that can be engineered by human or diabolical machination are brought to nothing, the king of the French arranged things prudently and providently in the first place, then determined and irrevocably decreed and ordained that, if living, he would set out on his pilgrimage after a complete year had elapsed from the feast of John the Baptist next coming [24 June], in order faithfully to fulfil his vow that he would worship the footsteps of the crucified one, who had restored him to life, in the Holy Land. He swore in public that he would most certainly do this and he made his people swear, unless they were hindered by some unexpected event which human frailty could not avoid, which God forbid. Anyone who opposed this admirable decree was to be excommunicated and reputed a public enemy. When this came to the knowledge of the Khorasmians and other Saracens who live on the Christian frontiers in the Holy Land in areas only recently taken over by the infidel, they strongly fortified their towns and castles.

Moreover the above-mentioned king, noticing that the English money, which was extremely useful to traders in his kingdom because of its metal, had been very much diminished in value and impaired by the swindlers who are called coin clippers, ordered that any sterlings found in his kingdom not to be of legal weight were to be melted down at once, so that neither the merchants nor the trade should any longer be troubled by such spurious money. The same thing was now feared in England owing to the considerable diminution in the value of the coins. Moreover it was said and discovered that the coins were being circumcised by circumcised people and infidel Jews who, because of the heavy royal taxes, were reduced to begging. Other crimes, too, were said to have originated with them.

Also in this year a peaceable agreement was made between the churches of Durham and St. Albans concerning the visitation of the parochial church in the monastery at Tynemouth. This was in the time of Bishop Nicholas of Durham and Abbot John II of St. Albans; it is more fully explained in the *Book of additamenta* at this sign.[2]

1. Psalm 115:16.
2. A fish is drawn here in the margin and the document in question is to be found at this sign in British Library Cotton MS. Nero D 1, f.63v. It is also copied out by Matthew Paris below, pp. 99–101. It is printed Riley 1867:390–1.

Frederick makes peace with many, and some of the Milanese pledge him their friendship

In the same year at about this time Frederick, realising that everyone was murmuring and rising against him, took the sensible advice of freely granting a peace to the Milanese, who requested it with due submission and respect. Indeed the citizens had no choice but to beg for it humbly because in their last battle with Frederick's son Conrad they were defeated and many of them were killed or taken prisoner by a body of men lying in ambush which attacked their rear. Frederick generously spared these prisoners, hoping that forbearance would subdue them where force had failed. He had ordered that, after they returned to their city, all the gates should be sealed off so that the citizens, whose lives depended on trade, were blockaded as if held in prison or besieged. They could travel freely neither to the markets, the ports, nor to neighbouring cities, without danger to their persons, their cattle or their property. Since many of them now returned to their allegiance to their former and natural lord, Frederick resolved to be merciful to them and thus, after a long and demanding struggle, he brought them back prudently into union and peace with the Empire. The peace was advantageous to them and to him, and from then on the Milanese did not trouble any longer to support the pope, who had deceived them with his false promises.

The death of [Henry Raspe], landgrave of Thuringia, in whom the pope had placed all his hopes

In this same Lent, lest the above-mentioned earthquake[1] should fail in its threatening significance, the lord pope, vainly trusting in the immense sums of money he had plundered from all directions, now believed that he would be able, without any difficulty or opposition, to promote the landgrave [of Thuringia], whom he had wished to make emperor, to be king of Germany, and to crown him solemnly and indubitably. But Frederick's son Conrad, informed of this by his spies, and having discovered all the details, suddenly arrived with a huge army recruited from far and wide at the place where the pope had arranged for the said landgrave to be crowned in great state and where everything necessary for such a solemnity had been prepared. But Conrad feared the doubtful outcome of a battle, so he placed fifteen thousand of his men in ambush in an out-of-the-way place not far off who might, if necessary, come to his aid at the sound of a trumpet. The festive joy, then, was unexpectedly interrupted and a most fierce and bloody battle ensued. At first the weight of battle swung against Conrad, who lost many of his noblest followers. But when the risk of defeat threatened him the signal was quickly given and the soldiers who had been waiting for it in their place of ambush advanced enthusiastically "swift as the rapid air"[2] and vigorously made up for the tedious delay by attacking the enemy, who were on the point of gaining a victory, and cutting everyone to pieces who resisted them. At their arrival Conrad breathed again

As energy restores the soul
Of him who freely quaffs the bowl.[3]

Now the battle revived. The very air seemed to be disturbed by the clanging of armour, the smashing of spears, the crash of blows, the neighing of horses, the yells of combatants encouraging one another, the cries of the wounded and the groans of the dying, not to mention the cloud of dust raised, the steam from panting bodies and the streams of blood. But the Germans and those with the landgrave could not withstand such a vigorous attack. They abandoned the fight either mortally wounded or disgracefully fleeing. Many were taken prisoner and committed to prison at the will of their enemies. After this pitiable slaughter and irreparable loss of Christian blood the landgrave fled and, taking refuge in a safe place, was there wasted away by grief. Now indeed the speech of Frederick's proctor Thaddeus [of Suessa] at the Council of Lyons was in large part justified. After the pope had fulminated the sentence against his lord, "Alas! Alas!", he had said, truly "this is a day of anger, of misery and of calamity." The landgrave, who had hoped to be crowned king of Germany on the following day, seeing his glory transformed into confusion, his friends and relatives with their followers cut to pieces and defeated, and all the money sent him by the pope seized by his enemies, was struck down by grief and lost faith in himself. Instead of being wounded by another's blow, he was smitten and suffocated by his own grief and he breathed out his effeminate soul, lamented by no one. The victor Conrad, wishing to be fully revenged for the injury and loss he had sustained in his recent flight after being defeated in Germany, either ignominiously hanged the prisoners who had escaped the sword, especially the relatives, kinsmen and friends of the landgrave, or ordered them to be imprisoned in fetters in gloomy dungeons, to be ransomed for large sums of money.

1.   Above p. 91.
2.   Ovid *Met* 3.209.
3.   Ovid *Epist. ex Ponto* 1.3.10.

The grief-stricken pope sends legates to the four quarters of Europe to defame Frederick more effectively

The lord pope was overcome with grief when he heard of these events and sent four cardinals, as solemn legates, to the four quarters of Christendom, armed with the fullness of power conceded to them, for the purpose of defaming Frederick and his son Conrad for having dared to attempt such things and to encourage all Christians, in remission of all their sins, to annoy and attack the said Frederick and, if possible, crush him, as effectively as possible. Also, they were to do him, as effectively as possible. Also, they were to do their best to extort[1] money on all sides using all the methods in which the Roman curia was experienced by cunning avarice and avaricious cunning[1] for the purpose of subduing the hated Frederick. So he sent one legate into Germany, one into Italy, another into Spain and the fourth into Norway, besides certain bogus[1] legates whom he deceitfully[1] sent into England invested with considerable powers, but without their insignia lest they should seem openly to infringe the royal privilege. These were Franciscans and Dominicans whom, as we believe, the pope made his tax-collectors and beadles against their will, not without causing harm and scandal to their order. The legate who was sent into Norway was Bishop William of S. Sabina. He was also sent to anoint and solemnly crown Haakon as king of Norway, and to act as legate in that kingdom and in Sweden to the injury of the aforesaid Frederick, not without reason and hope of gain.[1]

1. The words "extort", from "was" to "cunning", "bogus", "deceitfully" and "and hope of gain" have been erased in the MS., no doubt by Matthew Paris himself, but have been recovered from the fair copy, MS. C.

Frederick makes everyone in Calabria, Apulia and Sicily do homage to his son by the empress Isabella

While time proceded on its way Frederick of suspect memory, whom we are forbidden to name or call emperor, made all the Sicilians, Apulians and Calabrians do liege homage to his much loved son Henry, whom he had had by his most dear empress Isabella, the king of England's sister, in order to strengthen and consolidate his Empire. On hearing this the lord king, uncle of the said boy, was extremely delighted, not without reason.

When Frederick discovered that the said legates had been sent through the various parts of the world to undermine his fame and standing, he instructed his son Enzio, the king of Sardinia, to waylay and even put to death the Genoese and especially the relatives, kinsmen and friends of the pope. This order Enzio effectively carried out, so as not to seem disobedient to his father, and he seized and hanged a near relative of the pope whom the pope loved more than any of the others, though he was very fond of them all. When he heard of this the pope was choked with anger and, in his hatred, on Good Friday [29 March], he excommunicated the said Frederick, together with his son the perpetrator of such evil, in so horrible a manner that he terrified those present. When Frederick heard about this he groaned and said, "This is what the Jews did when they crucified Christ and then pierced him with a lance."

Concerning some new statutes made by the king in England

In the same year the lord king of the English, following the example of those barons who enacted statutes in France which the king of the French confirmed and sealed, decreed that the following articles should be inviolably observed in England, in order for the time being to restrain to some extent the insatiable greed of the Roman curia.

The articles

> Cases of breach of faith and perjury are prohibited by the king whenever in such cases lay people are summoned before an ecclesiastical judge.
> Ecclesiastical judges are forbidden to try any causes against laymen, except concerning marriage and wills.
> The king once again prescribes for the bishops a certain procedure in cases of bastardy, that is, whether a child is born before marriage or after.
> Clerks are forbidden by royal writ to initiate actions concerning tithes before an ecclesiastical judge. That writ is called *Indicavit*,

As to the oaths clerics are required to swear before the royal justices, in cases they are alleged to have initiated against the royal prohibition, clerics are not bound to swear except before an ecclesiastical judge, above all in spiritual cases.

Another article concerns clerics who are arrested by royal officials because of accusations made against them by laymen.

Concerning an agreement made between the bishop of Durham and the abbot of St. Albans

In this year the dispute between the bishop of Durham and the abbot of St. Albans was settled in the following terms:

> To all sons of the holy mother Church who see these letters Michael, archdeacon of Stowe, papal judge-delegate, and

Nicholas, chancellor of Lincoln, sub-delegate of the archdeacon of Northampton, colleagues of the said archdeacon of Stowe, greetings in the Lord. Be it known to you all that by apostolic authority a suit has been brought before us — the third judge, the treasurer of Lincoln, having been wholly excused — between the venerable father Nicholas, by the grace of God bishop of Durham, in the name of the church of Durham, on the one hand, and John, by the same grace of God abbot of St. Albans and the convent of that place together with the prior and convent of Tynemouth in the name of the cell of St. Albans at Tynemouth on the other hand, concerning the visitation of the parochial church of Tynemouth and the obedience demanded by the said bishop from the prior of Tynemouth by virtue of the said church of Tynemouth and the other parochial churches held in his diocese by the monks of Tynemouth. At length, with the agreement of the chapter of Durham, the dispute between the churches has been brought to an amicable conclusion in perpetuity, as follows. That is to say, that the aforesaid bishop of Durham and his successors shall either in person or through their diocesan officials exercise that office in that part of the church of Tynemouth in which divine services are performed for the parishioners, without demanding procuration, on condition that they on no account concern themselves with the monks nor with any other part of the church nor with the cell itself and saving always the other privileges and indulgences of the said monks. The prior of the cell [of St. Albans] at Tynemouth shall be appointed and dismissed by the abbot of St. Albans or, in the event of a vacancy, by the prior of St. Albans with the consent of the chapter, according to the tenor of their privileges. When he is appointed the prior shall go to the bishop to be presented to him, promising canonical obedience to him with respect of the parochial churches, as far as the privileges of the monastery of St. Albans allow, on condition that the priors of Tynemouth shall not be summoned to a synod, chapter or other ecclesiastical assembly against the tenor of their privileges. The vicars of the church of Tynemouth shall be successively appointed by the prior and convent of Tynemouth with the agreement of the abbot of St. Albans and presented to the aforementioned bishop and his successors. These vicars shall answer to the said bishop in spiritual matters and to the said monks in temporal affairs. In witness to the foregoing, which has been drawn up in the form of an indenture so that one copy remains with the above-mentioned abbot and convent of St. Albans and prior and convent of Tynemouth and the other with the church of Durham, the bishop and chapter of Durham and the abbot and convent of St. Albans and the prior and convent of Tynemouth have respectively affixed their seals together with our own. Done in May 1247 in the presence of the above-mentioned bishop and abbot, present also the abbot of Newminster, the archdeacons of Nottingham, of St. Albans, and of Salisbury, Master Hugh of Stanbridge, William de Burgo and Odo of Kilkenny and Dom John Francigena and many others.

Concerning the papal exactions made by John the Englishman, a brother of the order of Minors

In the same year at the beginning of Lent a certain Franciscan named J., mentioned above, arrived in England. At London, after the feast of the beheading of St. John the Baptist [29 August], he demanded four hundred marks from the church of St. Albans on papal authority, producing mandates from the apostolic see in support of this renewed demand, for the abbot had previously appealed to the pope and cardinals against such an insufferable exaction. So he cited the abbot, by virtue of the authority of this new papal mandate, to come to London on the third day following, namely the day after the feast of St. Giles [2 September], or to send a competent and properly empowered proctor in his place, to satisfy the said John concerning this long-standing demand of the pope. The abbot sent a proctor, namely his archdeacon, on that day, who immediately asked for a copy of the new papal document. He obtained it with some difficulty and transcribed it as follows:

The papal document

Innocent, bishop etc., to his beloved son John, abbot of St. Albans in the diocese of Lincoln, greetings and apostolic blessings. In order to resist the continual and violent provocations of the secular authorities we are forced for the good of the apostolic see to turn to our subjects for help. For this reason, on the advice of our brethren, we solemnly ask, exhort and warn you, and with these apostolic letters we command you, to give full credence to what our beloved son Brother John the Englishman, provincial minister of the Franciscans in Provence, our messenger and bearer of these presents, has to say to you on our behalf concerning the subsidy for our see, so that, by carefully considering that the Church, by making this stand, is protecting the interests of all churches and churchmen, you will appreciate the need to fulfil your obligations freely and generously, in such a way as to be acceptable to us and our brethren, and so that your good will is demonstrated by your actions, which constitute the best possible evidence of the truth. Given at Lyons, the fourth of the ides of October [12 October], in the fourth year of our pontificate [1246].

On this authority Brother J. ordered the abbot's proctors to appear in the place where they had appeared before on the eighth day following, to pay him three hundred marks of silver. Otherwise he would carry out the pope's order by excommunicating and interdicting them. The proctors replied that the abbot was sending his special messengers to the pope to explain his grievances and to satisfy him according to the means of his church and people, without withdrawing from the appeals he had made previously. These things happened towards the end of the year; we have related them out of chronological order, but of necessity. For the finger goes to where there is an itch.

The powers of this same brother are aggravated

To the greater subjection and annoyance of the English, the powers of this same Brother J. were increased and aggravated and the pope encouraged him to make greater demands in these letters:

Papal letters

Innocent etc. On considering the matters which you have intimated to me in your letters, we command you, by authority of these presents, to make the English prelates pay within a reasonable period of time to whoever you choose a larger sum of money than you oringinally asked for, even though a majority of them, when required to contribute to this subsidy for the Roman church sought by you on our behalf, replied that they were exempt from it. Those resisting should suffer ecclesiastical censure notwithstanding any privilege or indulgence they may have, even though they are not expressly mentioned in these presents. Given at Lyons, the sixteenth of the kalends of August [17 July], in the fifth year of our pontificate [1247].

Anyone who wants to see the original powers of this same Brother J. will find them in the *Book of letters* at this sign.[1]

1. British Library Cotton MS. Nero D 1, f.90b Luard 1882:119.

An imminent general danger

A good many people when these things came to their knowledge, namely that such frequent and violent[1] demands for money were being made by the pope and his pseudo[1]-legates and that the privileges and indulgences of the holy fathers were of no avail against them, began to fear that the laymen and secular princes and lords, or their ancestors, who had founded, endowed and enriched the churches by reason of which their possessions were in large measure now being mutilated and for the benefit of which they had issued their charters, might take back the goods and possessions of these churches notwithstanding the tenor of such and such a privilege, taking their example from the pope. This all the more since the pope and his people, against the intention of the founders, were fattening whoever they wished among the Italians and other foreigners on these churches, while the natives were going hungry.

1. The words "violent" and "pseudo" have been erased in the MS. probably by Matthew Paris himself, but recovered from the fair copy, C.

An unheard of oppression

When the convent of the above-mentioned church, namely St. Albans, advised by the abbot, saw itself oppressed on all sides, they appealed to the apostolic see, whose duty it was to relieve the oppressed from their burdens, and straight away sent a monk of theirs, Dom John Bulum, and Master Adam de Bern, to the pope at Lyons. But, before they returned, the aforesaid Brother John sent the following mandate to the abbot of St. Albans:

To the venerable man Lord John, by the grace of God abbot of St. Albans, Brother J. messenger of the lord pope in England, greetings in the Lord. Although we have already written to you several times, we have decided, encouraged by an urgent command, to write once more to ask and warn you and command you by virtue of your obedience to the papal authority, laying aside all excuses, to be in the Franciscan convent at Bedford on the Tuesday before the feast of St. Thomas the Apostle [17 December], to make full satisfaction concerning the subsidy for the Roman church. And see to it that you act in such a way that we do not have to proceed, though unwillingly, according to the tenor of the said mandate. Nor should you omit to do this because of your appeal, for we have received special instructions concerning that. Farewell. Please reply by the bearer of these presents to let us know what you propose to do about this.

How an appeal was made to the pope because of this oppression

And so an appeal was made to the lord pope, for both abbot and convent preferred to be tried by the pope and the most senior prelates than by a person who concealed such harsh severity behind a cloak of humility and poverty. But, while messengers were sent to the Roman curia [on 13 October] fifteen days after Michaelmas, the aforesaid Brother J. redoubled his threats. When the archdeacon of St. Albans and some of the monks were sent to him to mitigate his rigour, he replied that he would fully exercise whatever severity justice and his powers allowed because, when he was at St. Albans, the monks had not paid him the respect due to a legate or at least a papal messenger. Indeed he was rebuked by some of them for infringing the rules of his order by changing his habit, though he was received respectfully and courteously enough as regards eating and drinking and polite conversation. Only with difficulty then, after kneeling and making begging speeches, did they at length obtain a respite until something certain was heard from the messengers sent to the Roman curia. As to their business there, Brother J. assured them that they would obtain nothing good or favourable for he had written to the pope exasperating him considerably by asserting that, alone among all the abbots of England, the abbot of St. Albans had opposed and refused to obey the papal mandate; a fact that was plainly apparent since he had sent his messenger to the pope. Because of this, the messengers sent to the Roman curia, hampered by various obstacles thrown in their way, were delayed longer there and had more difficulty in expediting their business. At length, helped by the money and bribes of friends in the curia, they settled with the pope for a payment of two hundred marks, but reckoning all gifts and expenses, the insatiable Charybdis of that curia swallowed up three hundred marks, thus the church of St. Albans, which should have been able under papal protection to breathe more freely and safely than the others, was more incessantly and severely oppressed than the others. For the bishops in whose bishoprics our cells were situated, refusing to accept the papal letters as valid, harassed the priors of the cells, disregarding, or hiding their knowledge of, the contents of letters which expressly stated that the exempt abbeys were excused from the above-mentioned subsidy of eleven thousand marks, and that they and three clerics were set aside by the pope from that impoverishment. The entire contents of these letters is given in the *Book of additamenta*. At length, persuaded by the contents of these letters and by those of the said Brother John, the bishops desisted, though unwillingly, from further molestation of the cells of St. Albans. They did not, however, restore what they had already plundered from them.

Concerning the convocation of all the nobles of England to a great parliament

At this time, when the lord king realised that his whole kingdom was seriously endangered, he ordered all the nobility of the realm to be convoked at Oxford, on the day for chanting the Quasimodo [7 April], to consider carefully the manifestly critical state of affairs. To this parliament he more especially and strictly summoned the prelates, because he saw how often they were impoverished by papal extortions and how frequently English money was being exported, though no advantage followed to the Church, but rather disadvantage. Hence it was truly maintained that these extortions were extremely displeasing to the Creator. Moreover it was most confidently hoped that at this parliament, something would be decided which would be beneficial both to church and kingdom. But in this everyone's hopes were deceived, for although some of the prelates had planned beforehand to oppose this subsidy, yet at the parliament they all, with the exception of the exempt abbeys and the three clerics, agreed to the subsidy of eleven thousand marks. Because of their privilege, these three clerics made themselves objects of suspicion throughout the kingdom. The money was paid to and received by the bishops of Winchester and Norwich, who were armed with papal authority, and the clergy was compelled to pay it in full. The exempt abbots were exposed to the pope's will, who by no means spared them but exhausted them with losses and injuries at the hands of the above-mentioned Brother J. as described above. Nor did the pope act any more leniently towards the abbot of St. Albans because of his payment of eighty marks in the previous year. Moreover, since the pope had recently written to the English nobles on the king's behalf, to promote his cause in the collecting of money, it was feared that the king would, because of the mutual permission and connivance between himself and the lord pope, compel the church and indeed the kingdom to suffer a similar exaction.

The abbot of Westminster and John Mansel are sent to the duke of Brabant in Germany

At this same time the abbot of Westminster [Richard of Croxley] and Lord J. Mansel were sent by the lord king into Germany to negotiate a contract of marriage between the king's son Edward and the daughter of the said duke. For some unknown reason they returned sadly with empty saddle-bags and each of them complained that his efforts and expenses had been expended to no purpose.

Count Willliam of Holland is elected king of Germany with a view to his appointment as emperor

In these days the lord pope, by promising large sums of money which were to be extorted from the Church on all sides to effect the downfall of Frederick, arranged for William, count of Holland, to be elected king of Germany. He was in the prime of life and strength and of illustrious birth. He was a cousin of the bishop of Liège [Henry of Guelders], the duke of Brabant [Henry II] was his uncle, and the archbishop of Cologne [Konrad von Hochstaden] was his inseparable friend and in some way related to him. The pope realised that, in his support of the landgrave of Thuringia, who had died suddenly as mentioned above, he had lost no small amount of money, indeed it was a sum that would stupify those hearing about it, namely fifty thousand pounds of Viennese pence, each one of which is worth three farthings sterling, and the whole of it fell into the hands of his enemies. So now he tried to arrange matters more carefully, sending the money promised to the newly elected king, Count William, more prudently and secretly by the hands of circumspect rather than suspect messengers, and appointing the lord Octavianus, a cardinal, to supervise the business. He also sent messages of encouragement to the Milanese and the Parmans and to others whose loyalty he thought was wavering, in the hopes of removing all their doubts and despair. But, so that the joys of this world should not come unmixed with sorrows, the count of Savoy, who was an open enemy of the Church, waited under cover of a deceitful peace until the papal messengers with their escort of soldiers were passing peacefully through his territories along the rugged roads among mountains and valleys, and then treacherously contrived, when they were cut off from the possibility of retreat or escape, the seizure of the papal treasure and the defeat and dispersal of the soldiers who, besides their arrears of pay, had received sufficient money for two months' wages in advance. Thus again, disgracefully enough, all the money fell into the hands of the pope's enemies.

Concerning the new privilege of the Preachers[1]

In the same year the brothers Preachers obtained the privilege from the lord pope that no brother should be allowed to transfer from their order to another and that no abbot or prior should be allowed to receive such a person, even though they themselves received deserters from the monks. This is evidently illogical and contrary to the rule of St. Benedict, as well as to the natural law that "What you would not wish done to yourself you should not do to another." [It was obtained because] a number of people of distinguished morals, learning and descent, who had sought refuge from the world in this order, failed to experience there the kind of religion they sought, but found the whole wide world instead of a cloister. So, particularly because at the start of his rule St. Benedict condemns the itinerant monk, they began to complain and, regretting that they had entered such an order, they tried to find some way out of it. It is because of this that those persons are considered the greatest in their order who follow a moderate course.

1. This paragraph is in the margin in B.

Some nobles arrive to carry away generous gifts

Also at this time some hungry foreign nobles arrived in England with empty stomachs and open mouths gaping for the king's money, namely Baldwin, emperor of Constantinople, with some of his supporters, who had been expelled forcibly from the Greek territories. A few years before this said Baldwin, having sold all the holy relics he could lay his hands on and borrowed money from wherever he could, had fled ingloriously from that country a poor man and a refugee, despoiled of all his belongings, although the pope had begun to support him and had given him effective help in his war against Frederick's son-in-law [John III] Vatatzes [the emperor of Nicaea]. Now he was in need and sought financial help from the king of England, of whose generosity he had previous experience and, in the hopes of gaining greater favours, he asserted that he was a relative of the king.

The cardinal bishop of [S.] Sabina arrives in England with the king's permission

Similarly there arrived in England the bishop of [S.] Sabina, a cardinal of the Roman church, on his way as legate to the northern countries of Norway, Denmark and Sweden, and in order to anoint and crown King Haakon of Norway. At first, when about to arrive in England, he encountered some difficulty in obtaining leave from the king, because legates of whatever rank they were, and all papal messengers, invariably impoverished or in some way disturbed the kingdom they were entering. But then he swore on his soul that he was coming to England, not to do any harm to the king, the kingdom or the church, but merely to pass peaceably through the country from the port of Dover to the port of [King's] Lynn, so that he could continue at once to more distant kingdoms the moment he met with a good opportunity and a favourable wind. As soon as he had obtained permission in this way he entered the kingdom fearlessly and, having paid his respects to the king and accepted some presents from him, he hastened on his journey to Lynn. While staying there for nearly three months, however, he found it impossible to suppress the innate cupidity of the Romans and he sent furtive messengers to the bishops, abbots, and priors, demanding procurations and costly gifts while he stayed in a house on the bishop of Norwich's manor called Gaywood, so that his gains were said to amount to four thousand marks. To disguise his proceedings behind a mask of holiness he frequently preached to the people and, when about to embark on a ship, which he had richly stocked with a large quantity of corn and a great many casks of choice wine and other provisions, he ordered a Dominican brother to celebrate mass in it, which was done, to the astonishment of many people who had never seen this before. In this ship, just as is said of Noah's Ark, he had had passages and rooms and decks specially constructed. And thus, with a favourable wind, giving England and the prodigal English his blessing, and having made himself wealthy, he set sail on the North Sea.

Three half-brothers of the lord king arrive in England with the same legate

At that time three uterine brothers of the lord king arrived in England with the said legate, invited by the king to enrich themselves as plentifully as possible with the delights and wealth of England, namely Guy of Lusignan the eldest, a knight, William of Valence, a youth not yet knighted, and a cleric, Aethelmar. Besides them, there was the king's and their sister, Alesia, the daughter of Isabella, a former queen of England and countess of La Marche, by Hugh le Brun, earl of La Marche. They were tired and ashamed of staying in Poitou, which the French now began to oppress wretchedly, ignominiously despising the inhabitants, who used, under the protection of the lord king of England, to be extremely free and well off in everything, and pointing them out as wicked traitors with grimaces and laughter.[1] As I was saying, the lord king went to meet these brothers and his sister with great joy. With a fatherly embrace, he promised them handsome gifts and ample possessions, and this he fulfilled even more abundantly than he had promised, as the following narrative will plainly demonstrate.

1. This sentence is in the margin of B.

Certain young women are married to English nobles

At the beginning of May, the lord king having stayed at Woodstock from the feast of St. Vitalis to the day after the feast of the apostles Philip and Jacob [28 April to 2 May], two Provençal girls were married at the instigation of Peter of Savoy to two young nobles whom the lord king had brought up at court for some years, namely Edmund earl of Lincoln and Richard de Burgo. These marriages caused considerable murmur and indignation to reverberate round the kingdom for it was said that the women were ignoble[1], unknown to the nobles, and married to them against their will.

1. This word "ignoble" has been erased in B, probably by Matthew Paris, but is found in C.

Joan, daughter of Warin de Muntchensil, is married to William of Valence, the king's half-brother

In the same year on the ides of August [13 August], on the lord king's advice and recommendation, Joan, daughter of Warin de Muntchensil, was married to William of Valence, the lord king's uterine brother. Since the eldest son and heir of the above-mentioned Warin was dead, his daughter Joan, the only one still alive, was due for a very rich inheritance. Thus the nobility of England devolved in a large measure to unknown foreigners. Moreover Alesia, half-sister of the king, was married to John, the young earl of Warenne.

Odo, archbishop of Rouen, dies

Also in the same year Odo, archbishop of Rouen and formerly abbot of Saint-Denis, died suddenly, struck down, it is believed, by divine judgement when he had corruptly[1] presided over the archiepiscopal see for hardly a year after audaciously[1] usurping the name and office for himself. He had distributed the revenues to his predecessor Peter. He was an Englishman by birth and had formerly been abbot of Saint-Denis, but ambition and pride had unfortunately attracted him so much to the aforesaid archiepiscopal dignity that he left that house irremediably in debt and, to his own ruin, obtained the archiepiscopal dignity through simony.

1. The words "corruptly" and "audaciously" have been erased in B., probably by Matthew Paris, but have been recovered from C.

William Longespee and many other nobles take the sign of the cross

About the time of the Rogation days [6 May] this year the bishop of Winchester, with William Longespee and Geoffrey de Lucy from the bishopric of Worcester, and many other English nobles, took the cross, encouraged by the example of the king of the French and the nobles of that kingdom. But William Longespee, in the hopes of reaping where he had not sown[1] by quietly collecting money from people who had taken the cross in the same way as had Earl Richard, went to the papal curia and addressed the pope as follows. "My lord, as you see, I have taken the sign of the cross, and I am ready to fight for God by journeying with the king of the French. I have a great and famous name, William Longespee, but little property, for my relative and natural lord the king of the English has confiscated my property and my title of earl. However, he did this judicially and not in anger nor by arbitrary violence, so I do not blame him. But I am forced to apply to your paternal generosity and ask your help in my need. Considering the case of the noble Earl Richard [of Cornwall] who, though he himself had not taken the cross, was permitted by your favour, which was highly profitable for him, to harvest no small sum of money in England from people who had taken the cross, I venture to request that I, in need and having taken the cross, be granted the same favour." The lord pope, considering the eloquence of the speaker, the cogence of his reasoning, and the handsomeness of his person, was favourably disposed towards him and granted him part of what he asked, namely a thong from another man's skin.

1. Compare Luke 19:21.

William de Bueles is made seneschal of Gascony

In this year William de Bueles, a knight who had formerly been marshal of the king's household, was appointed seneschal of Gascony. As is usual with his countrymen, he was a Neustrian, he was great in talk but slow and weak in deeds, so that province was exposed to considerable danger and disturbed by numerous wars while in his care. The most active enemy of the king of England there was Gaston, son of the countess of Béarn. The king had granted him many favours, but he was the most ungrateful of all the men whom the king's lavish bounty had enriched.

The translation of the blessed confessor Edmund

During the ups and downs of this year the blessed Edmund, archbishop of Canterbury and confessor, was translated at Pontigny with great honours, in the abbey church of the Cistercian monks there in the presence of the most Christian lord King Louis of France and innumerable nobles, both prelates and others. Amongst everyone of both sexes present there, the most conspicuous in her devotion to God and Saint Edmund was Lady Blanche, the lord king of France's mother. She kept vigil with fasting and prayer and numerous candles, frequently repeating these words in her prayers: "Most holy lord confessor who, when alive and in exile, at my entreaty blessed me and my sons and who crossed over into France at my request, complete what you began with us and establish the kingdom of the French in the security of peace and success."

The next day [7 June], which was the date of the translation of the body of the most blessed bishop and confessor Wulfstan of Worcester (and I think this happened by God's will), the body of the glorious Edmund was translated at Pontigny many years later. It should be known and indeed published to the whole world that his body was found complete, uncorrupted and exuding a pleasant aroma and, what is incredible in a corpse, the limbs were flexible, as with someone asleep, and the hair and clothes were unaltered in colour and substance. From this time on it was decided, at the king of France's instigation, that permission should be given to the English, more freely than to the people of other nations, to visit his body to see it and say their prayers. It was also decided that his tomb should be honoured with offerings of lighted tapers and finely-wrought effigies, but what was done in this respect is described in the *Book of additamenta*, at this sign. . . .¹

1. See British Library Cotton MS. Nero D i, f.91. = Luard 1882:126–7.

Note a memorable miracle concerning Earl Richard [of Cornwall]'s disease

When Earl Richard heard about this from the reports of credible and trustworthy persons he said with a sigh, "Alas! that it was not ordained on high that my brother the king and I should have been present at such a joyful and solemn translation. For he was our saint in his birth, education and promotion, even if unfortunately, because of our sins, he withdrew from England. However, what I was not present to do there, I will do for him while absent. I will pay due reverence and homage to him". From that time he began to love the saint more sincerely and to honour him more devoutly and, since he was oppressed to death's door by a severe and secret illness, he confidently invoked the saint's aid. He was happily cured of his disease and, in gratitude to God and the saint, he agreed to provide a quarter, that is the front gable, of the shrine, most sumptuously worked.

Concerning an intolerable clipping of the English coinage

At that time the money of sterlings, because of its good metal, was spoilt and diminished in value by those falsifiers of money called clippers, who cut round the edges [of the coins] so that the inner circle was scarcely remaining and the lettered border wholly cut away. The authors of this fraud, namely the merchants of the countries bordering on England, especially the Flemings, were manifestly convicted of it more on the continent than on this side of the Channel, so the lord king of the French punished such people more in his lands than did the king of England in our country. As the money was now beyond measure vitiated and adulterated, the royal councillors began to consider some remedy, namely whether the coin should not be advantageously altered either in form or metal content, and many discreet people thought it would be better to change the metal than alter the form of the coin, since it was because of its metal, not shape, that the money suffered such mutilation and injury. The money of the French and many other princes witnesses to the evident truth of this.

Concerning the tournament between the earl of Gloucester and Guy, son of the earl of La Marche

Also at this same time a tournament, bloody sport indeed, was fixed between Earl Richard of Gloucester and Guy of Lusignan, son of the earl of La Marche, between Dunstable and Luton. The king, however, who favoured his brother Guy and his other Poitevin followers more than his natural English subjects, was very much afraid that, if the tournament took place, his brother and his supporters would be cut to pieces. So he strictly prohibited the tournament on penalty of disinheritance. The English patiently accepted this prohibition for many of them sincerely loved this Guy. It was he who had warned the king of England, in Saintonge, to withdraw at once because his father, the earl of La Marche, had sold the king to the king of France. And so that potentially dangerous tumult was with God's will pacified.

How the menace and strength of the Khorasmians in the Holy Land faded away

In the same year too, the entire race of the detestable Khorasmians after spreading fire and slaughter and bringing manifold destruction in the Holy Land, and after besieging and impoverishing Acre, was so weakened and enervated by God's vengeance that it faded away. For they had broken with the sultan of Babylon and, deprived of his help, they suffered from want and were attacked and defeated by their enemies on all sides until their name was completely wiped off the face of the earth and no trace of them remained, except that the stench of their footsteps had indelibly stained the Holy Land.

Conrad withdraws from Germany

At this time Frederick's son Conrad, wicked offspring of a wicked father, fled from Germany to his father in Italy, unable to withstand the attacks of his enemies and the daily increasing powers of the Church. For the papal legate, relying on the support of the archbishop of Cologne [Konrad von Hochstaden], after extorting an immense sum of money from the German church, brought with him some 10,000 armed mercenaries intent on fire and slaughter, for a non-stop attack on Frederick's partisans. Fulminating excommunications here and there, this legate amassed money wherever he could to pay for the archbishop's numerous army, by extorting it from bishops, abbots, priors, and other prelates, who were obliged to redeem even their bells. Frederick was perturbed and embittered when he heard of this and thought hard about revenge, and a good many discreet persons, weighing future dangers in the scales of reason, were afraid that, carried away with anger and indignation, he would either apostatize or summon the Tartars to his assistance from Russia, or treacherously permit the sultan of Babylon, with whom he was on the friendliest terms, to invade the Empire with a herd of his pagans, to the confusion of the whole of Christendom. Thus was to be seen suffering, scandal heaped upon scandal, evil crowded upon evil; for some supported Frederick as representing the commonwealth and the Empire, and others the pope, representing the Church, and in the process brought about contentions and bloody wars. So in Germany, as well as in Sicily and Calabria and Italy, the bishops and other holy men, who had been nourished in the bosom of the Church's maternal affection, were now ignominiously forced to beg, and to demand the necessaries of life by preaching in far-off foreign countries. But the people responded to their entreaties with refusals and insults, saying, "Go and ask your pope, who has plenty of plundered treasure." Indeed the pope never stopped amassing money both in the curia and in remote areas, turning the Dominicans and Franciscans, against their will, into fishers not of men, but of money. How they carried out this task is explained in the *Book of additamenta* at this sign. . . .[1]

1. British Library Cotton MS. Nero D i, f.90 = Luard 1882:134–8.

How Earl Richard collected a vast sum of money from those who had taken the cross

Also at this time Earl Richard, by authority of the pope whose demands he had secretly and astutely satisfied, collected endless sums of money from those who had taken the cross. So much so that from a simple archdeaconry he is said to have carried off £600, relying on the authority of his [papal] letters, which are to be found in the *Book of additamenta* at this sign . . . , and further on at this. . . .[1] By a similar trick, as mentioned above, William Longespee took 1,000 marks and more off would-be crusaders on the pretext of his pilgrimage, and this was more readily tolerated. A certain other nobleman did the same.

1. British Library Cotton MS Nero D i, fos. 90 and 93 = Luard 1882:134–8 and 91–2. The last sentence of this paragraph is in the margin of B.

On the extortion of money by Boniface, archbishop of Canterbury, and the penalty for those unwilling to pay

At this same time also Boniface, archbishop of Canterbury, suspended the bishops of the province of Canterbury on papal authority because they were unwilling to agree to the new and unprecedented contributions which he demanded on behalf of the pope. These were the payments to him of the revenues of vacant churches during the first year of their being vacant, to meet the cost of the debts and consequent heavy interest charges with which he claimed his predecessors had irremediably burdened the church of Canterbury. This was well known to be a fabrication, injurious to his immediate predecessor the blessed Edmund and to other holy men, but the bishops, unwilling and unable to resist the pope's authority and mandate, at last reluctantly consented, though against their will and with the utmost resentment, in order to be released from the suspension. Afterwards they received a mandate from the dean of Beauvais, who was acting in this affair, which states that anyone complaining about or opposing or fraudulently evading the above-mentioned privilege gladly conceded by the pope, except the king, his wife, and children and the noble Richard, earl of Cornwall, would be excommunicated by the pope and denounced as an excommunicated person throughout the province of Canterbury.

How Frederick made war on various Italian towns and besieged Parma

When the sun was moving towards the autumn equinox Frederick crossed the Alps and advanced with a massive army towards Lyons, where the pope was staying. Fear was aroused thereby that he might do violence against the persons of the pope, the cardinals and other ecclesiastics; but the lord pope, who had encouraged the Parmans and promised them effective help and a substantial sum of money, prudently arranged for Parma, which had hitherto firmly supported Frederick, to ally immediately with the Milanese and others who hated the emperor, and boldly get ready to resist him. Frederick could hardly contain his fury when he heard this, and was consumed with anger at being diverted from his purpose by these rebels. He returned, therefore, with the whole of his army in order, by besieging and assaulting Parma, to wreak the harshest vengeance on these traitors. The pope was in consequence somewhat relieved from the fear which had oppressed him. While Parma was closely invested, Frederick began to construct another city outside it which seemed to equal Parma itself in size and population. He called it Victoria and he swore that he would not withdraw thence until he had forcefully and violently occupied the besieged city. Within a short time he deprived them of the benefit of the river, nor could the Milanese or anyone else in whom they trusted give them any assistance. So, after three months, they resolved to offer their right hands to Frederick in reconciliation and asked him for peace terms, but he was suspicious and refused to accept their humiliation. They now began to feel the pressure, and said among themselves. "We deserve these sufferings for attacking the ruler who trusted us. We are being justifiably punished and are in imminent danger; for ours is the city in which that holy bishop of London, Roger [Niger], whom it is now said the Lord honours with miracles, was cruelly robbed of the necessaries for his journey and other valuables and never paid compensation, when he was travelling to the papal curia. When he left, next day, he placed a curse on the city and its inhabitants."

A pious deed of the lord king of the French

During this same autumn the most pious French king, Louis, sent Dominican and Franciscan brothers throughout his kingdom on a detailed enquiry and he got his bailiffs also to proclaim and assist in this investigation. Any trader or any other person who had suffered any damage by way of forced loan or extortion of money or provisions of the sort habitually practised by royal officials, was to submit a written statement or list of his grievances or give evidence or place himself on oath or legally prove the fact in some other way. For the king was ready to make full restitution of everything. And this was done.

Concerning the steadfast faith of the lord king during the illness of his son Edward

On St. Matthew's eve [20 September], since the lord king's eldest son and heir Edward had fallen ill, the lord king wrote to all ecclesiastics in the London area asking them to pray devoutly for his son's health. Among others, he wrote in particular to the abbot and convent of St. Albans, requesting that, in praying for him, all the monks would solemnly chant a mass, the first collect of which would be for St. Alban and the second, namely "Almighty and everlasting God, eternal hope of believers", for the sick boy. And by the grace of God he was restored to health. I have said this much because people complained at this time: "If laymen can pray to God and their prayers are granted, why cannot the pope pray not only for himself but also for us and the whole Church instead of gaping tirelessly after money?" It was also said and maintained, which I ought neither to write nor recite in any way without tears, that the pope trusted more in monetary treasure than in the prayers or alms of the faithful.[1]

1. The words from "instead" to "faithful" have been erased in B, probably by Matthew Paris himself, but recovered from the fair copy, C.

The magnates of Germany elect Count William of Holland as their king and also do liege homage to him

The day after Michaelmas day [30 September] the majority of the German magnates with electoral rights chose William, count of Holland, as king of Germany, a young man of about twenty, elegant, virtuous and magnanimous; and they did homage to him. But the duke of Saxony [Albert] and some other magnates would not accept this election, so that a major schism occurred among the people, who said: "Knighthood through pride is opposed to priesthood, and for the same reason the priesthood is against knighthood".

Some of Christ's blood is brought to London

About the same time the lord king wrote to all the magnates of the kingdom ordering them all to assemble on the feast, that is the translation, of St. Edward, which is a fortnight after Michaelmas [13 October], in order to hear most agreeable news of a holy benefit recently conferred by heaven on the English; secondly to honour the translation of that glorious king and martyr; and thirdly so that they could attend the initiation of the king's half-brother William of Valence, on whom he intended that day to confer the honour of knighthood, along with several other noble youths. For this multiple festivity would be more joyfully enlivened by the presence of the nobles, both prelates and others, to the honour of both king and kingdom.

When the magnates assembled in London at Westminster on the appointed day and were told about the feast of St. Edward and the knighting of the said William, they enquired about the good news they were going to hear, which was said to be true and worthy of complete acceptance. [It was that] the masters of the Templars and Hospitallers with the testimony of a good many seals, namely those of the patriarch of Jerusalem and the archbishops and bishops, abbots and other prelates, and magnates of the Holy Land, had sent some of the blood of our Lord, which he shed on the cross for the salvation of the world, in a most beautiful crystal container, in the care of a certain well known brother of the Templars. The king indeed, as a most Christian prince, exalting the cross after the example of the most pious and victorious Emperor Heraclius and of the then living king of the French, Louis, who was honouring it in Paris, kept vigil on St. Edward's eve devoutly and contritely, fasting on bread and water with numerous candles and devout prayers, to prepare himself suitably for the next day's solemnities.

The continuation of this holy and memorable occasion

The lord king ordered all London priests to assemble at St. Paul's in good order and reverence early next morning, which was St. Edward's day, festively dressed in hoods and surplices with their clerks suitably attired and with symbols, crosses and lighted candles. The king arrived there and, receiving the container with its treasure above-mentioned with the utmost honour, reverence and awe, he carried it publicly in front of his face, going on foot and wearing a humble dress consisting of a simple cloak without a hood. Preceded by the priests dressed as described above he went without stopping to Westminster Abbey, which is about a mile from St. Paul's. It should be pointed out, too, that he carried it with both hands and even when he came to a rough or uneven section of road, he kept his eyes fixed always either on heaven or on the container itself. The pall was carried on four spears, and two assistants supported the king's arms lest his strength should fail during his exertions. The convent of Westminster together with everyone who had assembled, bishops, abbots and monks to the number of a hundred or more, tearfully singing and exulting in the holy spirit, went out to meet the king as he arrived at the gates of the bishop of Durham's palace and then returned as they had come, in procession, to Westminster Abbey, which could hardly hold them all, there were so many of them. Nor even then did the king repose, but indefatigably continued, carrying the container round the church, his palace and his own rooms. Finally he presented and offered this priceless gift, which had made all England illustrious, to God, to the church of St. Peter at Westminster, to his beloved Edward, and to the holy monks who minister there to God and his saints.

The lord bishop of Norwich's sermon that day

The bishop of Norwich [Walter Suffield], who also solemnly celebrated mass that day, stated in preaching to the people that, of all things held sacred among men, the most sacred is the blood of Christ, for it is the price of the world's redemption, and its effusion was the salvation of the human race. And, in order to emphasise this the more, he quoted the philosopher's saying "Every end is more elevated than its means". True, the cross is a most holy thing, but only because of the sacred shedding on it of Christ's blood; nor is the blood holy because of the cross. He said that we believed this so that England might have as much joy and glory in the possession of this great treasure as France had in the possession of the holy cross which the lord king of the French justifiably reverenced and venerated and delighted in more than in gold or topaz. And he added that it was mainly because of the reverence and holiness of the lord king of the English, who was recognised as the most Christian of all Christian princes, that this incomparable treasure had been sent by the patriarch of Jerusalem, the certainty of which fact had been sufficiently proved. It would be venerated more in England than in Syria, which was now left more or less desolate, for in England, as everyone knows, faith and holiness flourish more than in any other part of the world.

When this affair was discussed some "slow of heart to believe"[1] still doubted, and Thierry, prior of the Hospitallers at Jerusalem, said to the bishops and others sitting round, "Dear lords, why do you still hesitate? Did any one of us, either a Templar or a Hospitaller or even the brother who brought it, demand any benefit for the same? Did he ask for any remuneration in gold or silver from the king or from anyone else; or any sort of reward?" "Certainly not", said the king. "Why", continued the prior, "should so many of such high rank risk their souls by testifying to a statement of this kind and fixing their seals to it, which are manifest pledges of good faith?" These words, though uttered by a layman, were approved by all the hearers, both bishops and others. But now let us return to our narrative.

When the above-mentioned bishop had finished his eloquent sermon he announced to the exulting people that whoever went to venerate the holy blood to be kept there would, by the spontaneous permission of all the prelates present, receive free remission from penances imposed on them for six years and 116 days.

After further discussion, some of those sitting round still remained doubtful. They put the question: "How could the Lord have left his blood on earth when he rose again full and entire in body on the third day after his passion?" This question was at once fully dealt with by [Robert Grosseteste] bishop of Lincoln, and [his reply] is set out in the *Book of additamenta* word for word as the writer of this page heard it and carefully wrote it down, at this sign. . . .[2]

1. Luke 24:25.
2. British Library Cotton MS. Nero D i, f.91 = Luard 1882:138–44.

The knighting of William of Valence, the king's half-brother

While this great solemnity was proceeding splendidly in Westminster Abbey, the lord king, dressed in cloth of gold made of the richest silk, wearing a gold crown commonly called a garland, and seated majestically on his royal throne, ordered his half-brother to be summoned together with a number of his companions. They arrived at once with him in order to receive their arms with suitable ceremony, and the king joyfully conferred the honour of knighthood on him and some of his companions.

The lord king's command about what has been described above

While the king was seated on his royal throne as mentioned above he saw the person who wrote this, called him to him, and told him to sit on the steps between the throne and the floor of the church. "You have seen all these things," said the king, "and you have firmly impressed what you have seen on your mind?" To which he replied, "Indeed yes, my lord, for they are worthy of retention; this day's proceedings have been truly magnificent". "I certify as a fact", continued the king, "that the Lord has actually deigned through his grace to work a glorious miracle today, as an earnest of more abundant kindness and future good works. It happened early this morning and I give thanks for it. I entreat you, and in entreating I command you, to write a clear and detailed account of all these proceedings to be entered indelibly in a book, so that their memory cannot on any account be lost to posterity down the ages." And he invited the person to whom he said this to dinner with his three companions. On the same day the king ordered all the monks who had come there to be sumptuously entertained in the refectory at the royal expense along with the monks of Westminster and some other people.

Bishop S. of Carlisle is consecrated

At this time Silvester the elect of Carlisle was consecrated bishop in St. Agatha's [church, Richmond].[1] On St. Edward's day [13 October] the earl of Leicester [Simon de Montfort] arrived from abroad, where he had gone on top secret royal business.

1.   Matthew Paris has written "on St. Agatha's day" in error here; see Luard 1877:645n.1.

The lord abbot of Westminster and John Mansel are sent abroad

At this same time the lord abbot of Westminster and Lord John Mansel the provost of Beverley were sent abroad on the same or some other secret affair of the king. It could be conjectured that this was for the marriage of Edward, the king's son and heir, to the daughter of the duke of Brabant, which had still not been finalized.

Earl Richard returns from the continent

Earl Richard of Cornwall returned from abroad on SS. Simon and Jude the apostles' day [28 October] having taken his son Henry there with him. It was said that he had had intimate and prolonged talks with the lord king of the French, who had firmly proposed setting out on his pilgrimage next Easter prudently prepared in both spiritual and temporal matters. Since he had also granted and resigned their legal rights to all claimants, and was ready and willing to make amends to the lord king of England, the earl earnestly demanded the restoration of the king of England's rights. The king of France would willingly have granted his request but for the objections raised by the envy and cupidity of his councillors, namely certain French nobles, in whom pride is innate. So the king of England's ambassadors were told to their face, especially as regards Normandy, that the king of the French had been in peaceful possession for a long time, that is about forty years. Nor had it been effectively claimed during that time by the king of England, nor vigorously demanded, nor had any appeal been made to the papal curia, which habitually determined difficult and complicated disputes. On this account it seemed to the French that the English king ought to be deprived of his rights, but this reasoning did not satisfy the delicate conscience of the king of France, who referred the determination of this difficulty to the bishops of Normandy. Closely interrogated on this matter, these prelates said that they were convinced that the king of France had a better right to Normandy than the king of England, especially as the latter had been judged against in this respect by his peers. But it seemed absurd, and against all justice and reason, for the king of England to be judged and condemned in this way by his enemies, especially when the Lord said that "the son", if he does not take after his father, "ought not to suffer for the iniquity of his father".[1] The above-mentioned earl left things in this state and, assuming a pilgrim's role, went to Pontigny to pray to St. Edmund and honour him with gifts and offerings, as well as gratefully to give thanks for the improvement in his health. On his arrival there, besides what he gave there and then and what he vowed and promised he would give in the future, he presented a very handsome collar, wider than a man's hand and ornamented with the most precious jewels, the like of which was not to be found among the king's treasures.

1. Ezekiel 18:20.

Wales is miserably oppressed at this time

Wales at this time experienced a cessation of arable and dairy farming and of commerce, and the inhabitants suffered from want. They accepted English rule unwillingly; their time-honoured aristocratic pride fell into decline; and the harps even of the churchmen turned to mourning and lamentation.[1] The bishop of Menai, that is St. David's, died as if he had pined away for grief, and William bishop of Llandaff was struck with blindness. The bishops of St. Asaph and Bangor were forced to beg and to live off others after their bishoprics had been ruined by fire and slaughter.

1. Compare Job 30:31.

Master Thomas is elected bishop of St. David's

After the Welsh had suffered innumerable tribulations through war and the deaths of their princes, the archdeacon of Lincoln, Master Thomas, called Wallensis because he was born in Wales, was elected to the vacant see of St. David's. Though the bishopric was in an impoverished state he consented to the election because the bishop of Lincoln was tyrannizing over his canons; because the post was in his native land and everyone is naturally attracted by pleasant recollections of their birthplace; and also because he hoped to comfort his wretched countrymen with his presence, advice and help. The king willingly consented to the election and accepted the bishop-elect; he made no difficulty because it was such an unimportant bishopric.

The city of Parma is miserably oppressed

Meanwhile the city of Parma, invested all round, was suffering terribly in all kinds of ways from famine and want. They could not leave their city on the side where the besiegers had built a large city instead of a camp, which Frederick called Victoria, nor could they by the river, which was closely guarded by Frederick. Nor could any help or advice reach them from the pope, who had encouraged them to rebel, because the roads and paths were under continuous surveillance. Since Frederick was prepared to winter there and prolong his stay till he had defeated his enemies, the hopes of the besieged faded. One day, therefore, impelled by privation and so as to avoid being accused of doing nothing, they decided to launch a sudden attack on the imperial army. So about 140 of the leading citizens suddenly sallied forth in arms, but their attack was imprudent because the enemy was forewarned. They were vigorously opposed at the point of the sword and, when they tried to return to their city their retreat was cut off by the enemy. Some were captured and the rest killed, for it was at that time decreed and acclaimed at Frederick's court on the advice of the judge Thaddeus that no captured enemies should be imprisoned and ransomed, but they should be beheaded at once: Frederick was so infuriated by the recent creation of a new king in Germany. And the dismayed citizens, finding themselves abandoned on all sides and completely deprived of the promised papal help, sent an embassy to request peace terms and seeking mercy rather than judgement. But the merciless Frederick, seething with anger and elated by arrogance, withheld his mercy from those entreating it and refused to lend the ear of kindness to those wretched people, thus incurring God's displeasure. Acting on secret and severe advice he sent an ironical message back to them to the effect that they should use their corn sparingly and prudently because they would get nothing more to eat while he was alive. This harsh message is thought to have emanated from Thaddeus.

Concerning the prohibition of a dangerous tournament

Also, in this same year about Martinmas [11 November], Earl Richard of Gloucester, relying on the concession he had obtained from the king which had been publicly proclaimed in the king's name on the day he knighted his half-brother William, namely a free and general permit to hold a tournament, got ready to meet the said William in the lists at Northampton in the week before Advent, so that William and his fellow novices could gain experience in the arts of chivalry. Moreover these Poitevins, emboldened by their relationship with the king and relying on his protection, had begun to consider themselves the equals of the English and even to despise some of them. But because it was feared that the arrogant boasting of these people and other foreigners might cause quarrelling and fighting, and that bloody swords might strike after the spears had been broken, the lord king forbade the tournament on the advice of prudent councillors and on penalty of the disinheritance of the children of any transgressors. So when people arrived at the place fixed for the tournament they were disappointed and went off annoyed after their unnecessary expenses, and deploring the king's change of mind. But the prohibition was by no means unnecessary, for the pride and insults of these foreigners had provoked the determined hatred of the English.

About this time Frederick gave his daughter in marriage to Thomas of Savoy, brother of the archbishop of Canterbury. He also gave him Vercelli and Turin and the surrounding territories, and entrusted to him the defences he had prepared to stop the pope and his supporters from passing through these provinces.[1]

1. This paragraph is in the margin of B.

How the lord king so enriched his half-brothers that he impoverished himself

When Guy of Lusignan the lord king's half-brother left England the king filled his saddle-bags with such a weight of new sterlings that he had to increase the number of his horses. To his other brother, namely William of Valence, the king gave the castle of Hertford with the honour belonging to it and a large sum of money. So much so that the king himself seemed to be in need and to have to plunder or beg his own food, and those who sincerely and truly loved him feared not a little that the curses of poor people heaped on his head would spoil the effect of his almsgiving and that his prayers would be transformed into sins.[1] The king provided for Aethelmar, the third of his brothers, from the rich and abundant revenues he had extorted with imperious demands from each bishop and abbot, one after another, so that he seemed to be outdoing the Romans in audacity and Aethelmar to be surpassing the bishops in wealth.

1. Compare Psalm 108:7.

Concerning the coronation of Haakon, king of Norway

Also in the same year, on the fourth of the kalends of August [29 July], which is the feast of the holy king and martyr Olaf, who is a very well known saint in the Norwegian territories and islands, King Haakon was solemnly crowned and anointed king at Bergen by [William] bishop of [S.] Sabina, at that time papal legate there. For this honour and benefit the king paid the pope 15,000 marks of sterlings. Moreover the legate, apart from the many valuable presents he received, extorted 500 marks from the Norwegian church. However, the said king, having taken the cross, obtained leave from the pope to make the ecclesiastics of his kingdom contribute one third of their revenues towards the expenses of his pilgrimage. When the king of France heard about this he wrote a friendly letter to King Haakon inviting him, out of affection and for the advancement of the Church's welfare, as well as for the honour of the holy cross, the sign of which he bore, to set out at once for the Holy Land with him. He would entrust to King Haakon, who was powerful and skilled at sea, his entire kingdom's fleet. Furthermore, the French army would to a large extent be placed under his command. When this letter, the bearer of which was the person who wrote this, reached the lord king of Norway, he replied as follows to the person who delivered it, after he had read the contents and taken him into his confidence: "I extend many thanks to the most pious French king for wanting my company on his pilgrimage, but I have some knowledge of the French character. The poet says "Everyone powerful is impatient of his fellow", but I say "Everyone proud is impatient of his fellow".[1] My people are impetuous and imprudent, impatient of any sort of injury or restraint. If therefore contention should arise between such people and [the French], who are proud, both of us would suffer irreparable injury. Therefore, let us each go by himself and act as the Lord disposes. However, I have written to the French king asking him kindly to grant me the privilege by his letters patent of landing peaceably on his territory and providing myself with necessaries if by chance I or any of my people fall ill or lack provisions or other things when sailing along the coast of his kingdom on my pilgrimage." On this the person with whom he was talking, namely the writer of this present work, gave him these letters patent.

The letters patent of the lord king of the French to the lord king of Norway

Louis by the grace of God king of the French, to all his friends and loyal subjects, bailiffs, mayors and provosts, who receive these presents, greeting. Since our dearest friend the illustrious King Haakon of Norway proposes to sail to the assistance of the Holy Land, as he has informed us by letter, we command you, if the said king or his fleet should happen to pass by our shores at sea or to land in territory of ours or dependent on us, to receive him and his people with kindness and honour, allowing them to buy provisions on our territory and lawfully to obtain necessaries.

Done at Saint-Germain-en-Laye, in the year of our Lord 1247.

When the lord king of Norway, who is a discreet, modest and perfectly literate man, read this letter, he was really delighted, and returned thanks to its bearer besides rewarding him with rich and royal presents.

---

1. Lucan *Phars*.1:93.

Concerning the danger the earl of Winchester was in

Also at this time Earl Roger of Winchester, who was living in his land of Galloway, which was his in right of his wife the daughter of Alan of Galloway, was suddenly besieged in one of his castles without warning. He had been acting more tyrannically than usual against the nobility of that country. Realising that he was threatened by an ignominious death and preferring to be killed in battle rather than die of hunger, the earl mounted an extra fine horse and, armed to the teeth, suddenly opened the castle gates and rushed with a few daring followers into the midst of his enemies who were gathered in strength. He opened a way through with his sword, striking them down on every side and, narrowly escaping death, he finally cut through and dispersed them. Nor did he rein in his horse until he reached the king of Scotland. When he complained to him, the king punished the rebels and reinstated the earl peaceably in his possessions.

The newly elected king of Germany was denied admission to Aachen

At this same time, the newly-elected king of Germany, Count William of Holland, was denied entry to the city of Aachen where he was to be crowned. So he could not be honourably received there and given the royal diadem according to the usual tradition in Germany. This was because Frederick's son Conrad, the deposed king of Germany, systematically organised opposition to him and, when he was advised in a friendly way by the lord Octavianus, papal legate there, the archbishop of Cologne, and other German magnates, not to take after his father by following the track of someone who had been excommunicated and deposed lest he should incur a similar punishment, Conrad replied, "Never shall I desert my father for traitors like you". The city was therefore besieged and a bloody war began between the supporters of either side. But the Church's strength increased because of the efforts of the Franciscans and Dominicans and because of the money collected by the lord pope from various parts of Germany and the neighbouring lands, while every day Conrad's power waned and his army diminished in strength. For the above-mentioned king-elect was related by blood to many of the leading German magnates: he and the bishop of Liège [Henry of Guelders] were cousins; the duke of Brabant [Henry II] was his uncle; and many other magnates were bound to him in various ways as well as by gifts.

A *plague causes many deaths*

In the dogdays, when the sun was declining in the zodiac, particularly in September, a plague which lasted three months caused many deaths; so many that one day nine or ten bodies were buried in the cemetery of a single church, namely that of St. Peter's in the town of St. Albans.

The death of the earl of Ferrers and several other nobles

In this same year several nobles died in England. About St. Catherine's day [25 November], William, earl of Ferrers, a peaceable and upright man, died at an advanced age. He was worn out after suffering for a long time from gout. He had been married to his wife M.[1] the countess by the blessed Thomas, archbishop of Canterbury. She died in the same month, similar in age, fame and goodness. The said earl was succeeded in the earldom by his eldest son and heir, William, a good and discreet man, but wretchedly afflicted with the same disease as his father. [Anselm], bishop of St. David's, also died. Born in Wales, he was a holy and pious man, an erstwhile Franciscan, among the most magnanimous of Welshmen, and of handsome person. He was worn out with grief and troubles occasioned by the slaughter of his countrymen and the destruction of his native land. Besides them, other nobles died, namely the knights Richard de Burgo and William FitzHamon.

1. Matthew Paris is in error here; her name was Agnes.

The conclusion of the annal

So this year passed, very abundant in corn but barren of fruit; harmful to England, tyrannical and oppressive for Wales, unfavourable in the Holy Land, a turbulent despoiler of the Church, bloody in Italy, belligerent and hostile to the Empire, the papal curia and especially to the kingdom of Germany; hatred was generated against the pope in the hearts of the prelates and many others because he forcibly despoiled their patrons and suspended them from the collation of benefices, something hitherto unheard of and against the king's interests, though he permitted it to happen.

[The Chronica majora 1248]

The king at Winchester

In the year of the lord 1248, which is the thirty-second year of the reign of the lord king Henry III, the king celebrated Christmas at Winchester with a numerous company of magnates. The next day, namely St. Stephen's day, he dined with Bishop William [Raleigh] of that city.

The earl of Leicester and many other nobles take the cross

At this time Earl S[imon de Montfort] of Leicester took the cross so that, absolved from his sins, he might deserve to ascend to heaven; this was because of pangs of conscience over his marriage, for his wife had formerly made an oath of chastity before the archbishop of Canterbury, St. Edmund. The countess too, apparently affected by the same qualms, rushed to take the cross as soon as she learned that her husband had done so. The knights and many others of their household also took the cross, to secure the benefit of eternal recompense. Among them were many nobles who planned to travel on crusade with the most Christian king of the French [Louis IX], whom the Lord had deigned to recall miraculously from death's door, or even from death itself. Nor does this seem to have been done without purpose, for it was claimed by way of a prognostic, or even asserted through prophetic inspiration as a fact, that the Lord had restored the king to life so that he could forcefully rescue his inheritance from the hands of the enemies of the cross.

The bishop of Bangor comes to St. Albans with a view to staying there

The impoverished lord bishop of Bangor, Richard, came at this time to

129

St. Albans seeking charity, so that he could stay there with the lord abbot until his bishopric, ravaged by war, had to some extent recovered, and he and his clergy could breathe again after the anxieties that had surrounded them; just as formerly Bishop John of Ardfert had been honourably maintained in the same place during a stay of about twenty years.

Richard Suard's mortal illness

At this time the distinguished knight Richard Suard[1], about whom much has already been written in this little book, seized by an incurable paralysis, took to his bed in a desperate state, hoping, through God's beneficence, that the sufferings of a protracted death might wash away his former sins so that he could more expeditiously migrate to eternal life.

1. His shield is drawn inverted in the margin: sable, a cross fleury argent between four plates.

Beatrice, widow of the count of Provence, comes to England

In the same year Beatrice, widow of the late count of Provence Raymond [Berengar], came to England accompanied by Thomas of Savoy, the former count of Flanders, as if on a visit to friends and relatives. For the benefit of those who wish to know the true cause of their coming, it should be explained that the countess and the above-mentioned Thomas went thirsting after a well-known spring: by the time they left they hoped to have filled their gaping and empty saddle-bags from the wealth and prodigality of the lord king.

The death of Roger [of Salisbury], bishop of Bath

Also at this time, namely about the feast of St. Hilary [13 January], Bishop Roger of Bath went the way of all flesh.[1] The lord king, as was his custom, laid his greedy hands on the episcopal property, hurriedly making off with whatever could be extorted from it.

1. A mitre and pastoral staff are drawn in the margin here, inverted. Bishop Roger died on 21 December 1247.

The king of the French re-assumes the cross

At this same time, the lord king of the French who, as was well known, had taken the cross, was reproached and seriously criticized, and indeed almost circumvented, by his magnates and courtiers, because he was unwilling to redeem or commute his vow in any way, in spite of their suggestions and advice. Among them his mother Blanche [of Castile] and the bishop of Paris [William of Auvergne], aware of the king's imbecility, boldly insisted and argued earnestly with him, the bishop addressing him as follows. "My lord king, remember that when you took the cross, making so important a vow hurriedly and without advice, you were ill and, to tell the truth, your mind was wandering. Blood had rushed to your brain so that you were not of sound mind and the words you then uttered lacked the weight of truth and authority. The lord pope will be good enough to grant a dispensation, knowing the critical state of the kingdom's affairs and your bodily weakness. On the one side the power of Frederick, now a schismatic, is to be feared; on the other the plots of the king of the English, who has plenty of money; here the treacherous deceit of the Poitevins, but recently subdued, there the suspect sophistries of the Albigensians. Germany is disturbed, Italy restless; access to the Holy Land is difficult, your reception there uncertain, while behind you would be the inexorable hatred and implacable enmity of the pope and Frederick, to which you would leave us abandoned".

Then the king's mother, adding her own suggestions, spoke to him with some effect. "Dearest son! Instead of resisting your own prudence, hear and pay attention to the advice of your discerning friends. Bear in mind what a virtue it is, and how pleasing to God, to obey and fall in with the wishes of a mother. Stay here, and the Holy land will suffer no detriment. An even more numerous military expedition could be sent there than that which would have accompanied your person. God neither plays tricks nor does he quibble. You, my son, are sufficiently excused by what happened during your illness: the deprivation of your reason, the dulling of your senses, the oncome of death itself, or the alienation of the mind."

To this the king, no little moved, replied: "You claim that the change in my senses was the cause of my assuming the cross; there now, as you wish and have argued, I shall lay down the cross, handing it over to you" and, raising his hand to his shoulder, he ripped off the cross with the words, "Lord bishop, here is the cross which I assumed; moreover, I resign it to you." At this, all those sitting around expressed their intense joy, but the lord king, altering his tone of voice and countenance, said: "My friends, certainly I am not now deprived of my reason or senses, nor am I powerless or infirm. Now I demand back my cross. He who ignores nothing knows that nothing edible will enter my mouth until I have again signed myself with it." When those present saw this they recognized that the hand of God was here[1] and that these things had been effected by a divine force from heaven. Nor did anyone dare raise any further questions about this affair. We have recorded this business fully and exactly so that everyone appreciates the constancy of the most Christian king of the French in the service of Christ.

1. Compare Exodus 8:19.

The general parliament held at London on the octave of the Purification of the blessed Mary

At the beginning of this year, namely on the octave of the Purification [9 February], the nobles throughout the kingdom of England were convoked to London by royal decree for a thorough and careful discussion with the king of the affairs of the kingdom, which was very much disturbed and impoverished and indeed at this time in a bad way. Besides a large number of other barons, knights, nobles, abbots, priors and clerics, nine bishops and nine earls attended, namely the archbishop of York [Walter de Gray], the bishops of Winchester, Lincoln, Norwich, Worcester, Chichester, Ely, Rochester, and Carlisle[1], and Earl Richard, the earls of Gloucester, Leicester, Winchester and Hereford[2], Earl Roger Bigod the marshal, the earl of Oxford[3] and besides them, the earl of Lincoln, Earl Ferrers, the earl of Warenne[4], and the earl of Richmond, namely P[eter] of Savoy. Not present at this great assembly were Archbishop B[oniface] of Canterbury, who was fighting for the pope abroad, the bishop of Durham, who was sick and far off, and the bishop of Bath, who had just died.

When the lord king explained that he was seeking financial aid, a fact which was not unknown to the community at large, he was severely reproached for unashamedly seeking such a subsidy, especially since, at the time of the last exaction, to which the nobles of England had with difficulty been induced to consent, he had drawn up a charter promising that he would not again cause his magnates such injury and damage. Not surprisingly, he was also most seriously criticised for indiscriminately admitting foreigners, to whom, indiscreetly, and in a prodigious and prodigal way, he had distributed and dispensed all the property of the kingdom; he had also married the nobles of the kingdom to ignoble foreigners, spurning and pushing aside his own natural and indigenous subjects, and without seeking their mutual consent, which is a prerequisite of marriage.[5]

The king was also blamed, not without reason, for taking by force whatever he needed by way of food, drink, especially wine, and even clothing, against the wishes of the sellers and true owners of these things. As a result, the native dealers withdrew and went into hiding, as did the foreign merchants, who would otherwise have brought their goods to sell in this country. Thus trade, which mutually assists and enriches the different nations, has been brought to a standstill; and thus we are diffamed and impoverished because they receive nothing but exactions and trifles from the king. Because of this the lord king is cursed by all and sundry, to the peril and disgrace of himself and the whole kingdom. Moreover, he has forcibly seized wax, silk cloths and other things from these same merchants, without payment, so that he can give alms freely and enjoy excessive illuminations. Thus he has brought opprobrium on himself, his kingdom, and all its inhabitants, not without seriously offending God, who hates "robbery for burnt offering".[6] In all these ways the king behaves in so tyrannical and arbitrary a manner that he does not even allow the herrings or other fish of the poor fishermen on the coast to be disposed of in the way they want, nor do they dare appear along the coast or in the towns for fear of being robbed, considering themselves safer in crossing the stormy waters to the farther shores. The wretched merchants are coerced and truculently forced by the royal agents, so that punishments are added to their losses and injury heaped on injury, and their persons, carts and horses are worn out when they are forced to transport their goods to remote places in inclement weather and over difficult roads.

The lord king was also rebuked for ruinously impoverishing the bishoprics and abbacies — not to mention the vacant wardships — founded by our holy and distinguished forefathers. He has been retaining these for long periods of time in his own hands, against the first and principal oath he swore at his coronation, yet he is supposed to be their protector and defender, hence the expression 'to be in his hands', meaning 'in his protection'. Serious complaints were also made to the lord king by one and all that, unlike his distinguished royal predecessors, he had appointed neither a justiciar, nor a chancellor, nor a treasurer, through the common counsel of the kingdom, as he should do and was expedient, but only people who would do his will whatever it was, so long as it was to their advantage, and who sought their own advancement, rather than that of the commonwealth, in amassing money and procuring wardships and rents for themselves.

1. Respectively William Raleigh, Robert Grosseteste, Walter Suffield, Walter Cantilupe, Richard Wich, Hugh of Northwold, Richard Wendene and Silvester Everdon.
2. Respectively Richard de Clare, Simon de Montfort, Roger de Quincy and Humphrey de Bohun.
3. Hugh de Vere.
4. Respectively Edmund de Lacy, William de Ferrières and John de Warenne.
5. The words from "and without" to "marriage" are in the margin in B.
6. Isaiah 61:8.

The lord king's shady[1] promise

The lord king was ashamed when he heard this, for he knew that all of it was perfectly true. He therefore promised most faithfully and definitely that he would gladly put right all these matters, hoping that, through such humility, even though it was false, he would the more readily persuade everyone to accept his demands. After considering this offer the community, which had often been ensnared by such promises, replied, "We shall look into this, and a solution will emerge shortly. We shall wait patiently and comply with the lord king in all matters according to the way he treats us." So everything was put off and deferred until the quindene of the nativity of St. John the Baptist [8 July]. But in the meanwhile the lord king, either of his own accord or on the advice of his courtiers, who were unwilling to see their power weakened, became hardened against and even exasperated with his own subjects, and did next to nothing to make amends to his loyal subjects for the above-mentioned excesses, in spite of his promise.

1. The word *umbratilis*, erased in B, has been supplied from the copy C.

How the bishop of Durham unjustly oppressed the church of Tynemouth

At this time the lord bishop Nicholas of Durham, contrary to his honour and to the agreement and fraternity enjoyed between himself and the house of St. Albans since the settlement of the dispute over the visitation of the church of Tynemouth, began to harass that church outrageously[1] in temporal matters and, not without causing injury and expense to both parties, to infringe its liberties, which had been granted and confirmed in the charters of distinguished kings, and had been in force for many years. One of the brothers of the church of St. Albans was therefore sent to persuade him to desist from this molestation but he, disdaining both the warnings and entreaties of this brother and the letters from the abbot and convent of St. Albans which he took with him, insisted that he had a just cause in this dispute. But this was evidently not true, though he maintained that it had been decided by his twelve knights, who had not, however, been freely elected with the full consent of both parties. This must be clear to any careful reader of the privileges of the church of St. Albans. We have decided to set down briefly in this work which privileges he had infringed as regards spiritual and which in temporal matters.

A summary of certain privileges which the above-mentioned bishop has presumed to infringe

The church of St. Albans, its cells, and all its appurtenances shall be free of all tribute to the king, bishop, earl, duke, judge or official and from all services which are customarily imposed.

We do not wish them to have to respond to anyone in any matter except to the Roman pontiff.

Item, we prohibit any archbishop or bishop from daring to make any exactions in your cells, and from presuming to exercise any right or episcopal function there.

Item, those of your chapels and cemeteries in which you do not have pontifical rights shall be free and immune from every exaction, and in these churches or chapels you and your brethren shall be allowed to elect your priests, so long as they assume the care of souls, without any payment, from the bishop or his vicar. After you have assigned sufficient for these priests to provide for their reasonable needs in food and clothing, you may convert whatever balance remains to your own uses.

Since we have sent orders in our apostolic letters to you and other prelates to contribute aid for the assistance of the Holy Land and you, as we understand, moved by our persuasion, have allocated a tenth of the revenues of your church and those of your cells and subjects to this pious purpose, we regard your laudable project as ratified and gratifying and by authority of these present letters, on pain of anathema, we strictly forbid any ecclesiastic or secular person to dare to compel you or your church, on pretext of this pious and necessary deed, to undertake in future either this or anything similar, or to molest you, your church, or its cells in any way lest,which God forbid, you are some day compelled against your will to submit to something which you are known to have begun in pure generosity and for reasons of piety.[2]

To all prelates throughout England etc. Because the church of St. Alban belongs to the jurisdiction and ownership of St. Peter etc., if any person or priest belonging to that church refuses to answer to the aforesaid abbot and brothers in a matter or to pay the pension they owe, we grant to the said abbot and brethren full powers to take away from them whatever they have in their churches and chapels that they are witholding from them without any possibility or opposition or appeal, until they are forced to answer in temporal matters and to pay the moneys owing.[3]

In willing agreement to your just requests, we confirm by apostolic authority through these present letters to you and through you to your church, which is a cell of the aforesaid monastery, the possessions donated to you through the pious generosity of the faithful, also the liberties and other benefits conferred on your church by King Richard of glorious memory and by our well beloved son in Christ the illustrious John, king of England, as you justly and pacifically possess them and as is more fully set out in their charters, also the churches and their pensions confirmed in the letters of the metropolitan and diocesan bishop, and the liberties and immunities granted to the abbey of St. Albans for its cells. Let no one therefore etc. and whoever etc.

However, after peace had been re-established on these terms, between the aforesaid bishop, who had rashly infringed the above-mentioned privileges, and the convent of Tynemouth, which had been harassed in many ways, the said bishop applied himself to annoying and damaging the prior and convent in temporal matters, and to undermining the special privileges granted to them by those glorious kings. How damaging this rash presumption was everyone can plainly see, from the following letter of the lord king, to whom the complaining lament [of that church] had ascended.

Letters of the lord king addressed to the bishop of Durham[4]

Henry by the grace of God etc. to the bishop of Durham, salutations. We cannot contain our astonishment that, even though we have asked you in full affection once and again to desist from harassing our beloved in Christ the prior of Tynemouth who, as you know, is under our special protection and defence, yet you have taken no notice whatsoever of our entreaties on his behalf. We reluctantly remind you that it was in deference to you that we put this matter off, firmly believing and hoping that your goodwill and discretion would induce you freely to accomplish what you should have done by the law of the realm and through royal authority. To make it manifestly clear to you that so far in this affair we have been willing to defer to you, we have decided to appeal earnestly a third time to your goodwill, in consideration of our entreaties and out of respect for the respect you owe to your prince, to hand over without any delay the belongings of the said prior which you took against the law of the land and are unjustly detaining, as can readily be proved by the liberties he holds by charters of our predecessors kings of England, especially the charter of our uncle King Richard, which they freely enjoyed in the time of our predecessors. Rest assured that, unless you arrange for these entreaties of ours to have their full effect by the octave of St. Hilary [20 January] next however much we have deferred to you and still wish to defer to you, as we rightly should, we shall thereupon cause the aforesaid belongings to be handed over and the damages suffered by the prior, as a result of the injuries done him by you, to be made good to him, and we shall compel you to do him full justice. This notwithstanding your privileges, by reason of which your damages to others cannot and should not be passed by without the intervention of royal authority. Witness etc.

It thus appears from this letter that both the prior and his convent have been grossly wronged. They enjoyed the same privileges and liberties as the church of the blessed Alban, to which has been granted every possible privilege by the pope in spiritual matters, and by its most pious founder Offa and other English kings whatever royal authority could grant in temporal matters.

1. The word "outrageously" is erased in B and "to his utmost" written into the space by Matthew Paris.
2. In the margin here in MS. B Matthew Paris has written, "Yet the bishop compelled the church of Tynemouth, along with all the other ecclesiastics in his diocese, to contribute to the Durham Cathedral fabric fund."
3. In the margin of MS B here Matthew Paris has written, "Yet the said bishop forbade some of the vicars to pay the pensions they owed to the church of Tynemouth"; and, with reference to the next paragraph: "Innocent [III] to the prior of Tynemouth and the monks of that place."
4. This letter is also copied into the *Book of additamenta*, BL Cotton MS. Nero D i, f93.

Frederick's defeat and the liberation of the city of Parma

While fortune was thus playing or rather sporting with worldly affairs, the people of Parma took counsel together in the common cause and humbled themselves to God and the blessed Bishop Roger of London, who had been so gloriously dignified by God with splendid miracles. When on his way to the Roman curia this bishop was furtively robbed at night of all his money while staying at Parma. Because of this, after leaving the city, on his return from Rome, he cursed it in the bitterness of his heart. However, the citizens took the trouble to find out how much money the bishop claimed to have lost, which amounted to . . . marks, and made a vow that they would in all humility make satisfaction to God and his saint for that amount, either by building a church in London or in the giving of alms, or in some other way pleasing to the holy man. I report all this because the Parmans had heard that Frederick, who was closely besieging their town, had at that time gone off on some business leaving most of his army there. Since the army was thus diminished and its commander absent, the citizens decided to launch a surprise attack on their enemies. One day, therefore, after invoking help from above and devoutly making the above-mentioned vow, they carefully organized their forces, for one and all were determined to prosecute the war for the liberation of their city, their wives and their children. Then, throwing open the city gates, they rushed at the enemy unexpectedly and suddenly, like lightning, preferring to be killed with weapons in their hands rather than die slowly of hunger.

When Frederick's close adviser, Thaddeus [of Suessa], to whom he had confidently entrusted both his army and his treasure, realised what was happening, he exclaimed arrogantly and insultingly, "The mice have dared to come out of their holes". However, the citizens made a most spirited assault and in a very short time routed the entire imperial army, many thousands being either massacred or put to shameful flight. Thus splendidly, they gained the longed-for victory over their enemies. After this they demolished, scattered or burned all the fortifications which Frederick had made round the city to maintain the siege, and took Thaddeus prisoner together with the immense treasure he had been entrusted with. He was a judge of the imperial palace, expert at pleading difficult cases and circumspect in deciding them, but, unwilling to wait to be trapped by the ambiguities of words and honeyed or well-oiled speeches,[1] they butchered him. The men of Cremona, who had joined the siege on Frederick's side, were put to flight and, to the confusion and disgrace of Cremona, their standard was captured. After they had defeated and dispersed Frederick's army, the victors returned joyfully to their city, taking with them arms, treasure, supplies of food, tents and utensils. Not to mention the vast amount of other booty, in this battle the triumphant citizens carried off with them some 15,000 animals including valuable war horses, riding horses, pack horses, mules and oxen, so that their city unexpectedly abounded in all good things.

When news of this reached the papal curia, the lord pope was beyond measure jubilant and spoke the following words: "In the name of Christ, Victoria, you have succumbed to a victory"[2] – for Frederick had called his siege-works by that name. When he learned about this Frederick groaned both inwardly and out loud, as if deeply wounded, lamenting with cruel sighs, for the death of Thaddeus and the pope's insult weighed on his mind and made him more bitter than all his other losses. Indeed, those of us who have read the succession of historical annals have found no other instance of such intense and inexorable hatred as existed between the lord pope and Frederick. When Frederick had recalled his forces from all directions he again took the offensive against the citizens with redoubled threats. These events are described more at length in the *Book of additamenta* at this sign. . . .[3]

1. See Psalm 54:22. There is play here on the words *mellitos*, honeyed, and *mollitos*, softened.
2. The original rhymes: *Ad laudem Christi, Victoria victa fuisti.*
3. BL Cotton MS. Nero D i, f.93v is here referred to, though a different sign is given there = Luard 1882:146–7.

The restoration of the coinage, which had been debased by too much clipping

At this time, the English money was so intolerably debased by money-clippers and forgers that neither the inhabitants nor even foreigners could contemplate it with a serene eye or an even temper. The coins were clipped almost to the inner circle and the inscription round the border either completely deleted or very badly defaced. It was there-fore proclaimed in the king's name by public criers in towns, fairs and markets that no one should accept a penny that was not of legal weight and circumference nor should such a coin in any way be used by a vendor, buyer or in exchange; violators of this decree to be punished. Some trouble was taken to discover these falsifiers so that, if judicially convicted of the crime, they might be suitably punished. After a most thorough enquiry, some Jews and notorious Cahorsins, and a few

Flemish wool merchants, were found culpable. The lord king of the French ordered all such people found in his kingdom to be exposed to the winds by being suspended on gibbets.

The death of Walter Mauclerc, former bishop of Carlisle, and of some other brothers of the order of Preachers

In this year too, around the time of the feast of the apostles Simon and Jude [28 October], Walter surnamed Mauclerc, formerly bishop of Carlisle, eluding the canker of worldly affairs and riches, came to the end of his days in laudable fashion and went the way of all flesh. And in the same year two brothers of the same order departed to God from this world; namely Brother Robert Bacon and Brother Richard Fishacre. During their lives, it is believed, no one surpassed or even equalled them in theology and other sciences. They had lectured brilliantly on theology for many years and were famous for preaching the word of God to the people.

Frederick and his son Conrad are married

Also in this year, to strengthen and further consolidate his cause in the struggle he had embarked on with the pope, Frederick, having made an alliance with certain princes, took as wife a woman rich in treasure, pleasing in appearance and illustrious in birth.[1] His son, prompted by the same idea, married [Elizabeth], daughter of the duke of Bavaria [Otto II]. When he heard this the archbishop of Cologne [Konrad von Hochstaden] and the supporters of the newly-elected king of Germany insisted more than ever on the plenary and solemn coronation of the said King W[illiam] at Aachen. But, because of the opposition of Frederick and his son Conrad, he was prevented and altogether precluded from entering that city. So the archbishop of Cologne and the legate [Peter Capoccio, cardinal-deacon of S. Giorgio in Velabro], together with innumerable prelates and nobles who supported the Church, most of whom had received the sign of the cross from the brothers Preacher and Minor, besieged the city of Cologne with the utmost enthusiasm. Frequent conflicts occurred between the two sides and many were killed. The siege continued, damaging and bloody to both sides, and the number of besiegers increased daily, as a river is swollen by torrents, while letters frequently sent by Frederick and his con Conrad encouraged the besieged not to tire and despair; the splendid consolation of their liberation, so the letters asserted, was near at hand.

1. This marriage, to a daughter of Duke Albert of Saxony, was proposed only, see below p. 147.

A *certain tournament well consummated*

On Ash Wednesday [4 March] a grand tournament among the knights of England, strenuously to test their military skill, was held at Newbury. Since the lord king was in favour of it, it started and ended admirably. William of Valence, half-brother of the king, a novice intent on acquiring knightly renown, took part there, advancing with audacious spirit, but his tender age and imperfect strength not allowing him to resist the impetus of hardened and warlike knights, he was prostrated and, as an initiation to knighthood, thoroughly beaten.

Distress and trouble caused by the changing of the coinage

Also at this time, various precepts of the lord king, concisely promulgated by public criers through the cities of England, concerning the issue of coins, so troubled the people that they would have preferred a measure of corn to have cost more than twenty shillings. For exchange was only permitted in a few cities. When they got there, they were given a certain weight of new money for a certain weight of old, but, on every pound they had to pay thirteen pence for the silversmith's work, namely for moneyage, which is commonly called blanching. This money differed from the old in that a double cross intersected the border with the inscription. Otherwise, that is in weight, impression and inscription, it was the same as before.[1] Thus the people were constrained and suffered no small damage, for they could scarcely bring back twenty shillings from the money-changer's table, in exchange for their thirty, and had the labour and expense of several days of wasteful and tedious waiting.

Unbounded profits accrued to the lord king because of this and Earl Richard his brother, to whom the king was deeply in debt, went to him like another Jacob and underhand usurper, and said to him, "My lord king and brother, will you pay me the debts that you owe me?" And when he most pressingly pressed his demand, the king replied, "My only brother by the same parents, you see my needs on every side.

Look at that little fragment of territory which remains to me beyond the seas, threatened by crisis and diminution. Only the shield of Bordeaux defends Gascony, for the liberation of which I must spend no small sum of money." But the earl, impudently raising his voice, demanded the profits of the newly minted coinage as satisfaction for the king's debt to him, nor did he cease repeatedly to demand this opportunely and importunely, until he obtained an assurance that he could take over the profits of the coinage. According to the estimate of some of the money-changers, normal proceeds of this would continue for seven years and amount to twenty thousand pounds, only one third of them being reserved for the lord king. Thus the lord king would be released from the entanglements of the debts which bound him to the earl. The earl, having obtained this, demanded letters of instruction from the lord king, that no clipped pennies should be accepted in the kingdom of England, and that all clipped coins should be perforated. If any money-changer were anywhere discovered giving two pence for one, or three for two, he should be arrested and severely punished in person and property as a criminal and transgressor against the royal precepts. The form of this writ sent to the sheriffs can be found in full in the *Book of additamenta* at this sign. . . .[2]

1. A rough diagram of a coin is drawn here showing the cross and border.
2. These "urgent letters of the lord king condemning the clipping of coins" are to be found on f.92 of BL Cotton MS. Nero D i. at the correct sign. See Luard 1882:150–1.

An eclipse of the moon

In the same year on the kalends of June [1 June] the moon was almost totally eclipsed just after sunset.[1]

1. An error. The eclipse was on 7 June at nine o'clock p.m.

Another great parliament on the quindene of the nativity of St. John the Baptist [8 July]

On the approach of the quindene of St. John the Baptist's day in June, the nobility of the whole of England assembled in London, firmly believing, from a certain promise of the lord king,[1] that he would be prepared to amend his errors and, with the help of God's grace, follow wiser counsels. When all the principal men of the kingdom had assembled, the following response came from the lord king:

All of you, chief men of England, have tried to bend your lord king to your unmannerly will and to force him into a position of subjection, while what is allowed to any one of you is bluntly denied to him. A person may follow what and whose advice he chooses; any father of a family can appoint anyone from his household to this or that office, or suspend or dismiss them, something indeed which you are rashly presuming to deny to your lord king, especially since servants should by no means presume to judge or lay down conditions upon their master, nor vassals their prince. On the contrary, whoever is thought of as inferior should rather be guided and ruled by the pleasure and will of the lord. "The disciple is not above his master nor the servant above his lord".[2] Indeed, your king would become more like a slave if he were thus to incline to your will. For this reason he will dismiss neither the justiciar nor the treasurer, as you have proposed he should, nor will he appoint others in their places.

The reply to the other points, beneficial to the king himself, was similarly captious,[3] namely "He askes financial aid from you to recover his rights overseas, in which you are also involved."

When the magnates heard this it was clearer than daylight to them that it emanated from his present council, namely from those whose flimsy authority would be wholly extinguished if the community of barons was listened to. Seeing that they were being answered and opposed with cunning, they all replied with one accord that they would on no account further uselessly impoverish themselves so that foreigners could take pride in their possessions, and enemies, both of the king and the kingdom, be strengthened, as had recently happened in Poitou as well as in Gascony, where the king had hastened precipitately and indiscreetly and against their wishes and advice, so that things had turned out to his disadvantage. For we may well believe, and so it appears from the king's greed and necessity, that he was secretly seized and held in custody but, having quietly paid a fine, pledged his faith and issued charters under oath, was carefully released and allowed to depart, ingloriously and in disgrace, dismissed after being deprived of honour, treasure and territories. Thus the council was dissolved with indignation on all sides, and everyone, deceived in the hope that they had vainly attached for so long a time to this parliament and having wasted their efforts and money, brought back as so often happened, nothing but worthless replies and mockery.

1. Above p. 134.
2. Matthew 10:24.
3. The words from "The reply" to "captious" are written in the margin.

How the king ordered his treasure to be sold because of lack of money

When the king realized what had happened, he lost his temper and said to his councillors: "It is your fault that the magnates have been alienated from me. Look! I am on the point of losing Gascony and have been robbed of Poitou. My treasury is empty! What can I do?" A weak-minded council was held and it was improvidently decided that the vessels, utensils, and jewels of the royal treasury should be sold by weight, without regard for the gold, with which silver things were made to gleam, nor for the intricate works of art in which "the work excelled the material,"[1] so that at all events money could be raised. Moreover, the royal councillors added a shameful consolation, to sooth the king, insinuating to him that "just as all rivers flow into the sea, so all the things now sold will certainly return to you at some time in the form of gifts; therefore, our lord king has no need to worry." After the sale the king enquired where, and to whom, the plate had been sold and, when he was told "London", he said, "I know. I know. If Octavianus's treasure was for sale the city of London would buy up the whole lot, for these coarse Londoners, who call themselves barons, are rolling in money; that city is an inexhaustible well." And he immediately conceived the idea, as soon as occasion arose, of plundering the citizens of their goods. Subsequent events clearly demonstrated this, as will be fully explained in what follows.

1. Slightly misquoted from Ovid *Met*. 2:5.

The king of the French crosses the sea on pilgrimage

As the equinoctial season offered pleasant weather and the autumn provided abundant fruit and new wine, the lord king of the French, having solemnly received permission at Saint-Denis and other holy places in his kingdom and having made a vow, set out for Jerusalem. Travelling via Lyons, where the pope was staying, he greeted him with humility and devotion and humbly implored him, saving in everything the honour of the Church, to condescend to grant the favour of a reconciliation, and to extend his fatherly affection, to a penitent, the humiliated Frederick. "So that at least my passage on pilgrimage will be safer." Seeing the look of disapproval on the pope's face, the king dejectedly withdrew with the words: "I fear that, once I have gone, hostile moves will be made against the kingdom of France because of your inexorable obstinacy. If the business of the Holy Land is held up, it will be through your fault. But I shall [guard] France like the pupil of my eye because on its situation depends your prosperity and that of the whole of Christendom". To which the pope replied: "As long as I live I shall stand by France against the schismatical Frederick, condemned by the Church and cast down by a general council from the imperial eminence, as also against our vassal the king of England if he dares anything against the kingdom of the French or its appurtenances, and all the enemies of the aforesaid kingdom". Calmed a little by these words, the king replied, "Since you make these promises I entrust to you the reins of government of my kingdom of France". It was therefore immediately arranged that a special nuncio be sent to the king of England to prohibit him from in any way hostilely attacking or molesting any appurtenances of the French kingdom. To this end Masters Albert and Paul were specially sent, and they reached the king of England at Windsor on the feast of the Exaltation of the Cross [14 September], to announce this to him. But it was kept secret, so that the lord king could more freely demand money for the recovery and restoration of his rights by force of arms. The king of the French, having said farewell [to the pope] and receiving from him the remission of his sins after he had made a rather morose confession, left Lyons and, with the pope's blessing, directed his reins and standard toward Marseilles. As he approached Avignon, the citizens, their hatred and anger aroused by a long-standing enmity, and unable to endure the insults of the haughty French, who called them Albigensians, traitors and poisoners, attacked them in a narrow pass they knew of, robbed some members of the French army, and even killed some who resisted them. Consequently, some of the French magnates proposed to the lord king of the French that he should lay siege to the city, so that at least he could justly and effectively take revenge for the death of his father, who had been poisoned there; alternatively, if he went on his way, they should do it with his approval. The king had difficulty in restraining their ardour. "I am leaving France," he said, "to avenge neither my father, nor my mother, nor my own injuries, but rather those of my Lord Jesus Christ".

The most Christian king of the French put up with much greater injuries at Marseilles, so that the French magnates would have been provoked into laying siege to that city with all their force and great indignation, had not the moderation and holy restraint of the king prevented them. For the king told them, "It is nearly time for us to set out; God forbid that Satan should prevail. He is annoyed about our passage and is trying to impede it by interposing obstacles." And so the king, having quietened the tumult, took with him some picked soldiers on the eve of St. Bartholemew [25 August], leaving behind more than a thousand crossbowmen and many more knights and attendants. These returned with great shame and indignation and could hardly restrain themselves from joining the supporters of the king of the English in battle against the king of the French, but, weighing future peril in the scales of reason and providence, they returned quietly via the lord pope. They offered themselves in his service, to fight at his command against anyone, but, circumvented by the reasoning of the pope and the people at the curia, who knew they had plenty of money, and having deposited the symbols of the cross and handed over their savings to the pope in return for remission from their vows of pilgrimage, they returned home with empty pockets that they might travel more lightly, scarcely keeping sufficient for their expenses on the way. Meanwhile the lord king of the French, committing himself to Neptune, with spreading sails and a favourable wind set course for Cyprus, an island abounding in all good things, to pass a restful winter there.

In the same year in the summer it was reported that the noble city of Seville, in Spain, had been conquered by the most victorious king of Castile. This city was worth 9,000 talents daily during the week to its lord, but on the sixth day, 11,000.[1]

---

1. These two sentences have been added, separately, in the margin by Matthew Paris.

The city of Aachen is taken, and Count W. of Holland is crowned king

As winter's cold became imminent in the frozen world, those besieged in the city of Aachen were severely constrained. On all sides they were denied ingress and egress, every kind of help and counsel, and supplies of provisions. Running out of wheat, their bread was coarse and mossy, their meat was putrid, their weapons broken and eaten with rust, their clothes worn out. The nature of women changed; children searched for food but there was no one to prepare it or give it to them. The besiegers, namely the magnates of Germany, together with the legate [Peter Capoccio], the archbishop of Cologne [Konrad von Hochstaden], and the bishop of Liège [Henry of Guelders], having with them a huge army, as well as other people who had taken the cross at the hands of the brothers Preacher and daily flocked to them from many parts of the world, assiduously prosecuted their purpose. This numerous army assembled by the prelates covered the country like a swarm of locusts. One section by night, another by day, in turn unceasingly battered the walls and towers of the city with mangonels, petraries, and other siege engines for hurling stones installed on all sides. They smashed the exposed and defenceless defenders to pieces, transfixed them with javelins, and did every possible harm to them. So the city, with no hope of rescue, was compelled by necessity to deliver itself up and submit to the enemy. Once it had been thus vigorously and violently conquered, Count William of Holland, the king-elect of Germany, was solemnly crowned there, namely where the most ancient kings of Germany were by right crowned, at the hands of Archbishop Konrad of Cologne, on All Saint's day [1 November]. Meanwhile many people, thin and only half alive from lack of food, fled from the captured, ruined and impoverished city, both inhabitants and the foreign mercenaries stationed there for its defence by Frederick and his son Conrad.

This coronation, however, was considered by many to be invalid, because the electors were not all present there, nor had they all consented to it. For example, neither the duke of the Saxons [Albert I], who was allied to Frederick, if he could be reconciled [with the Church], nor the duke of Bavaria [Otto II] whose daughter [Elizabeth] was to marry Conrad, Frederick's son, agreed, and nor did many others.[1]

1. This paragraph has been added in the margin of B by Matthew Paris. For the marriages, see above p. 140.

Conrad is powerfully resisted while hurrying to the aid of the besieged

Just as the archbishops, bishops, prelates and other magnates who supported the Church had achieved their aim, Conrad, Frederick's son, now suppressed and supplanted as king, was hurrying powerfully to the rescue of the city, but the other German army raised by the legate, more numerous and very strong, moved more powerfully towards him and attacked him fiercely at the point of the sword. In command of this army were the archbishops of Mainz [Siegfried III], of Metz in Lorraine [James of Lorraine], and of Strasbourg [Henry of Stahleck],[1] with their innumerable forces, and the infinite legions of Frisia, Gotia, Russia, Dacia and regions of Germany or next to Germany, who had taken the cross. They all with one intent, indeed as one man, impetuously repelled Conrad, who had Frederick's army and his own, and triumphantly forced them to take flight. And thus the son, not sparing his horse's flanks, withdrew in confusion at top speed to his father, without the consolation of the Holy Spirit.

1. Matthew is mistaken here; Metz and Strasbourg were bishoprics only.

The warren on the land of St. Alban is repeatedly molested but at length freed

In this same year the church of St. Albans suffered persecution and losses with injury from the knights whom it had confidently believed were its friends and allies. For while to some of them in particular hunting was denied under pain of a ten pound fine, it seemed to others not named that they ought to enjoy licence to hunt hares in the said warren. For they claimed that what was to the detriment or advantage of others should not redound to their prejudice. By consent of the parties, therefore, twenty belted knights were elected to bring the controversy to an end by stating the truth of the matter. But five of them, who were dim witted, ignorant of the truth, and shifty, being sworn in, said that they were uncertain of the truth of the affair, but they believed that the abbot's opponents did indeed have the right they were demanding, unless the abbot had obtained another charter of which they knew nothing. When they were certified of the charter in the abbot's possession issued by the present king, besides the ancient ones, all his opponents were confused and silenced. And if they had not been mercifully protected by a provision of the then justiciar Henry of Bath, they would have suffered a sentence of disinheritance; with the abbot's consent he put off this sentence. This was the last relic of the persecution which the church of St. Albans had suffered in the year of our Lord 1240, where, for anyone wishing to read it, it is fully set out.[1]

1. In the *Chronica majora*, Luard 1877:50–4.

A new fair instituted at Westminster

Also in the same year, when the lord king was hastening to London for the feast of St. Edward, that is the translation of that saint in the quindene of Michaelmas, namely the third of the ides of October [13 October], he intimated to a great many of the prelates and magnates, on the pretext of friendship and devotion, that they should come in person with him to Westminster devoutly and solemnly to celebrate the feast of the blessed Edward. In response to this summons Earl Richard, Earl Roger Bigod the marshall, the earl of Hereford, various barons with a number of knights, the bishops of Winchester, London, Ely, Worcester and Carlisle, together with numerous abbots and priors, came there. And the lord king ordered it to be officially announced and proclaimed throughout the whole city of London and elsewhere by public crier that he had instituted a new fair to be held at Westminster to continue for a full fortnight, and, in order that the Westminster fair should more copiously abound with people and merchandise, he absolutely forbade on penalty of weighty forfeiture and fine all markets usually held in England for such a period of time, for instance the fairs at Ely and elsewhere, as well as all trade normally carried on in London both in and out of doors. As a result, a vast crowd of people flocked there as if to the most famous fair, and so the translation of the blessed Edward and the blood of Christ was amazingly venerated by the people assembled there. But all those who exhibited their goods for sale there suffered great inconvenience because of the lack of roofs apart from canvas awnings; for the variable gusts of wind, usual at that time of year, battered the merchants so that they were cold, wet, hungry and thirsty. Their feet were dirtied by the mud and their merchandise spoilt by rain. When they sat down there at table, those who normally took their meals at home by the family fireside could not stand this discomfort. The bishop of Ely, because of the loss of his fair at Ely, which the royal edict had suspended, made a very serious complaint about this to the king for introducing such novelties to the detriment of his subjects. But he gained nothing except empty words and comforting promises of future consolation.

An amazing surge of the sea

In the same year, on the eighth of the kalends of December [24 November], the sea exceeded its normal height by a long way and caused irreparable damage to those living near it. When the moon was in its fourth quarter, according to the calendar reckoning, the sea rose three times with a tremendous surge, without any appreciable decrease or ebb. Although it seemed likely that this was due to the force of the wind, which was blowing from the sea at the time with extreme violence, nevertheless because it often happened that the wind raged from the sea and yet the sea did not rise as violently as this, older people were astonished at this unheard of novelty.

A horrifying event in the territories
of the count of Savoy

At this same time, in the region of Savoy, namely in the valley of Maurienne, certain towns, five in fact, were overwhelmed and swallowed up, with their cowsheds, sheepcotes and mills, by the neighbouring mountains and crags, which, as a result of a horrible earthquake in some caverns inside them, were torn away and pulled out from their normal place. Many say that three religious houses were struck down there, but one chapel escaped.[1] It is not known if the destruction of the mountains which raged so horribly in that place occurred miraculously or naturally, but because about nine thousand persons and an incalculable number of animals were destroyed, it seems to have happened miraculously rather than through natural causes. It was indeed said that the severity of divine judgement deservedly raged on the dwellings of those people because, sullied with disgraceful greed, they were impudently and indiscriminately carrying on the infamous business of usury, and that, to give their vice an appearance of virtue, they did not blush to describe themselves ambiguously as 'money merchants'. They were not opposed to simony, nor did they fear to engage in merciless robbery and plunder. They never failed to poison or cut the throats of scholars or merchants who passed through or stayed with them on their way, when compelled to go to the Roman curia. They did not realise that the slower the divine vengeance is, the more severely is it said to vent its rage; witness the blessed Gregory, who says "Divine wrath moves with a slow step toward punishment, but later makes up for its slowness by its severity".[2]

1. The words "Many" to "escaped" are written by Matthew Paris in the margin of B; they are not in C.
2. Nearly word for word from Valerius Maximus 1.1.3.

A scandal arises through the death of the prior of Thetford, a Provençal

In order to fulfil what is written in the gospel "It must needs be", that is, it is inevitable, "that scandals come; woe unto the world because of scandals!"[1], in the same year, in December, the prior of Thetford, a Savoyard by birth, a monk of Cluny who claimed to be a blood relative, or kinsman, or at least compatriot, of the queen and who rode the high horse as a result, summoned his brothers, a knight called Bernard and a beastly cleric called Guiscard, to come to his house at Thetford. There, forgetful of matins, he remained all night till cock-crow with them, according to custom, indulging in immoderate feasting and drinking. He seldom went to mass, was seldom present at the canonical hours; and in the morning, drunk, he vomited forth his nocturnal potations. If the cries of the hungry poor came to him, "These things were a minor care in his mind".[2] And if one of the aforesaid brothers, namely Bernard, went away, the other, Guiscard, whose belly was like a bladder in frosty weather and whose body was a cart-load, stayed longer; and all the monks' provisions were engulfed in the Charybdis of his belly. Afterwards, thoroughly gorged, he despised and insulted them.

While the aforesaid prior was entertaining his brothers, who had "borne the burden and heat of the day",[3] in a manner unbecoming to him and unprofitable, disgracefully squandering the substance of his little church and, as it was said, exceeding the bounds of moderation in his cups, a dispute and quarrel arose between him and a certain monk, Welsh by birth. The prior was trying uncharitably and spitefully to send this monk, whom he had summoned from Cluny shortly before, back to Cluny against his will and in spite of his perfectly reasonable excuses for not wanting to go. But when the prior yelled at him fearfully, swearing that, willy nilly, he should go on pilgrimage with a pilgrim's wallet, this devil of a monk, in a fit of violent anger or rather seized with madness, drew a knife and disembowelled him, without any fear of perpetrating such a crime within the church precincts. When the wounded prior, with the death-rattle sounding in his throat, tried by shouting to summon the monks, or at least to arouse them, he could not do so because his windpipe had closed. Again the monk rushed at him and with frantic blows, three or four times repeated, buried the knife right up to the hilt in his lifeless body. Thus this wretch, not without great dishonour and harm to the monastic order, and with the anger and vengeance of God on both sides, sent another wretch to Tartarus.

I have narrated all this in full so that the reader, warned and prevented, will stear clear of such crimes, lest he be precipitated into a similar confusion by an angry God. The author of the crime was seized by those arriving at the place and taken into custody tightly bound. When this came to the notice of the lord king, urged by the queen's complaints, he ordered the miscreant to be committed to the lowest dungeon of Norwich Castle, where he would be deprived of all light, notwithstanding the cause of the blessed Thomas [Becket], the martyr, who constantly held to and maintained, even to the shedding of his own blood and brains, on behalf of a certain homicidal priest, the principle that a cleric, and especially a priest, should not be condemned by the judgement of a secular court nor hanged after being deprived of holy orders. He accepted martyrdom for the principle that God does not punish twice for the same offence, mitigating the punishment of sinners and rewarding beyond merit, and that a single misdeed ought to be adequately reprieved by a single reasonable penalty.

When these things were related by an enemy of the monks as a reproach to the religious, a particular supporter and lover of religion replied that "The Lord found a rebel among the angels, a deviator among the seven deacons,[4] and a traitor among the apostles. On no account can the sin of one or a few taint the entire community. This notion is taught by the heathen poet, who said 'Forbear to attribute to all the crime of a few' "[5]

In the same year, when a quarrel arose between the monks of Selby and the royal clerk J[ohn] Francis over the collection of hay and corn, one monk was killed and several were wounded and beaten. And, lest a single scandal come unaccompanied, at the same time in the priory of Canterbury one monk mortally wounded another.

1. Matthew 18:7.
2. Misquoted from Ovid *Epist. ex Ponto* 1.2.76.
3. Matthew 20:12.
4. See Acts 6.
5. Misquoted from Ovid *Art. am.* 3.9. The paragraph which follows is written by Matthew Paris in the margin of B.

The miserable death of the prior of Bentley [near Harrow]

In this same unfortunate month a certain prior of the canons of a small church not far from the monastery of St. Albans was inspecting a pile of corn, commonly known as a rick, in order to estimate its value, when the rick, which was ill-constructed and leaning over, suddenly fell on him. Before the sheaves piled over him could be removed, this same prior, a plain fellow of little substance, died, miserably suffocated.

Others, his companions and servants, escaped because fewer sheaves fell on them.

The sad and ignominious case of a certain knight

In case lamentable scandals be imputed only to the religious, I must not omit to mention, even if it seems ridiculous, the disgrace and irreparable harm which happened in this same most unlucky month to the knights. For a certain Norfolk knight of noble birth and accomplished prowess, named Godfrey de Millers, wretchedly led astray, one night secretly entered the house of a knight called John Brito to sleep with his daughter. But he was prevented by some people placed in ambush with the connivance of the whore, who was afraid of being found out. He was seized, savagely thrown to the ground and badly wounded. Then he was suspended from a beam by his feet with his legs stretched apart, so that he was completely at the mercy of his enemies, who disgracefully mutilated him by cutting off his genital organs, though he would have preferred to be beheaded. Thus wounded and castrated, he was thrown out half dead. The noise of complaint reached the king, the authors of this cruelty were arrested, and John Brito was convicted and sentenced to irrecoverable disinheritance and irrevocable exile. The adulteress managed to avoid death by going into hiding so that she could not be found. All who were present at this flagrant deed were dispersed and banished, exiles and fugitives, so that this inhuman and in every way merciless crime involved many nobles in a miserable calamity.

At this same time a certain extremely elegant cleric, rector of a wealthy church, who surpassed all the local knights in the manifold honours of generosity and hospitality, was caught up in a similar misfortune. However the lord king, compassionate and sorrowful to the extent of sighs and tears, ordered it to be proclaimed as a law by public crier that no one should presume to mutilate the genital organs of an adulterer, except if his own wife was involved.

Some accidental fires

In this year too something happened which was noteworthy because it was so amazing; we think it should be included in this work, for we do not remember having seen such a thing before. In many countries in turn, owing to God's anger, extremely destructive fires raged, reducing towns and cities to ashes, but were caused neither by heat nor drought. Thus in Germany, besides other damages caused by the devouring flames, the cathedral church of St. Peter in Cologne, which is as it were the mother and matron of all the German churches, was consumed by fire down to the walls. In France and Normandy, too, uncontrollable fire caused irreparable damage to cities and towns. In England, indeed, not to mention other fires, the greater part of the borough of Newcastle-upon-Tyne, together with the bridge, was consumed by a raging fire.

In Norway destructive fires raged to such an extent in the three principal cities that wonder and astonishment was universally aroused. One of these, Bergen, was totally reduced to ashes except for four religious houses and the palace, chapel and lodgings of the lord king. For in this city eleven parishes were burnt down together with some houses belonging to the bishop, and the sin-avenging flame flew like a fire-breathing dragon dragging its tail after it as far as the royal castle which was then in the city five arrow shots distant. Nothing was plainer or more manifest to the inhabitants than that this was due to the severity of divine vengeance. The castle indeed, which was constructed of the largest and hardest stones, was for the most part reduced to ashes. On the following day the Lord thundered horribly and terrifyingly over the site of the city and a sudden flash of lightning struck the largest ship, which had come from England and arrived that same night, killing one man in it and wounding or badly hurting everyone else in the ship. The mast was smashed into tiny fragments which fell into the sea, and all the ships in the port, two hundred or more, were shaken. The writer of this had been in the ship whose mast was broken, but at that time he was in a certain church near the shore celebrating mass, as it were reciting a nautical hymn to give thanks to God for his escape from the perils of the sea. When all this came to the notice of the lord king [Haakon IV], on account of his regard for the person who had been aboard that ship, he ordered a larger and better mast to be provided for it.

The bishop of Norwich goes abroad

After Michaelmas the bishop of Norwich went abroad for certain secret reasons.

A thoroughly abusive order of the archbishop of Canterbury[1]

At this time the archbishop of Canterbury Boniface, oblivious of[2] his church so far as the care of souls was concerned, and busy fighting for

the pope in the area of Lyons, extorted no small treasure from the vacant
churches in his province which, relying on the apostolic authority, he
retained in his own hands for a year. Thus wretched England became like
the vineyard wasted "by the boar out of the wood" and plucked "by all
they which pass by the way".[3] And in order still more to wound the
feelings of the despoiled, he had it announced by the dean of Beauvais,
his agent in this matter, that anyone, except for the lord king and queen
and their children and the celebrated Earl Richard, who publicly or
privately criticised or blamed the favour which the lord pope had
granted and conceded to the archbishop, or in any way opposed it or
subtracted anything from its proceeds, or acted fraudulently with
respect to it, would be excommunicated. This order, published in each
and every church in England, roused indignation in the hearts of many,
as much because of the greedy, damaging and unprecedented extortion
of money, as because of the adulation that went with it, and they heartily
cursed the lord king for tolerating and agreeing to such things.[4]

1. This heading has been erased in B. and is taken from C.
2. The words "oblivious of", from the fair copy of C and therefore originally in B, have
    been erased there and the words "less solicitious for" substituted.
3. See Psalm 80:13, 12. The words from "thus" to "despoiled", erased in B, have been
    supplied from C.
4. The words from "and" to "things" have been erased in B but have been recovered
    from the copy C.

Two envoys from the Tartars come to the pope

In this same summer two envoys came from the Tartars, sent to the
lord pope by their prince; but the cause of their arrival was kept so
secret from everyone at the curia that it was unknown to clerks,
notaries and others, even those familiar with the pope. The letters they
brought with them for the pope were three times translated from an
unknown to a better known language as the envoys approached the
region of the West. But many suspected from certain indications in the
letters that the proposition and advice of the Tartars was that they
should shortly make war on [John] Vatatzes, Frederick's Greek
son-in-law, a schismatic, and disobedient to the Roman curia. It was
believed that this offer was not displeasing to the lord pope; he gave
them some costly clothes, which we commonly call robes, of choice
scarlet, together with cloaks, and furs made from the pelts of squirrels.
He conversed freely, favourably and frequently with them through
interpreters, and he secretly gave them precious gifts of gold and silver.

Concerning the outrages caused daily and with increasing frequency in England by the Roman curia

In this same year the outrages which were devised in multiplex ways and which proceeded daily from the Roman curia to the wretched kingdom of England, were multiplied with increment. Besides the hardship and unaccustomed servitude due to the suspension of ecclesiastics from the collation to benefices until Roman avarice was satisfied, against which the puny king in his weakness did not protest, the fruits of detestable new oppressions sprouted forth daily. Although not all the injuries — which would be difficult if not impossible to describe — can be mentioned, we have thought it right to include some of them in this little work, so that the reader may deplore them and complain to God in the hope of some future release from them by Him, and so that the miserable misery of England, which alas lacks good rulers and defenders, is apparent to all.

The abbot of Abingdon [John de Blomevil] had received a mandate from the lord pope to make provision without delay for a certain Roman, but this Roman, unwilling to accept any church but only a rich one, waited quietly, dissembling, until a noble and opulent church should fall vacant. This was St. Helen's church in the town of Abingdon which was valued at a hundred marks and had every advantage, for it was in a borough subject to the above-mentioned monastery. The Roman, who had remained quiet for a long time, at once demanded this church and importunately insisted that it should be given him on apostolic authority. On the very same day that the church became vacant, the abbot received a most urgent mandate from the lord king, composed of threats mixed with prayers and promises, to the effect that he should grant the church in question to his half-brother Aethelmar, even though this Aethelmar had such an abundance of churches and rents that it would not surprise us if he was ignorant of their number and value. The perplexed abbot, as it were crushed between two revolving millstones, consulted his monks and loyal and discreet friends, who replied that "Things are hard either way. Still, if the lord king will protect you from papal pressure, we think it better to confer the church on the brother of the lord king, who is your prince and patron, rather than on the Roman, who as your neighbour would always be a vigilant plotter against you and a tireless nuisance and, as it were, a permanent thorn in your flesh". This was signified to the lord king at the proper time, and he immediately promised the abbot his assured protection and every kind of indemnity. The abbot therefore, relying on these deceitful words, gave the church to Aethelmar at the king's request. The Roman, very annoyed, went at once to the pope and, making a serious complaint, fully related the whole matter, adding some further provocations. So the lord pope cited the abbot to appear in person before him to answer a charge of disobedience and the abbot, obtaining not the least help from the lord king in spite of repeated requests, although old and an invalid, went to the Roman curia in much sorrow, fear and bitterness of heart. There, after many difficulties and no little expense, he had to satisfy the said Roman at the will of the pope, by paying him fifty marks annually from his treasury, to the great prejudice of his church.

Another grievous injury

Also in the same year, after the death of the abbot of St. Edmunds, the king, heedless of fear and reverence for God and the holy martyr whom he was bound for many reasons particularly to venerate, took so much money from that house while it was vacant that he seemed to have wholly lost the bowels of compassion, for, not counting the pay of the royal bailiffs, he harshly extorted 1,200 marks from it.[1] When the brothers had elected another person, Edmund de Walpole, to take the place of the dead abbot, they sent some of the brothers to the Roman curia to secure confirmation of his election. But a quibbling enquiry was made into it and both the election and the elect were rejected, in such a way that the injured party, ensnared by a merciless person, should become the object of mercy. For as the monks went sadly and shamefully away, the lord pope called them back and said, "Since the wretched are in need of compassion, merely out of favour and so that you should not be upset, we will for the moment accept the abbot-elect, freely and graciously handing over the monastery of St. Edmund to him. But he will have to look around for 800 marks and answer for this sum to a certain merchant we shall assign to him, to whom we owe that amount." Thus ensnared, the monks went away but, exasperated by so much abuse and injury, they grieved inconsolably. One of them died at Lyons before they left the papal curia; the other went the way of all flesh, not without bitterness of heart, at Dover, on his way back from that discourteous court.

1. The words from "not" to "from it" have been erased in B and have been taken from the copy C.

The abbot of Waltham dies

And, as the days passed by at this time, the abbot of Waltham of most pious memory died, a man of uncommon sanctity, of the order of canons of St. Augustine.

Master Simon Langton dies

During the course of this same year Master Simon Langton died. He was the brother of Stephen, the archbishop of Canterbury of illustrious memory, and archdeacon of the church of Canterbury. It is not surprising that he was a persecutor and perturber of his church at Canterbury, for he perturbed, disturbed and troubled the kingdom of the French, as well as the kingdom of the English when it was vexed by manifold warfare, as has been explained above in its place.[1]

Also in this year died Master John Blund, chancellor of the church of York, a distinguished theologian and at one time elected archbishop of Canterbury, but the election was quashed by the above-mentioned S. Thus at one and the same time persecutor and persecuted passed on to join the crowds of the dead.

Earl Patrick [of Dunbar] also died, who was reckoned the most powerful Scottish magnate. He died bearing the sign of the cross, a pilgrim in company with the lord king of the French, and is believed to have taken the cross in order to be reconciled with God and St. Oswin. For he had unjustly harassed and injured the monastery of Tynemouth, a cell of St. Albans especially devoted to the blessed king and martyr Oswin, and where his body is known to lie.

1. See Luard 1874:628, 654–5 and 1876:31. The two following paragraphs are written by Matthew Paris in the margin.

How Brother Matthew was sent to Norway

In the same year a crisis occurred in a certain noble monastery in Norway, which is called the monastery of St. Benedict of Holm, founded by the most noble king Cnut, who had also founded a monastery of the same name and order in England.[1] For it was much impoverished, the monks were dispersed, almost the entire monastery with its appurtenances was destroyed, and the abbot had gone off, having left the order. He furtively removed the seal of the chapter and, under the pretence of loyalty, he either sold or, having drawn up charters to this effect, fraudulently mortgaged almost all the monastery's possessions. He had with him one of the brothers, the sacristan, who was keeper of the seal, knew what was going on, and was a party to the abbot's crimes; he was indeed an apostate and a fugitive. Because of this the archbishop of Nidaros,[2] in whose diocese this monastery was, took it into his own hands with all its appurtenances, accusing the monks of being monks only in their monk's habits, of being wholly ignorant of the order and rule of St. Benedict, of being manifest violators of the monastic statutes, and some of them thieves and fugitives. The monks, though they had no abbot, still stood by God as best they could under the rule of their prior; they took refuge in an appeal to the supreme pontiff, for it would be unworthy and irrational for the fault of one or two or a few to redound on the whole community. Pending the appeal the archbishop did not dare to interfere with them any further or make any new moves.

The prior, having prudently recovered some of the monastery's possessions and raised some money, now went to the Roman curia. But —who would have thought it! — the apostate abbot with his accomplice had been there a short time before and, having drawn up and signed charters with the stolen seal, had placed the monastery under an obligation for around 500 marks. The prior returned home sad and confused but, before he got back, news was brought to him that this wretch of an abbot had died in a monastery of St. Alban at Seljord in Norway. So the prior and convent, having confirmed this, elected a new abbot for themselves, and the prior was sent off with one of the monks to accompany him, together with the sum of 300 marks, and with letters of the lord king [Haakon] addressed to Brother Matthew Paris, asking him to direct his efforts towards freeing them from their debts. The release of the monastery was happily settled by the repayment of the principal sum only, and, having taken possession of all the documents and instruments by which the monastery of Holm was indebted to the Cahorsins then established in London, the prior returned home within a year, free of debt and in all prosperity. However, although they could breathe freely in temporal affairs, they were still in difficulties in spiritual matters, lying low, having obtained by means of repeated gifts a truce and brief respite, in order to prevent the archbishop from taking over the entire island, which belonged to the monastery, and the monastery itself, which was on the island, with all its appurtenances, having expelled the monks, who indeed, according to him, were monks only in name.

Now it happened about this time, as has been said before,[3] that the bishop of [S.] Sabina [William], cardinal of the Roman see, came to Norway as legate and the monks, much harassed by their archbishop and hoping to be consoled over their trouble, at once went to the legate. To them he replied. "My sons, I am wholly ignorant of the statutes and observances of monks and of the rule of St. Benedict, but I advise you in good faith to go to the Roman curia and request the lord pope to provide you with a reformer and suitable instructor for your order, and I will write to him affectionately on your behalf to ask him to hear you with favour. Nor should this matter be delayed, for your archbishop is vehemently insisting that he should expel you because of your ignorance". The abbot therefore went to the Roman curia on this business, accompanied by the prior, and when they had fully explained their wishes to the lord pope, they showed him letters of petition from the lord king and the legate on this matter. The lord pope replied to them. "My sons, if you are ignorant of things which you ought to know about, you should with due deliberation choose someone from any region or monastery you like, to inform you of them, whoever you prefer, and your request shall be granted. You should instruct yourselves, or your adversary will prevail against you". The following day, after discussing the matter carefully with other prudent men, they replied to the lord pope as follows. "My lord, we have learnt from experience that the monks of our order are nowhere throughout the entire world, we believe, so well regulated as in England. Nor is there, we hear by report, so well-ordered a monastery in the kingdom of England as that of St. Alban, protomartyr of the English. We therefore request a certain monk of that house called Matthew, of whose prudence and loyalty we have experience, as our reformer and instructor. Moreover he is very friendly with and well known to our king, so that he will be able through the king's help, if necessary, to subdue anyone rebelling against him." Since this reply was sufficiently pleasing to the pope, the monks obtained the following warrant, to be presented to the abbot of St. Albans.

1. St. Benet's of Holme, Norfolk. The Norwegian monastery was on the island of Nidarholm near Trondheim.
2. That is, Trondheim. His name was Sigurd.
3. Above p. 108.

The pope's warrant to the abbot of St. Albans[1]

Innocent etc. to his well beloved son the abbot of St. Albans of the order of St. Benedict in England etc. Since, as has been put to us by our well beloved son the abbot of the monastery of Holm of the order of St. Benedict, in the diocese of Nidaros, the said monastery, because of the negligence of his predecessors has become disordered in matters concerning the monastic order, nor is there to be found in that region anyone who is familar with the statutes and observances of the order, we, on the request of the said abbot, earnestly ask and exhort you, and by virtue of these apostolic letters command you, to send our well beloved son Brother Matthew your monk, who is said to be of approved way of life and thoroughly religious, to this same monastery to inform and instruct the said abbot and his monks in the regular discipline and statutes pertaining to that order. Out of reverence to God and the apostolic see you shall not delay this. Given at Lyons etc.

1. The date of this document is 27 February 1247. It is also copied out by Matthew Paris in the *Book of additamenta*, BL Cotton MS. Nero D i, f.92v, preceded by the words, "Papal warrant by which the writer of this, Dom Matthew Paris, though reluctant, was appointed and sent as reformer of the Benedictine order and visitor of the Benedictine abbots and monks in the kingdom of Norway".

The conclusion of this affair

Since, as was right, the abbot of St. Albans complied with the lord pope's wishes and the above-mentioned monk was obedient to his abbot, the affair was undertaken with success, so that the abbot of Holm in Norway continued in peace and prosperity, and through God's grace the monastic order, though exposed to danger, breathed more easily, as did other monasteries in that region.

An earthquake in England[1]

In the same year, in Advent, that is to say on the fourth day before Christmas [21 December], there was an earthquake in England which, as the bishop of Bath [William of Bitton], in whose diocese it happened, informed the writer, disrupted the walls of buildings, tearing away stones from their places in the walls and causing gaps and chinks in the ruined walls. Moreover, a stone dome of great size and weight, which had been set up on the top of the cathedral church of Wells through the perseverance of the builders, was hurled from its place and fell on the church, causing considerable damage and, as it fell from on high, making a terrifying noise, which frightened those who heard it out of their wits. In this earthquake a remarkable thing happened: the tops of chimneys, battlements and pillars were brought down, but not their bases and foundations, yet the reverse ought naturally to have happaned. This earthquake was the third which occurred in three years this side of the Alps; one in the region of Savoy and two in England; which is all the more terrible because such a thing had never been heard of since the beginning of the world.

1.   This paragraph is in the margin in B; it comes at the end of the annal in C.

The conclusion of the annal

So the year passed, with temperate and serene weather, filling the barns with abundance of corn and producing a redundance of wine from the presses, so that a measure of corn fell in price to two shillings and a cask of choice wine was sold here and there for two marks. Orchard fruit was extremely copious in some places but barren in others, the gourd-worms almost entirely destroying all the green leaves wherever the pest made its way. The year was most unfavourable to the Holy Land, inimical to Italy, deadly to Germany, adverse in England, destructive to France. To conclude in a few words, it was wasteful of money in almost every Christian region. The end of the world was indicated in manifold prophecies; for instance, "Nation shall rise against nation", and "Great earthquakes shall be in divers places",[1] and others similar. In particular, the year was infamous to the Roman curia, pernicious and pestiferous and clearly threatening divine anger. The entire winter was turned into spring in temperature, so that the earth was covered neither by frost nor by snow, or not for more than two days together. You could see trees sprouting in February and birds singing and courting in April.

1.   Luke 21: 10, 11.

[The Chronica majora 1249]

The lord king was at London for Christmas

In the year of the lord 1249, which is the thirty-third year of the reign of King H. III, the same lord king was at London for Christmas; Earl Richard his brother was at Wallingford to celebrate this festival with a large gathering of magnates staying with him; and the earl of Gloucester held court at the same time with no less worldly magnificence on the Welsh border near Gloucester. But the king, shamelessly exceeding the limits of royal authority, on the day of the Circumcision [1 January], demanded from each of the citizens of London individually whom he knew to be among the more wealthy, those earliest presents of the year which common people are wont superstitiously to call New Year's gifts.

A grand feast of St. Edward

On the approach of the feast of the blessed Edward, which is on the eve of the Epiphany [5 January], the lord king summoned by letter a large number of magnates to celebrate that feast with him splendidly in St. Peter's church, Westminster. He himself, on the eve of the feast, that is the Monday, fasted on bread and water wearing woollen clothes, as was his custom. A good many magnates gathered together there who had previously been dispersed, either out of love and devotion for the saint, or to venerate the recently-obtained holy blood of Christ and obtain the remission granted thereby, or out of reverence for the king who summoned them. So now the king, the queen, Earl Richard and the marshal R[oger], with four other earls and as many bishops were assembled there.

163

The earl of Leicester S[imon] returns from Gascony

While the king was staying at Westminster for this feast, namely Christmas, Earl S. of Leicester returned from the region of Gascony with some magnates, knights and attendants who had been loyally fighting there for the lord king. Their arrival gladdened the king himself and his entire court in no small measure. For the earl had forced a certain traitor, Gaston, son of the countess of Béarn, to accept a truce against his will. Causing a great deal of harm there by excessive plotting against the king, he had almost completely ruined and corrupted Gascony, and had fraudulently and treacherously turned it aside from loyalty to the king. For this Gaston was rolling in money, which he had obtained from the king by false promises when he was in Gascony. His deceitful mother was a party to her deceitful son's behaviour. She too, at the same time, had basely obtained an infinite treasure from the bewitched king, which was emptied out of England to the subversion and impoverishment of the kingdom and its nobles and prelates. Moreover, the aforesaid earl, strengthened with the help of those loyal to the king, had captured a certain public robber named William Bertram of Aigremont, a traitor to the king and his most bloodthirsty enemy, who had likewise done much harm in and around Gascony, and consigned him in chains for safe keeping to the tower of La Réole until, if the lord king's council agreed, the said earl returned to Gascony to crush him and all the king's other enemies.

Money is imperiously extorted from the citizens of London

The king, however, did not, as he should have done, give glory to God the Lord of hosts for the victory granted to him according to his wish. He now carefully thought out how he could wholly dry up the inexhaustible well of England. For having experienced a just repulse from the community of magnates of England, as above-mentioned, who had refused any further to squander their goods to the ruin of the kingdom, he cunningly applied himself to overflowing the bucket of his avarice through other devices. So, immediately after the delights of the aforesaid festivities, he set about harassing the citizens of London in the following way. As has been mentioned above, he had suspended trade in the city for a fortnight, having instituted a new fair at Westminster to the harm and prejudice of many, and directly after this he sent letters by his satellites containing detailed and peremptory prayers asking the citizens to help him with substantial financial aid. At this they grumbled heartily, saying, "Alas for us! Alas! Where is the liberty of London, so often bought, so often conceded, so often written down, so often sworn to? For almost every year, like vile slaves of the lowest status, we are impoverished by different taxes and injuriously attacked with fox-like cunning. Nor can we find out into what whirlpool the goods we are despoiled of are submerged." What more can be said? Although incalculable sums were demanded, the citizens at length, unwillingly and not without bitter resentment, agreed to a contribution of two thousand pounds, to be paid to the lord king over a short period. Moreover his habitual oppression raged without any restraint, for all saleable articles, especially meat and drink, if not hidden away as if stolen, were seized for the king's use. His household, however, derived no increase in hospitality from this, but rather, discarding all shame, he daily stinted himself with reprehensible parsimony so that, having eliminated the ancient bounty of the lord king of England, the customs of the Roman table now sneaked in, and to the no small detriment of the royal fame and honour.

An ingenious trick of the lord king for extorting money[1]

At this time the lord king, since he could not persuade all the nobles of the kingdom assembled together to accept his demands, had recourse to the habitual cavillings of the Romans and accosted them individually, summoning them to him, or writing to them, with impertinent entreaties, saying, "I am a poor man, completely broke. It is essential that each of you gives me substantial aid, for I am indebted, by charter, in the sum of thirty thousand marks. However, I demand nothing except as a favour. If anyone does me a favour, I shall return it to him when the time comes; and if anyone denies me a favour, I shall deny it to him." He held out a fictitious reason for this, namely that he was about to make war on the king of the French, since the truce was expiring, in order to recover his rights by force. But he aroused nothing from circumspect people except derision and contempt because he had lately been prohibited by the lord pope through Master Albert from in any way interfering in any territory held by whatever title from the lord king of the French, who was fighting for God and the universal [Church] in the Holy Land as a crusader. Even if he had not been prohibited, it was rightly thought that he could by no means muster the military skill or strength, or indeed sufficient cash extorted on every side, to deprive the king of the French of even a single tiny possession. For it was not thought that France was wholly lacking in money or men. But, in order to conceal the aforesaid master's message from everyone, the king did not allow it to be published in any way. It was also said that this same Master A. had been empowered to lay an interdict on the territory of England if the king disobeyed the papal mandate. But this was all covered up, hidden like some grand mystery, so that the cunning king could get round people kept in ignorance.

1.   This heading has been erased in B, no doubt by Matthew Paris, and is taken from C.

The abbot of Ramsey is defrauded

While the king with open gape thus gaped after financial gain, he happened to go to Huntingdon about the feast of St. Hilary [14 January]. Sending for the abbot of Ramsey and speaking confidentially with him, he said, "My friend, I earnestly request you to help me by giving or at least lending me one hundred pounds. I am in need, and must have that sum immediately". The abbot, who could not honourably reply otherwise, said, "A donor I have sometimes been, but never have I lent you anything, nor shall I;" and he immediately borrowed that sum from the Cahorsins at an exorbitant rate of interest, to satisfy this pitiful beggar of a king.[1]

At the same time the lord king disquieted the abbot of Peterborough with a similar request, demanding financial assistance and maintaining that it would be more charitable to give money to him than to any beggar at the door. The abbot excused himself, and would not listen to his entreaties, but he was [thereafter] so exasperated by abuse that he secretly left the king's household. At the same time, with a similar harangue, the king extorted sixty marks from the abbot of St. Albans, although this year and also last year he had casuistically cheated him of a by no means insignificant sum. When the lord king saw that nobody could or would contradict him, he entertained the hope that none of the abbots or priors would resist him and, since the magnates had placed a barricade of opposition in his way, he wrote as follows to the prelates who, though unwillingly, had been "turned aside like a deceitful bow".[2]

1.   The words *regulo mendicandi*, erased in B, have been recovered from C.
2.   Psalm 78:57. The letter that follows is also in the *Book of additamenta*, BL Cotton MS. Nero D i, f93. The words supplied in square brackets, missing in B, are from that copy.

Letters of the lord king

H[enry] by the grace of God etc. greetings to all the abbots and priors in the counties of Essex and Hertfordshire. It is not surprising that the dignity of the royal majesty should wish to test the friendship of devoted and loyal subjects in defence of the rights of the kingdom, nor that they should often at suitable moments honour their prince, under whose protective wings they breathe freely, with bodily service or the offer of gifts. Now that the [truces] between us and the lord king of the French have expired, we, for the recuperation and defence of our rights both on this side of the Channel, and overseas, where we have recently sent an army, must needs [incur] considerable expense and for various reasons extend the hand of liberality to many persons. So we are sending our loyal and well beloved subject Simon Passelew together with the sheriff of each of the aforesaid counties, and we earnestly entreat you to hear them favourably when they expound our business to you on our behalf, so that you can generously help us with your money to meet the above-mentioned expenses; and we shall make [due] recompense for what we thereby owe to you.

[Witnessed by myself at Windsor, 18 December, in the thirty-third year of our reign.]

When this came to the attention of prudent persons, they realised clearer than daylight that when [the king] was in Poitou and Gascony, as if trapped and imprisoned, the people to whom he had inadvisedly committed himself, loaded as he was with cash and without the watchfulness of his loyal English subjects, had outrageously impoverished him, villainously extorting whatever he possessed or would possess, that is, irrevocably obliging him by oath and charter to hand over to them whatever could be scraped up from England. Thus the groans and sighs of the English increased day by day.

The bishop of Durham resigned his bishopric

On the approach of the Purification of the blessed Mary [2 February], the bishop of Durham Nicholas [of Farnham], realising that he was aged and infirm and preferring to relinquish his wealth rather than be relinquished by it, resigned his bishopric of Durham after obtaining papal permission. The archbishop of York and the bishops of London and Worcester being appointed provisors in this matter, three manors were assigned to him, namely Hoveden with its appurtenances, Stockton and Easington. After taking leave of the brethren, he left Durham to stay at one or other of these manors, where he was free to be at leisure in peace, without the bustle of courts and cases, putting aside worldly cares and wholly devoting himself to prayer and meditation until the transformation he was awaiting should come upon him. When he was informed of this, the lord king, by no means slowly or unwillingly, took everything remaining into his own power and possession so that, hungry and greedy as always, he could swallow down the juicy financial fruits. To take over and collect them for himself he sent one of his clerks there, namely Thomas of Newark.

A tournament arranged at Northampton is prevented

At this time a general tournament was planned at Northampton on Ash Wednesday [19 February], [but] it was put off by a royal prohibition with threats, and by bad weather. When the knights deplored this, especially the novices, who were eager to put their knightly expertise to the test of combat, William of Valence, the king's half-brother and a novice, intimated that they should not fail to hold the tournament if they were favoured with fine weather, in spite of the king's prohibition and inept suspicions. He would interpose himself as a pledge between them and his brother the king in case he was angry with them. Because of this statement, honour and claims to knighthood were attributed to the said W. in no small measure. However on that day, namely Ash Wednesday, such great masses of snow fell that for two days the surface of the ground was everywhere covered to a depth of a foot, and the loaded branches of the trees were broken down. When it melted, the furrows of the fields, cavernously enlarged, were filled with water. Thus doubly hampered, the tournament came to nothing.

The king importunately tries to have his brother Aethelmar elected and promoted to the bishopric of Durham

Meanwhile the king, vigilant and untiring in his quest for lucre and disregarding the fear of God, improperly sent request after request by prudent and circumspect messengers, experienced in getting round people, to the convent of Durham, to whom the right of election is recognised as belonging, advising, imploring and insisting with threats that his half-brother Aethelmar should be unanimously elected with approbation the pastor of their souls and bishop of Durham. In order to achieve this happily, as the poet has it, "He mingled together authority, promises and prayers"[1]. The convent humbly replied, "Lord king, most Christian of kings, be pleased to bear in mind the first and foremost oath you swore on being crowned, to allow the holy Church — at least sometimes — to enjoy its liberty so that we can, with God's help, elect for ourselves a suitable father and pastor of our souls. You know and the world knows that your brother is insufficient in wisdom and in years to undertake the burden of so arduous a spiritual office". To which the king is said to have replied, "And I am well able, and perfectly willing, to keep the bishopric in my hands for eight or nine years or longer, so that at least then he will be old enough for you to accept him."

1. Slightly misquoted from Ovid *Met.* 4:471.

The extraordinary disorders which happened at Winchester and the country around not undeservedly

As Lent drew near and the lord king had happily arrived at Winchester, two merchants from Brabant came to him with complaints and grievances. Weeping and lamenting, they said to the lord king, "Peaceful and just king, we are merchants of Brabant who were passing defenceless through your territories, which we thought were peaceful, for purposes of trading, when some thieves and robbers, whose faces we have recognised at your court, attacked us by the way and, basely and thievishly, took two hundred marks from us by force. If they presume to deny this by refusing to confess, we are prepared to dispute and prove the truth by means of a judicial duel against them". The suspects were seized, but when it was decided that their case should depend on the report of the local people, the oath of the country freed them. No wonder! That country was like them, tainted throughout with robbery. But as the aforesaid merchants still pressed their charge and still opportunely and importunely demanded their money at the hands of the king, he began to get worried and, having gathered his councillors, said to them, "What is to be done? The wretchedness of these men is most upsetting". And they replied to him, "My lord, we have heard and we know that all parts of England are similarly suspect. For travellers here are very frequently despoiled, wounded, kidnapped and murdered, so that we are amazed that your itinerant justices, whose especial duty this is, have not cleansed the country of such infamy. We believe that the robbers, who are so numerous in this country, have cunningly made a conspiratorial pact that no one of them shall on any account accuse another. Thus their conspiracy and ingenuity has escaped you, your justices and your bailiffs. Your judge Henry de Mara was here with his colleagues, but did no good. The persons he chose as inquisitors were consorts and abettors of robbers. We must proceed cautiously, so that the skill of such manifold traitors can be beguiled by skill. Large numbers of merchants, especially from overseas, come and go through this area, as well on account of the neighbouring ports, the presence of this royal city, and the fairs. And these men recently robbed maintain that if their money — on account of which they are prepared to submit to judgement by combat — is not restored to them, they will recoup it by force from the merchants of your kingdom travelling in their country, to their loss and your dishonour; thus deservedly arousing the disdain of the duke of Brabant, whose friendship we desire".

So the lord king had the bailiffs and free men of that county, namely Southampton, summoned, and addressed them with a grim look. "What is this that I hear about you? The complaints of plundered people have reached me, and I have to listen to them. There is no county or district in the entire breadth of England so infamous as this one, nor stained by so many crimes. Even where I am present in the city itself or the suburbs or in neighbouring places, robberies and murders are committed. Nor are these evils enough, for my own wines, open to robbery and pillage, are carried off in stolen carts by these malefactors, guffawing and inebriated thereby. How can such things be tolerated any further? To eradicate these and similar things I have appointed wise men to rule and look after my kingdom with me. I am only one man; I do not wish, nor am I able, to support the burden of the whole kingdom without the comfort of helpers. The stink of this city and the adjacent parts ashames and wearies me. I was born in this city, but never was such dishonour inflicted on me as here. It seems probable and even credible, indeed it is now clear, that you, citizens and compatriots, are infamous accomplices and confederates. I shall convoke all the counties of England so that, judging you as traitors to me, they can uncover your crimes; nor will astute argument be of any further use to you."

This was in the hall of Winchester Castle, in the presence of W[illiam] bishop of that city. Suddenly the king exclaimed with a fearful shout, "Shut the gates of the castle! Shut them at once!" The bishop then rose and said, "Hold on, my lord, stay a little, listen to me patiently please! There are some strangers in this castle, good men of unimpaired fame, and your friends, whom you ought not to shut in, for you are only accusing Winchester people and their abettors". Then, continuing his speech, the bishop turned towards the people and said, "I am your pastor and spiritual father, having power over your souls in spiritual matters and in large measure in temporal matters. I excommunicate all conspirators in this infamy and crime, and anyone who, when questioned, shall in any way depart from the truth, whether out of fear, favour or for a reward."

Twelve people were therefore elected from Winchester and the county of Southampton to declare under oath the names of any thieves they knew. Withdrawing apart, they discussed this for a long time. They were carefully guarded but, when summoned after a lengthy deliberation, were absolutely unwilling to make any mention of the thieves. This annoyed the king a great deal, for he knew that they knew something about the robbers. So the king, as if in a frenzy of anger, said, "Arrest these deceitful traitors and throw them into the lower dungeon, tightly bound, for they will not speak, and are hiding what they ought to declare. Without doubt they have been excommunicated by their bishop; just look at the favour and agreement they find with [the thieves]. Choose me another twelve, from among the citizens of Winchester and the county of Southampton, who will in no way be opposed to the truth, so that they can reveal the truth to me on matters put to them."

Another twelve were sent for, but, when they realised that the first twelve, who had suppressed the truth, had been imprisoned and were to be hanged, they began to be very frightened, saying to each other, "We shall be similarly judged if we suppress any of the truth about what we are asked". And, after a lengthy and secret discussion among themselves they came out into the middle of the assembly and, giving tongue, they revealed the thefts and crimes of numerous people, many of whom were from neighbouring parts, especially Alton and the bishop's liberty at Taunton. Hearing this, some citizens and many of their compatriots, who were reputed good law-worthy men of some substance, enjoying possession of horses and precious clothes, houses and families, and fifty or eighty librates of land, whom the king had appointed custodians and bailiffs to look after that country and arrest or expel robbers, and others too, who were officials and crossbowmen of the king's household, were arrested, convicted and hanged. Some took refuge in churches, others fled secretly and abruptly and appeared no more. Some indeed from the city itself, present at the time and acting as royal ushers to keep back the crowd thickly assembled there because of the novelty of the affair, cunningly intermingled with the people and, leaving the castle at once, either went into hiding or fled to the nearest churches. When more closely questioned, those arrested confessed to unheard of crimes, both robberies and murders, perpetrated with the advice and assistance of others. Out of those accused and manifestly convicted, about thirty were hanged, and as many or more imprisoned, to await a similar punishment.[1] Those who had been in the king's household, when about to be hanged, said to the officials in charge, "You can tell our lord king that he is our death and the foremost cause of it, because for a long time he withheld the pay due to us when we were in need, so that we were forced to become thieves or plunderers, or to sell our horses, arms and clothes, which we could not possibly do without." When the king heard this he was distressed and sorrowful and full of lament for a long time.

Among these detestable thieves a certain William, surnamed Pope, who was arrested, made an appeal. He was rich in household belongings and his house was superbly furnished; so much so that, after he was arrested, a search revealed about fifteen casks of wine in his cellar. He appealed. Those who were convicted were immediately hanged. One man had served the king well in battle and had freed the country of six thieves. Thus were these malefactors driven out of the region they had wretchedly dishonoured, with the merciful help of an avenging God. But Winchester, Southampton and the whole of that county incurred opprobrium and an indelible reputation for infamy from this.

I have set all this out at length and in detail to make it clear to everyone how weak pacts are and how easily dispersable is a conspiracy of malefactors, who, moving in a circle, in times of crisis promote their own destruction, so that a severer punishment follows in the end.

1. The words from "and" to "punishment" are in the margin.

A horrible rumour

In these days the fame of Frederick began to be so much despised throughout the different regions of the world that he was now reckoned worse than Herod, Judas or Nero. For the deadly stench given out by his deeds, as is apparent from the following letter, exasperated the ears and hearts of the faithful, to the astonishment and grief of very many people.

The tenor of the letters sent by Cardinal Reiner
of Viterbo to the lord pope on the suspension of the bishop
of Arezzo and Frederick's manifold villainies

Great crime, nefarious presumption, savage cruelty, unheard of wickedness, and execrable baseness, making a horrifying spectacle, have been perpetrated these days in front of God, the angels and the human race.[1] At this the sky ought to grow pale, the sun should be dimmed by cloud, the stars obscured with darkness and as it were closed with a clasp, the earth should tremble, the sea swell up, the ears of listeners ring, the hearts of the faithful be agitated and Christians' kidneys quake, and the hearts of all kings, princes and knights, and of all the faithful who profess Christianity, should be roused to vengeance. See how the devil's herald, the vicar of Satan, the forerunner of Antichrist, the maker and minister of all evils, has raged against and attacked the anointed of the Lord, the high pontiffs anointed with the holy chrism.

When Marcellinus, lord bishop of Arezzo of honoured memory, found that the pot of persecution with its face toward the north was vigorously seething against him in his own city,[2] he yielded to the force of its fury and for many years lived in exile and penury at Ancona, a most devoted daughter of the apostolic see. At length, on receipt of an apostolic precept, he worked hard to rescue the people of the March [of Ancona] from the jaws of the virulent dragon, from the snares of the demons pursuing them and from the yoke of tyranny; in all this he appeared, by God's grace, to have made some little progress. It happened, however, that God permitted him to fall into his enemies' hands, and he was harshly treated in prison and in chains for three months and more by the satellites of Pharaoh. At length that man of blood Frederick, who, raging like a dragon, "as a roaring lion walketh about, seeking whom he may devour",[3] drenched with the blood of innocent people and "drunken with the blood of the saints", was extremely pleased on hearing about this, conceived the idea in his bestial mind of killing this prefect of God. This impious, profane leader, doubtless, like his father the devil, "having great wrath" against the Church of God "because he knoweth that he has but a short time",[4] instantly bursting into fury, thundered a hurried sentence of hanging and throat-cutting against this anointed of God at Victoria, founded by him, but the name of which ought to be ascribed to the faithful. By an amazing miracle, this was done on the third day before the triumphant overthrow of him and that city; for this Victoria, against the wishes of the madman who gave it its name, by the happy auspice of this name presaged the bestowal from itself of the trophies of victory on the cause of the Church.

To return to the point, the hellish Cyclops and satellites of Vulcan, obeying orders received from their prince, urged the bishop to excommunicate the lord pope, the cardinals, and the other prelates of the Church, publicly in front of all the people, and to swear allegiance to the perfidious Frederick, promising him impunity for himself in this affair and a substantial reward. But he, strengthened by the Holy Spirit, boldly asserted that he had frequently excommunicated this Frederick, the progeny and pupil of Satan, and his people, and there and then repeated this same sentence of anathema against him. And when this pontiff was led to martyrdom he fortified himself first, as much with tears of repentance as with all the church sacraments. Then when he thought he was about to be thrown into the abyss, but heard from the bystanders that he was to be dragged through the town and then die by hanging, he began to sing, "We praise thee, o Lord" and the hymn of the angels at the top of his voice. He wanted to be dragged to the gibbet like Christ to the cross, but, because of the weeping women and children around him he was not allowed to be entirely stripped. The Saracens bound his holy hands and feet, covered his eyes, and placed his head near the tail of the animal dragging him, so that this holy head would be fouled by any emission.[5] But that brute beast, though goaded with spurs, could not be made to move until God's champion had finished the psalm and prayer he had begun, and had himself given leave for it to move on. And so the Saracens dragged him to the gallows through Castel Planio as if he were plebeian and ignoble, or the foulest of all refuse or a perfidious parricide, an assassin, a kidnapper or a nocturnal ravager of the fields. Among other things, he honestly confessed to the Lord Christ, and to some brothers Minor who were standing here and there, that human frailty prompted him to escape martyrdom if he could, though he had wished for it when he was free. He did not cease to confess this publicly, as well as some other trifles that came to his mind, and, dismissing all feelings of offence against those harming him, he patiently endured whatever they did to him. He was hanged from the gibbet on the first Sunday of this present Lent [21 February], almost at the same time as our redeemer ascended the cross. Guards having been posted nearby, he remained suspended on the gallows for three days, when at last the brothers Minor stole his corpse.[6] But the executioners disinterred it and, dragging it through the mud, again suspended it, not to be taken down without the express permission of the new Pilate, to the great shame of Christianity, the contumely of the clergy, the perpetual ignominy of the order of priesthood, and the detriment of the honour of the pope.

The corpse of the martyr, at first wasted by the treatment it received, is now lustrous with miracles, as is testified by some religious brothers coming from there who positively assert that, although a decade, namely ten days[7], has now elapsed, there is no foul smell. The same is said by reliable people of that illustrious and most praiseworthy man Dom Hugelino Rainocius, who was recently taken in battle after being thrown from his horse, stripped by impious enemies, and cruelly put to death. "Behold", Christian people, "and see if there be any sorrow like unto"[8] the sorrow of the Church, or indeed your own. For who has ever heard of such a deed or seen anything like it? What loyal servant of Christ confronted with this, can contain his tears or control his groans and sighs? Surely there is no one so hard hearted as not to be saddened by the blows of so much cruelty? Are there any stony Christian hearts that will not be broken, or adamantine feelings not torn apart and reduced to compassion? Where is the seal of the Christian faith? Where the burning love of Christ, who is now suspended in the person of his pontiff and minister? For he said to Peter, "I will go to Rome to be crucified again", and to Saul, "Saul, Saul, why persecutest thou me?"[9] And in the gospel, about his disciples, he said, "He that despiseth you despiseth me", and "he who touches you, touches the pupil of my eye". This wicked [Frederick], adding to the store of his damnation, and in reproof of the hardness of our hearts, which were scarcely moved by such horrid crimes, had no hesitation in repeating these offences frequently, for he maintained that his iniquities abounded without retaliation, the charity of many waxed cold,[10] that heartfelt piety had deserted them, and that every kind of zeal for the faith was lacking.

In the space of two years [Frederick] had the bishop of Gerace in Calabria drowned and, in the same year in the city [of Rome] at the Lateran, he caused the bishop of Cefalù in Sicily, of blessed memory, who had now been expelled from his see for fifteen years by this impious man, to be put to the sword by a Sicilian official.[11] That white-haired and venerated prelate, already bordering on old age, was in any case hastening to the grave after being baked for so

long in the furnace of poverty and crippled by the frosts of a
lengthy exile. The above-mentioned executioner was sent not only
for this purpose but also, if possible, to lay his blood-stained hands
on one of the great pillars of the Church. It is not surprising that
[Frederick] put to death less distinguished prelates, for he had
previously sent his hired assassins and cut-throats to murder the
supreme vicar of Christ and some of his brothers,[12] and he has
already made similar attempts on certain princes. Alas! How the
fear of God has languished among Christian princes and the love
of the Saviour has everywhere grown tepid! Formerly in the time
of the gentiles, if anyone refused to worship a demon giving
oracles he was torn apart and killed with all kinds of torture. But
now faith is despised and heretics are on the increase and are
protected by this impious man. Heresies are preached in the
territories of this wicked potentate, apostates multiply there, the
Lord's enemies are protected, the sacraments and authority of the
Church are held in contempt, the liberty of the Church is trampled
on, nor is there any care of souls. Some time ago, when the
Christian army intent on the conquest of Cairo was cut off by the
Nile flood, was it not through the kindness of the sultan supplied
with provisions and protected, and sent back home unharmed?[13]
With that army were the bishops of Albano and Acre[14] of
illustrious memory, some other bishops and prelates, and the king
of Jerusalem John of Brienne, of illustrious memory. Was not the
lord cardinal priest John of Colonna of distinguished repute, who
had gone with the emperor of Constantinople to recover Greece
and was taken prisoner by Theodore Comnenus,[15] respectfully
treated and set free? Look how the madness of this most ferocious
enemy, not content with these evils, has caused Saracens to
profane the churches, altars to be demolished, relics to be
dispersed, and Christian virgins, widows and married women to
be violated in holy places.[16] Moreover on his orders the brothers
Minor and other religious men who were at work behind the
Christian lines imposing penances and burying the bodies of the
slain, were killed by the swords of impious men.

Besides this, to make the Lord's fury burn more fiercely against
this evil man, at Narni recently the Saracens, in front of a crowd of
people, dragged a crucifix and images of the blessed Mary and
other saints at the tail of an ass. Then, having cut off the legs and
arms from the crucifix, they fitted it and other images to their
shields so that, in battle, the Christians would be forced to assault
them with spears and arrows. Why on earth do the crusaders

ignore these insane deeds and direct their efforts either by swimming rivers or crossing the sea to conquering the Saracens or Tartars whose fury is far distant and whose cruelty is considered far less than that of these? This Saracen garbage should be eliminated first, together with its instigators and authors, and thereafter the other should be dealt with, for the cause which is being sought after abroad exists here at home. Now persecution by pagans has been introduced into the bowels of the Church, in the cloisters of the faithful, and within the boundaries of Christendom. It is right that the perpetrators of such enormities should first be driven out from Italy, lest a serpent in the sleeve, a mouse in the corn sack or a fire in the bosom be nurtured. Afterwards, matters further off should be dealt with. The Lord does not choose people according to place, but rather the reverse, as appears from the dispersal of the blessed Peter and the other apostles from Jerusalem to the various nations. Consider, finally, since "The Lord looked down from heaven upon the children of men, to see if there were any that did understand',[17] if there is anyone who mourns his death or cares about injuries done to his ministers. Let every Christian ponder the fact that he will be answerable to the Lord at the last judgement if he leaves such villainies unnoticed. Prosecute therefore the cause of the son of the most high, the cause of God, so that your own may prosper. Protect his spouse with the right hand of your power, so that on the judgement day the just judge may place you at his right hand to enter into everlasting glory.

---

1. Near here Matthew Paris has written in the margin "Note this dreadful letter".
2. See Jeremiah 1:13; and, for what immediately follows, Ovid *Remed. amoris*, 119.
3. 1 Peter 5:8; the following quotation is from Revelation 17:6.
4. Revelation 12:12.
5. "Note this inhuman and impious crime" writes Matthew Paris in the margin here.
6. Matthew Paris has written in the margin here "Note the ferocity against the already defunct."
7. The words "namely ten days" are in the margin. "Note the miracle" is written in the margin near here.
8. Lamentations 1:12.
9. Acts 9:4. What follows is partly from Luke 10:16.
10. See Matthew 24:12. Near here Matthew Paris has written in the margin "Note another similar crime".
11. Near here Matthew Paris has written "Note another crime as bad as the others" in the margin.
12. "Note another crime worse than the others" comments Matthew Paris in the margin near here.

13. Hereabouts in the margin Matthew Paris has written "F. prefers the sultan of Cairo" and, further down, "Comnenus too is preferred".
14. Payo Gaya, papal legate at Damietta, and James of Vitry.
15. He was despot of Epirus; the date was 1217.
16. The word "Abominations" is written in the margin here and, at the start of the next paragraph, "Detestable things".
17. Psalm 14:2.

How many people would have been roused against Frederick by this letter, had it not been for the vices of the Roman curia

When this shocking letter came to the notice of the public with telling effect, it would have roused its hearers against Frederick but for the fact that the papalists, enemies of this same Frederick, were defiled with avarice, simony, usury and other vices. Amongst other crazy things, they shamelessly harassed people who had taken the cross, urging them under penalty of excommunication now to set out for the Holy Land, now for the Byzantine Empire, and now suggesting that they attack Frederick. And, what was thought detestable, making the brothers Minor and Preacher their tax collectors, they extorted the necessary funds for an expedition on whatever pretext from these crusaders. Because of this, although the tyrant Frederick did shameful things, yet alas, to the disgrace of the Romans, he found large numbers of open as well as secret supporters and abettors in his crimes.

Disputes at Cambridge between scholars and townspeople

At this time, too, namely in Lent, a dispute over some minor matter arose at Cambridge between town and gown. From it ensued litigation and fights, housebreaking, wounding and homicide. Noise of this came to the king's ears, along with serious complaints, and both sides suffered not a little from the damage, and the scandal spread abroad. This too I consider worth mentioning and bearing in mind, namely that, at the habitual instigation of the enemy of the human race, as has frequently been mentioned before in this book, a gory quarrel was stirred up in Lent between scholars and laymen both here and overseas, in order that people should be injured at this holy time.[1]

1. The words from "in order that" to the end of the paragraph are from C, where they are written between the lines.

Frederick escapes a deadly drink prepared by Peter de Vinea

In this same year Frederick, everywhere harassed by formidable difficulties, advanced to this side of the mountains to attack the pope, then returned to Apulia, poisoned, as it is said. Being seriously ill, he was advised by his doctors to take a purgative and, afterwards, a specially prepared bath. Now Master Peter de Vinea, who was the most intimate councillor of the said Frederick and who had special care of his soul, had a certain doctor with him who, on the orders both of Frederick and the said Peter, was to prepare the things necessary for this purging. He undertook this with treacherous intent, for, at the instigation of this Peter, he mixed a deadly and most efficacious poison with the medicine and in the bath in order to do away with their trusting lord. According to the enemies of the Church the lord pope had corrupted Peter with gifts and great, even the greatest possible, promises, to induce him to perpetrate this crime. At the very moment when he was about to take this drink, Frederick was secretly warned and fully informed about the intended crime by a friend of his. When the doctor and Peter showed him the drink he said, "Friends, my soul confides in you. Take care, I pray you, not to give me, trustful as I am in you, poison in place of medicine." To which Peter replied, "My lord, this doctor of mine has often given you wholesome medicine, why should you be afraid now?" Frederick, however, having placed a guard behind the traitors so that they could not escape, with a grim look said to the doctor offering him the cup, "Drink half the medicine with me". The doctor was dumbfounded and, conscious of his crime, pretending that he had been tripped up, fell on his face and spilled most of the medicine. The small amount left over Frederick ordered to be given to some condemned criminals brought from prison; the wretches expired instantly. Thus certified of the deadly treachery prepared against him, Frederick ordered the doctor to be hanged and Peter, deservedly deprived of his eyes, he had led through many of the cities of Italy and Apulia so that he could publicly confess his crime to everybody. Finally, Frederick ordered him to be handed over for execution to the Pisans, who inexorably loathed this Peter. When he heard this, lest he should suffer death at the will of his enemies – for, as Seneca says "To die at the will of an enemy is to die twice"[1] – Peter struck his head forcefully against the pillar to which he was tied and brained himself.

---

1. This does not appear to be from Seneca; see Luard 1876: 27n.5.

Frederick's grief

After this Frederick was broken-hearted and wept abundantly and bitterly, and "Rivers of waters ran down his eyes",[1] which was pitiable to see in a man of such an age and of so great authority. Wringing his hands together in grief, he exclaimed "Woe is me, for my own flesh and blood fight against me! Peter, whom I believed to be a rock and half my soul, has plotted to kill me. The lord pope, whom the Empire, under my noble predecessors, created and enriched from nothing, is trying to destroy it and is plotting to exterminate me, the ruler of this now disturbed Empire. In whom can I confide? Where can I be safe? Where happy? Friends sitting around him shared his grief with sighs and tears. The fame of the lord pope was no little sullied by this incident, but God, the infallible investigator of secrets, alone knows the truth.

1. Psalm 119:136, misquoted.

Victuals are brought to the needy French wintering in Cyprus

At this same time, when the king of the French, Louis IX, who was staying the winter in Cyprus, was suffering from a serious shortage of provisions, he sent the count of Bar [Theobald II], a discreet and eloquent man, and [Imbert] lord of Beaujeu, a most energetic knight, to the Venetians and to other inhabitants of neighbouring islands and cities, humbly requesting them charitably to come to his aid, since he was fighting for the Church universal, by selling him provisions. To this the Venetians responded favourably; they generously sent six large ships loaded with corn, wine and other victuals, as well as military aid and many crusaders. Likewise some other cities and islands, whose assistance he had sought, sent various supplies. Frederick not only permitted this, but kindly persuaded them to help, and he himself likewise, lest he should seem inferior to the others, sent a most abundant supply of different sorts of food. Thus the king had plenty. He thanked Frederick and wrote to the lord pope asking him to admit Frederick to his favour and no longer defame or make war on so great a friend and benefactor of the Church, thanks to whom he and the entire Christian army had been saved from imminent danger of starvation. When the king's noble mother Blanche heard this she thanked Frederick repeatedly and sent him priceless gifts, declaring that he had preserved the life and honour of her son and the whole Christian army. She too wrote to the lord pope to ask him to mitigate his rancour against Frederick. However, the lord pope, spurning all such requests, became daily more and more hostile to Frederick, but everywhere had the worst of things.

The king of France arbitrates many disputes

Meanwhile the king of the French, following sane and saintly advice, fully pacified many nobles in dispute, including the Templars and Hospitallers, both in Cyprus and in other parts of Christendom, so that, by leaving no grounds for offence behind him, he could resume with greater security the journey he had begun.

Frederick's son Henry writes on the king of England's behalf

Also at the same time, at the instigation, it is thought, of the king of England, Henry, the son of Frederick and the empress Isabella and nephew of the said king, urged the lord king of the French with repeated requests and gifts, by means of solemn ambassadors, for the salvation of his soul and because of his pilgrimage, like a pious and just man to hand over to his uncle the lord king of the English the possessions which belonged to him by right of his grandfather, lest the sin of Louis, king of the French, should be transferred by an angry God to his innocent son. Likewise, Frederick himself is said to have applied to the king of the French in the same matter but not pressingly, lest he should seem, in this way, to be demanding payment for the gifts [he had recently sent Louis]. To these requests the king replied: "By the holy cross which I bear, I would willingly do this if my council would allow it, for I love the king of England sincerely, like a kinsman, but it would be a serious matter for me, in the middle of my pilgrimage, to disturb the whole community of my kingdom by rejecting the advice of my mother and magnates, even though the petitioners are dear to me."

The archbishop of Rouen comes to England for his own benefit

Also in the same year, about Easter, the archbishop of Rouen [Odo Rigaud], a brother of the order of Minors and French by birth, came to England with the king's permission to collect some revenues pertaining to the rights of his church. When he had taken care of this, he did homage to the king for these receipts, for they were in England, and returned home.

At the same time the bishop of Tortosa, whose bishopric is in Syria, an Englishman and a brother of the order of Preachers, came to England to visit his native soil and any relatives that might still be alive. He was born near Reading of humble parents, but he returned unsuccessful and sorrowful when, because of poverty and the lapse of time, he could find no trace either of his family home or of his parents. He most positively asserted to the assembled monks in the monastery of Reading, where he celebrated high mass on the day of the Invention of the holy cross [3 May], that the Khorasmians remaining in the Holy Land, aroused to battle by the sultan of Cairo and the vengeance of God, had slaughtered one another. Moreover, the more powerful Saracen princes, who had been wearing themselves out by fighting each other, because of the pride of the said sultan, made peace and joined in an alliance when they heard of the hostile approach against them of the lord king of the French. This sultan, who is known to be chief or one of the chief of all the eastern Saracens, let the said king know that the Saracen princes in the East were eagerly awaiting him, so that they could all fight a pitched battle with him. They in no way feared his advance; and they sent other haughty and ironical messages.

The crusaders assembled in London

At the close of Easter [11 April] the magnates of England, as had previously been agreed among themselves, assembled in London for the lord king to do what he had at all events often promised, namely to appoint a chancellor, justiciar and treasurer on their advice. But just as they believed themselves certainly on the point of achieving everything, the absence of Earl Richard, who appeared to be their leader, entirely prevented any progress in this matter. He had gone to Cornwall some time before as if on business and was thus far off. So the deluded magnates returned home.

The brothers Preacher and Minor become the pope's tax-collectors[1]

At this time the brothers Preacher and Minor, on the pope's orders, which they obediently complied with, set about preaching eagerly and diligently. To increase the devotion of the faithful, they went with great solemnity to the places appointed beforehand for their preaching and granted many days of indulgence to the people who came. They were met by priests and clerks in white vestments, with crosses and banners, bringing with them no small numbers of the faithful, just as happens on Rogation days. Preaching the crusade, they bestowed the sign of the cross on people of any age, sex, condition or worth, even on male and female invalids, sick people and those incapacitated by age. Then, the next day or even directly afterwards, receiving the sign of the cross back from those who had taken it, they absolved them from their vows to go on pilgrimage for whatever sum they could obtain. To many this seemed unbefitting and absurd, because, not many days later, Earl Richard heaped together all these grapes gathered by Master Berard, an Italian clerk, into his treasury. Because of this, no small scandal arose in the Church of God and among the entire populace, and the devotion of the faithful manifestly cooled.

1. Erased in B, probably by Matthew Paris himself, this heading is from C.

The death of the archbishop of Mainz, Frederick's great opponent

Also at this time died [Siegfried], archbishop of Mainz, a great opponent of Frederick. But, so that Frederick would not rejoice over his death for long, the lord pope handed over the care, administration and rule of that archbishopric to the archbishop of Cologne [Konrad von Hochstaden], because he battled steadfastly for the Church against Frederick and his son Conrad. Moreover, the lord pope handed over a very well known vacant abbey to the same archbishop of Cologne. There is said to be no more rich or famous abbey in the world; it is called Wolsa.[1] This abbey has been obliged since ancient times to find one thousand knights for each new emperor after his coronation at Aachen. The aforesaid archbishop of Cologne so impoverished these two noble bereaved churches, using everything for the pay of his soldiers that, the monks and clerics having been dispersed, the few remaining priests scarcely had sufficient to sustain a meagre existence. For he plundered and snatched away anything these churches had of value, in gold, silver, gems, and costly vestments, as well as the rich revenues. The narrative that follows will explain to what end all this rapine came. Moreover this same martial and belligerent archbishop obtained a privilege from the lord pope to extort an infinite sum of money in support of his wars, from poor people throughout his archbishopric, whose complaining lament is believed to have ascended to heaven.

1. Surely an error for Fulda, in Hessen.

Enzio, Frederick's son, harasses the Parmans but does not prevail

At this same time the Parmans, to comfort and support whom against Frederick the lord pope had sent a large sum of money and military help, despatched two hundred knights for the defence of a certain castle they had constructed not far from their city for its defence. But Frederick's son, Enzio, king of Sardinia, secretly warned of this, having laid an ambush, seized them all unawares. When he was about to hang them in view of the city, the citizens let him know that, if he hanged them, they would immediately retaliate by consigning all their prisoners from Frederick's army to the gallows. Enzio therefore spared his captives, keeping them for the time being for ransom or exchange. When the lord pope heard this [he deplored the fact that] the money he had sent to the Parmans had produced no result.[1]

1. This sentence remains unfinished in the MSS.

An extraordinary flood caused by rain

At the beginning of June such a huge deluge of rain fell, mostly around Abingdon, that willows and other trees and houses near the rivers and streams, and even sheepcotes and the sheep in them, salt-works and mills with bridges, and a chapel not far from Abingdon, were carried away. The green corn with its sprouting ears coming into flower was levelled to the ground so that the bread afterwards seemed to have been made from bran rather than wheat.

Concerning the second translation of the blessed Edmund, archbishop and confessor

In this same year the venerable and uncorrupted body of the blessed Archbishop Edmund of Canterbury was translated a second time, at Pontigny, in a shrine most beautifully made of gold and silver, inlaid with gems and fitted with crystal panels. On the same day that it was brought up from the ground, namely the fifth of the ides of June, the feast of SS. Primus and Felicianus [9 June], the venerable body, thanks to God still entire and undecayed, was reverently replaced in the same tomb, in the presence of a large crowd of prelates and magnates, to the honour of God and the Church universal and especially of the kingdoms of the French and the English.

Many English nobles take the cross

At this same time many nobles from the kingdom of the English, namely William Longespee, Robert de Vere his standard-bearer, and many others, who were reckoned to number two hundred knights in all, prepared to go on crusade. William therefore, the leader of all the crusaders from the kingdom of England, with the permission and blessing of his noble and holy mother [Ela, countess of Salisbury], the abbess of Laycock, set out in July without further delay and joined the French army safe and sound. The most Christian king of the French received him and his men with respect and enrolled them among his picked troops, thanking them for coming to his aid; and he most earnestly entreated all his men not to permit the usual pride and envy of the French to arouse discord between them and the English, as was said to have happened in the time of King Richard. But, by the instigation of the devil, who from ancient times has always envied the successes of men, when the French later saw the pre-eminence of the English, and their success in acquiring things and fame, they began to be jealous and insulted them, coming out with their habitual sarcasms, together with sneers and blasphemous oaths. As the poet has it: "Every power is impatient of a partner." Likewise one could say: "Every proud man is impatient of a partner."[1] Moreover, pride aroused mutual hatred and envy among these Frenchmen, so that their ruler's progress was much hindered, as will be more fully related in what follows.

1. Lucan *Phars.* 1:93–4.

The Gascons are conquered by the earl of Leicester

In these days also the earl of Leicester Simon de Montfort, after altering or deferring his vow to go on pilgrimage, for he had taken the cross, crossed the sea to subdue the king's enemies in Gascony. With a large contingent of troops and a large sum of royal money, he arrived in force and forcefully attacked the enemies of the lord king, who had seditiously lifted up their heel against him.[1] He subdued Gaston [de Béarn], Rustan and William de Solers and all the principal men of Bordeaux and conducted himself so bravely and loyally that he earned the praise and favour of all the king's friends, and was said to take after his father in everything.

1. Misquoted from John 13:18.

Frederick's son Enzio is captured by the Bolognese

In the same year, in May, while Enzio, king of Sardinia and natural son of Frederick, was campaigning against his enemies near Bologna with some people from Cremona and Reggio, the Bolognese, forewarned, having prepared a secret ambush, made a surprise attack on him as he was incautiously advancing towards the bridge at S. Ambrogio, which is half-way between Bologna and Cremona. A fierce encounter ensued and no slight slaughter. Enzio was defeated and captured and, with him, the principal men of his retinue, some two hundred knights, many citizens of Cremona and Reggio, and a large number of common soldiers. They were taken to Bologna and imprisoned and, since they were cruelly and inhumanly treated at the will of their enemies, the prisoners gave the Bolognese eighteen thousand imperial pounds, which are worth almost as much as pounds sterling, to be treated more leniently and be less tightly chained.

Frederick is taken ill and another son of his dies

At this same time another natural son of Frederick died in Apulia[1]. He himself was struck down with a skin disease called 'holy fire' and, oppressed with so many adversities, grieved inconsolably. Humbled, according to David's words, "Fill their faces with shame; that they may seek thy name, o Lord,"[2] he offered honourable terms of peace to the lord pope. But the pope, rejoicing in his troubles, would not accept his offer, and, because of this, he incurred the indignation and rancour of many nobles, who began to sympathise with F. and support him, detesting the pride of the servant of the servants of God.

1. This was Richard, count of Chieti.
2. Psalm 83:16.

Peter Capoccio, legate in Apulia, is expelled from there in confusion

In the course of those days Peter Capoccio, a clerk and influential friend of the lord pope, was sent to Apulia by the lord pope as legate, armed with extensive powers to remit sins, so that he could oppose the said Frederick and the Frederickites. With increased power, which he obtained on all sides through giving money and granting plenary indulgence for the remission of sins, he harmed this same Frederick and recalled many nobles from their loyalty to him.

The Cistercian monks engage in teaching in the universities

At this same time the Cistercian monks, so as no longer to be held in contempt by the brothers Minor and Preachers, and secular scholars, especially legists and decretalists, obtained a new privilege. In connection with this, they put up fine buildings in Paris and elsewhere, where schools flourished, so that, by organising teaching in theology, decretals and law, they could study more freely, and so that they would not seem inferior to others. For the world has now become elated with pride and despises the religion of the cloisters, aiming at despoiling the monks of their property. And so, because of the wickedness of the world, the vigour of the monastic order has been somewhat enervated. For we do not read that this originated in the rule of St. Benedict, who is said, witness St. Gregory[1], to have had in him the spirit of all saints. What is more, we read and sing of him, that, abandoning literary studies, he resolved to seek the desert.

1. *Dialogues* 2:8, Migne, *Pat. lat.* 66, col. 150.

The archbishop of Canterbury Boniface is enthroned

On All Saints day Archbishop Boniface of Canterbury was enthroned rather ostentatiously[1], the king and queen and almost all the English prelates having been summoned for this great solemnity.

While the lord king was hastening there with his household, his special councillor John Mansel fell seriously ill at Maidstone, infected with poison, it was said. He was listless for two days and was only just saved from the gates of death by the care of the doctors.

1. The words *fastigiose nimis* have been taken from C. They have been erased in B and Matthew Paris has written *cum magno honore* "with great honour" in their place.

Various rumours are spread around

At this same time rumour spread, but we do not know if it is true, although a well-composed letter was sent to the king on the subject, that the king of the Tartars had been converted to Christianity. The painstaking reader can find it in the *Book of additamenta*.[1]

1. BL Cotton MS. Nero D i, f.98b = Luard 1882:163–5. See too below, p.193.

The bishop of Norwich returns from the Roman curia

Also at this time Bishop Walter of Norwich returned from the Roman curia. It was said that he had obtained an infamous privilege for extorting money from his bishopric.

Most welcome rumours of the capture of Damietta

About Michaelmas and afterwards a very welcome rumour spread about through the whole of the West. The first person to bring it to England was Archbishop Boniface of Canterbury, who arrived on St. Matthew's day [21 September]. It was, namely, that the most Christian king of the French, having landed on the coast in strength and repelled and defeated the Saracens, had taken Damietta. In confirmation of this, the lord king of England received a letter, which can be found in the *Book of additamenta*.[1]

1. BL Cotton MS. Nero D i f.93 = Luard 1882:152–4.

Concerning the provincial chapter at which the reform of the Black order was thoroughly discussed

About this same time the abbots of the order of Black monks, or their proctors, convened at Bermondsey on St. Calixtus's day [14 October]. By common consent and with the inspiration of God a reformation was agreed on which may be read at this sign in the *Book of additamenta*.[1] . . . One thing worthy of record which I do not think should be passed by without mention, and which is by no means included in these statutes, is that the lord king obtained from all of them an agreement that, at the mass which is daily chanted in their churches in honour of the blessed Virgin, the collect beginning "O God, in whose hands are the hearts of kings", should be said daily for himself and the queen; but he made no allowance to them for this.

1. BL Cotton MS. Nero D i f.95b = Luard 1882:175–85.

Concerning a white marble stone on which our Lord's footprint appeared

At this same time the brothers Preacher brought from the Holy Land a certain stone of white marble which, since the time of Christ, had carried an impression of the saviour's footstep. It quite plainly showed the form of half a human foot, as if it had been made in soft wax. The inhabitants of the Holy Land maintained that this form or impression was the footprint made by Christ at the Ascension, when he took leave of his disciples, so that, by this token, he could perpetuate his memory with them; he whom they were then looking at for the last time, not to see again until he should come to judge the world. In the same way, Christ is said to have made the impression of his face, which is called the 'Veronica', namely so that a record of it would remain on earth.[1] The lord king presented this [stone] as a noble gift to the church of Westminster, as he recently had the blood of Christ.

1. Matthew Paris made a painting of this miraculous impression of Christ's face in the annal for 1216, see James 1926:25–6 and Plate 29. Veronica was the name of a woman said to have handed Jesus a handkerchief with which to wipe his face when he was on his way to the cross.

Concerning a mannikin and a giant

At this same time a sort of mannikin, eighteen years old, John by name, was found in the Isle of Wight. He was not a dwarf, for his limbs were of just proportions; he was hardly three feet tall but had ceased to grow. The queen ordered him to be taken around with her as a freak of nature to arouse the astonishment of onlookers. The length of his tiny body is sixteen times that of this line.

At the same time a male child was born, begotten it was said by a demon, on the Welsh border in the earl of Hereford's territories. Within half a year his teeth were full grown and he was as tall as a youth of about seventeen. His mother was taken ill after the birth, pined away, and died miserably.[1] Both of these were freaks of nature, the latter exceeding man's natural size, the former not attaining it.

1. The last three words are in the margin.

A tournament is held at Brackley

Also at this time a tournament was held at Brackley at which many knights of the community of the realm, who call themselves bachelors, were injured. Earl Richard of Gloucester, who always opposed the foreigners and supported the natives, joined the foreigners at this tournament, to the enormous detriment of his fame and honour. Because of this the English side was defeated. In this conflict the lord king's brother William of Valence, with the said earl's help, got the better of William de Odingesseles, and badly wounded him. He was a powerful knight who was counted among the bachelors.

Walter of Kirkham, dean of York, is consecrated bishop of Durham

On the first Sunday in Advent [28 November], Walter of Kirkham, the elect of Durham, was consecrated at York by Archbishop Walter of York, whose suffragan bishop he was.

On the quarrel between the abbot of Westminster and his convent

At this same time dissension arose between the abbot of Westminster [Richard of Croxley] and the monks of this convent, to the disgrace and scandal of the entire order of Black monks. The cause and details of this are more fully recorded in the *Book of additamenta*.[1] However, as a result of the intervention of the king, who is known to be specially fond of this convent, peace and concord of some kind or other were re-established between them.

1. BL Cotton MS. Nero D i f.62b, has two relevant writs. See Luard 1882:152, 175.

A dissension between the abbot of Peterborough and his convent

To increase the scandal from this, strife arose at the very same time between Abbot William of Peterborough and the convent there. He was reproved for extravagance and for enriching his relatives – he was surrounded by an excessive number of them – to the enormous loss of his church, but did not correct the fault. The monks were unhappy about this and laid a serious complaint about their abbot's excesses before the bishop of Lincoln, who was always ready and willing to punish transgressors. The abbot was convicted and, since his deposition was imminent, he resigned the office and dignity of abbot, as if spontaneously, into the hands of the bishop. He was then assigned a certain part of the abbacy, namely a single manor, though he did not deserve it, where he might live honestly and honourably, like a hermit, in repentance. On this the royal officials, sent there forthwith by the king, agape after profits and greedy for the abbey's revenues, set about its plundering and extermination. For the king was extremely annoyed and wanted a pretext to move against that house because he had been told that the monks were persecuting, and had accused, their abbot, because he had been favourable and bountiful to the lord king.

Robert Passelew shuns the court

On the fifth day before the feast of the blessed Lucy [9 December], Robert Passelew, about whom much has been written in this book, detesting the fickleness of the court, fled to the fruits of a better life and was promoted to the rank of priest. On this the lord bishop Robert of Ely gave him the fine church of Dereham which had belonged to Jeremiah [de Caxton], a recently deceased royal clerk. The lord king pursued both the giver, the bishop, and the recipient, Robert, with inexorable hatred, because the bishop would not voluntarily bestow that church on Aethelmar, the king's brother.

Concerning the passage toll of the count of Guines

In the same year, when the count of Guines [Arnaud] was travelling across England to see the king, Earl Roger Bigod, hearing about this, ordered him to be seized. When this became known to the count of Guines he made a serious complaint about it to the king. Earl Roger was therefore summoned and replied publicly as follows:

My lord king, when I was sent to the Council of Lyons as the envoy of yourself and of the whole kingdom, I passed through the territories of the lord count of Guines peacefully and at some expense. I felt sure that I would be courteously received with honour and hospitality both out of respect for you and in return for the many kindnesses many times done him by us. But he acted very differently, for he forcibly halted my horses and men, to my loss and dishonour or rather yours, until he had extorted for passage money whatever amount his officials chose to demand, I do not know for what reason or on what grounds. Nor did he spare me either on account of politeness or respect for you. When therefore this same count came to this side of the Channel and was passing through my territories, he deservedly received similar treatment. For I hold my land as freely from you, my lord king, and I am an earl just as he is. What right has he to practise such forcible plundering, by selling the roads and the air to travellers?

The count of Guines, when he heard this, was shamed into silence, nor could he reasonably reply to the charges. When this affair came to the notice of the most pious king of the French, which was soon after the Council, having granted an income to the count so that he should incur no loss, he ordered the aforesaid passage toll, as shameful as it was harmful, to be abolished.

The church at Beaulieu is dedicated with great solemnity

In the same year the abbot of Beaulieu had his church, which King John had raised from its foundations, dedicated with the utmost solemnity in the presence of King Henry, son of the said King J., Earl Richard his brother, and many other magnates and prelates. On this solemnity he spent two hundred marks and more; nor did the king spare him on that account, but he had to pay the maximum fine for an offence which it was said he had committed against the king by occupying some forest land. What is more, the abovesaid abbot sent twenty picked monks and thirty brethren to inhabit a new house of the

Cistercian order which Earl Richard had recently founded not far from Winchcomb[1] to fulfil a vow he had made at sea.

1.   At Hailes in Gloucestershire.

Rumours about the conversion of the Tartars reach the lord king

During those days very welcome rumours spread about, namely that a most powerful Tartar king, as a result of the preaching and painstaking persuasion of Peter, an Indian monk of the Black order, of whom much mention has been made above in the letters about the Tartars, was converted to the Christian faith and baptised, on account of the purity, honesty and manifold holiness which are preached and taught in it. This king sent encouraging and friendly letters to the lord king of the French then at Damietta, urging and persuading him to attack the Saracens powerfully and confidently to purge the lands of the East of their filth. As a loyal catholic and baptised recruit of Christ, he also offered prompt and effective help. A letter on all this, translated from Arabic into Latin and French, sent to the lord king, is fully set out in the *Book of additamenta*.[1] The lord king of the French, overjoyed at this addition to the Christian faith, sent him a costly portable chapel with some most precious relics, as well as some Preachers and Minors to inform himself more fully.

At the same time too other rumours, doubtful and fictitious, to encourage the Christians and perhaps to persuade crusaders to cross over and join the king of France, circulated through the kingdoms on this side of the sea. The chief disseminator of these reports was the bishop of Marseilles [Benedict of Alignano], and likewise certain well known Templars. These fables were more credible because issued under their seals, but when the truth of the matter became known, they caused anxiety and harm. However, they seemed to contain so much truth that the Saracens and their princes, dumbfounded after the Christian capture of Damietta, offered the Christians whatever territory had ever been Christian, and more, if they would restore Damietta and their recent conquests and pay an indemnity. But the pride of the count of Artois would not permit this, nor would he accept the humiliation of the Saracens unless the Christians could have and peaceably retain Damietta and also receive Alexandria. The Saracens would in no way accept these harsh peace terms. We believe that God was offended by this, for the Christians ought not to have crossed the sea with any intention other than to gain possession of Christ's inheritance. The Saracens, discussing this among themselves, said, "Let us wait awhile. Pride and avarice, which Christ Jesus their God especially detests, will destroy them all." And so in truth it turned out, as the following account will fully elucidate.

1. See above, p. 188.

On the lamentable death of Alexander, king of the Scots

During the course of this same year, on the fifth of the nones of July [3 July], died Alexander [II], king of the Scots, a wise and modest man who, after he had reigned justly, happily and in peace for many years, is said in his last days to have been diverted by greed from the path of justice. Seeking an occasion to vent his spontaneous anger, he flared up against one of the principal nobles of his kingdom, Owen of Argyll by name, a zealous and most accomplished knight. As he planned to disinherit him, he accused him of treachery because in the previous year he had done homage to the king of Norway for the tenure of a certain island which Owen's father had held from the same king and had peaceably possessed for many years in return for homage. The island is situated between Scotland and the Orkneys.[1] Owen, fearing the threats of his lord the king of Scotland, let him know that he would fully render the service he owed, both to the king of the Scots and the king of the Norwegians. But when the king of the Scots retorted that "No man can serve two masters,"[2] he received the reply from Owen that it was easy to serve two lords well, provided they were not hostile to each other. The king raised an army and advanced against Owen, who, unwilling to offend his lord the king of Scotland, entreated him to grant him a truce so that he could resign to the king of Norway both his homage and the aforesaid island. When the king of the Scots denied him this, his hatred became apparent, and so he offended both God and St. Columba, who is buried and honoured in those parts, and many of the nobles. The king defied this Owen and pursued him by sea as far as Argyll, encouraged, it is said, by the importunate instigation of a certain indiscreet bishop of Strathearn, a brother of the order of Preachers.[3] But the king, on disembarking from his ship, before he could mount his horse, as if by divine vengeance, was struck down by a sudden and deadly attack of illness. Thus he abruptly expired in the arms of his nobles while trying to disinherit an innocent man.

1. Stroma seems to be meant. Norwegian sovereignty over the Orkneys was retained until their incorporation into the kingdom of Scotland in the fifteenth century.
2. Matthew 7:24.
3. Clement, bishop of Dunblane. The see of Dunblane was at first called Strathearn, being probably coterminous with the earldom of that name.

The death of Hugh le Brun, count of La Marche

In the same year Hugh, surnamed Brun, count of La Marche, was released from the affairs of the world after the king of the French had landed at Damietta. He deserved to be lamented the less because he treacherously plotted in Poitou against his son-in-law, the king of the English, who trusted him. For he summoned the king there, and then deceitfully sold him to the king of France.[1] However, it is to be charitably believed that he prudently expiated this crime and all his other sins on this pilgrimage.

1. See Luard 1877:211, 216. A reference to Henry III's expedition to Poitou in 1242.

William of Holland the new king of Germany is defeated by F.'s son Conrad

In the same year, as summer drew to an end, the fortunes of the pope's party in the struggle begun against Frederick declined and were diminished in no small way. Besides this William of Holland, who had ascended to the dignity of king of Germany with the lord pope's help, was defeated by F.'s son Conrad and had retreated into hiding.

Raymond count of Saint-Gilles or Toulouse, a courageous and circumspect knight and a great friend of the lord pope, who was seriously and indeed mortally ill, sent back the money entrusted to him by the pope for waging war on the enemies of the Church and especially on the count of Savoy [Amadeus IV], asserting that he was so oppressed by a grave and mortal sickness that he was expecting only death, and all that was left to him was the tomb. Solemnly making his will, he ordered his body to be buried in the house of nuns at Fontevrault, at the feet of King Richard, whose kinsman he was; and with his body he bequeathed five thousand pounds of silver to that house.

The death of Peter de Geneure, whom the king had endowed in Ireland

Moreover in the same year died Peter de Geneure, a Provençal by birth, and, though of humble origin, a great friend of the lord king, who demonstrated this by his actions. For he granted to this P. the noble young lady Matilda, the beautiful daughter of Walter de Lacy, together with her entire inheritance and the honour pertaining to it. By her he had a son and a daughter.

The death of Simon the Norman

In the same year too died Master Simon the Norman, formerly a special councillor of the lord king and keeper and master of the seal. Although he had been proud, nevertheless in the end he incurred the king's indignation because of the honesty he believed in. For when the lord king wanted to concede and confer to Thomas, count of Flanders, a certain charter, drawn up against the interests of the crown and to the enormous harm of the kingdom of England, the said Simon would on no account do this. This was loyal and commendable, and all his other vehement acts were thereby excused.

The death of Master William of Durham, an excellent cleric

In the same year too Master William of Durham died at Rouen on his way back from the Roman curia, a man very eminent for his learning and abounding in riches, though he was agape for more. He was rector of the fine church of Wearmouth, situated not far from the sea, and on his death the king at once successfully arranged for this same church to be given to his brother Aethelmar of Valence without any enquiry. This Aethelmar, because of the abundance of his revenues, especially in the north, appointed as his seneschal Martin de Sainte-Croix, a cleric and a most prudent man.

The death of Roger FitzJohn in a tournament

In the course of this same year around Pentecost [23 May] one of the more illustrious of the northern barons, Roger FitzJohn, died, leaving a small boy as heir. The king there and then granted his wardship to his brother William of Valence, though the mother wanted to purchase the wardship of the boy for two hundred [marks]. Her name was Ada de Baliol; the child's name was . . . .

Many French nobles die in the island.

In the island of Cyprus, while the king of the French was wintering there, some illustrious French crusaders migrated to the Lord. It would be a lengthy business to enumerate them and irrelevant to the history of the English. Many died on the journey, both on land and sea, but that illustrious man the bishop of Noyon [Peter Charlot], count palatine and one of the twelve peers of France, died on board ship not far off Cyprus.

The death of Count H.

Before the king of the French set sail, Hugh de Châtillon, count of Saint-Pol and of Blois, died at Avignon,[1] crushed by a stone shot from a mangonel, in a battle which the king of the French fought there. This was an unfortunate presage for the success of the crusade, for there was no one more renowned nor more expert in arms in the whole army of the French. In his retinue he had fifty picked knights as his standard-bearers in battle; but on his death they were all demoralised and dispersed. This Count Hugh had had a splendid ship fitted out at Inverness in the kingdom of Scotland, namely in Moray, in which he could boldly cross the sea with the men from Boulogne and Flanders and those commonly known as 'from the Low Countries'.[2] But all these preparations were cut short, as a weaver cuts his web.

John [count] of Dreux also died in Cyprus, a young man most accomplished in war and the flower of all his family, of most noble blood. This was a fateful and lamentable prognostic of the future. There died moreover nobles of both sexes who, falling sick because of the changes in diet and climate usually abhorred by nature, flew like martyrs to the celestial kingdoms. We have been induced to mention them in this book because they happily ended their lives in the cause of the universal Church and the service of the cross.

1. Matthew Paris is wrong here. It was Hugh's father Guy II who was killed in this way at Avignon, and with Louis VIII, not Louis IX.
2. *De avalterris*, B.

The conclusion of the annal

So passed the year, not very productive of fruit though the trees were covered with blossom almost throughout the spring, but producing corn in abundance. At the end of the summer, to the provocation of mankind, the crops that had offered good hopes were spoiled, and yielded wheaten bread that was bran-like and dark. The year was, I say, infamous for the Roman curia, turbulent for France and England.

[The Chronica majora 1250]

The king was at Winchester for Christmas and with the bishop on the day after Christmas

In the year of the lord 1250, which is the thirty-fourth year of the lord king H. III, the said lord king was at Winchester for Christmas, where the feast of the Nativity was, as usual, celebrated magnificently. On the day after, he was the distinguished and now customary guest of Bishop W[illiam] of that city at dinner, for he courteously wanted to please the bishop by the honour of his presence. Then he set out in haste for London, where he solemnly consummated the feast of the blessed Edward, having summoned B. archbishop of Canterbury, who celebrated mass there, seven bishops and very many of the magnates of the kingdom.

The countess of Cornwall gives birth to a son

At the same time, namely in Christmas week, Sanchia, countess of Cornwall, wife of Earl Richard, bore him a son at Berkhamstead. The earl summoned the archbishop of Canterbury, the child's uncle, to baptize him, and he was called Edmund, in honour of the blessed Edmund, archbishop of Canterbury and confessor.

The death of the royal councillor Jeremiah

In these same days the clerk and special councillor of the lord king Jeremiah Caxton died. The bishop of Ely at once gave his fine church to Robert Passelew in the hope that, after a long and childless life, he would become a holy priest.

199

The rash transgression of Walter Clifford and the king's anger

At this same time Walter Clifford, not the least of the barons of the Welsh march in power, wealth and liberties, was gravely accused before the lord king of treating a messenger of the said king bringing royal letters to him violently and improperly, in contempt of the lord king, and of forcing him to eat the royal letters together with the wax seal. Walter, convicted before the king, did not dare to stand trial, but, submitting to the mercy of the lord king, barely escaped death or disinheritance. He lost his liberty and all the money he had or could have, namely one thousand marks,[1] and was then allowed to return home without being imprisoned, on the pledge of some chosen securities.

1. The words from "namely" to "marks" are in the margin of B.

Peace is re-established between the abbot of Westminster and the convent

During the above-mentioned festivities the lord king did his best to re-establish peace between the abbot of Westminster and the convent of that place, for the scandal of this dispute spread throughout the religious community, indeed it had infected the entire region. The king was even told that he would have laid himself out to no purpose on the rebuilding of the church at Westminster, namely in carving and fitting the stones, if the personnel of the church, that is the pastor and his flock or abbot and convent, who are the "living stones"[1] in the make-up of such a noble building, were so improperly in dispute. Thus, by the efforts of the lord king, who was fond of that church, peace was re-established between them.

1. 1 Peter 2:5.

The monks in the diocese of Lincoln are cited before Bishop R.

Also at this same time that indefatigable persecutor of monks, the bishop of Lincoln Robert [Grosseteste], had all the monks in his diocese summoned to assemble at Leicester on the feast of St. Hilary [13 January], there to hear a mandate from the lord pope. For this bishop was puffing and blowing his utmost to get back into his own hands the churches and revenues of the monks established throughout his diocese, which would have been extremely harmful to many people. Moreover, the monks had neither the assent of the chapter to this nor the documents providing clear evidence about it. To this end he had at the greatest expense sent his clerk, Master Leonard, who was a frequent messenger to Rome, to the papal curia. This curia, I must say, like an abyss, had the power and the practice of swallowing up everyone's income, even nearly everything that the bishops and abbots possessed. The letters containing this grant can be found at this sign . . ., that is to say in the *Book of additamenta*.[1]

1. BL Cotton MS. Nero D i, f.94b = Luard 1882:152.

Many English nobles cross the sea

At the same time many nobles from the kingdom of England crossed the sea, but nobody knew the reason why. They were Earl Richard, the earl of Gloucester, Henry Hastings a baron, Roger Thirkeby, and many other nobles with them. Furthermore, from among the prelates, were the bishops of Lincoln, London and Worcester, and, from the bishopric of Lincoln, the archdeacons of Oxford and Bedford,[1] and many other clerics. Earl Richard crossed the kingdom of France in the greatest splendour with a magnificent retinue of forty uniformed knights newly fitted out on superb horses, their harness glittering with gold, together with many waggons and fifty cart horses. With him was a numerous suite, including the countess his wife and his eldest son, Henry. This was designed to present a wonderful and glorious show to the French onlookers and admirers. The honourable lady Blanche met him on his arrival with the utmost respect, welcoming him with handsome presents, as one relative to another, or rather as a mother might a specially loved son.

The reason why the bishop of Lincoln crossed the sea was the only one known to everyone.

1. Robert de Marisco and John Crakehall respectively.

Bishop R. of Lincoln crosses the sea to bring his plan to the desired effect

Although he was an old man, the aforesaid bishop of Lincoln worked assiduously to subject strictly to his will the monks who, summoned to hear the papal mandate as before mentioned, had appealed to the apostolic see against his unheard of exactions. For the exempt abbots, the Templars, Hospitallers and many others had appealed; afterwards they carefully made peace with the lord pope with the aid of money, for, as the moralist says, "When the law is iniquitous the judge's aid is sought". When, after great expense and wasted labour, the bishop heard about this, he went to the lord pope in sorrow and confusion and said: "My lord and holy father, I blush at the frustration of my intentions because I relied confidently on your letters and promises, but now I am deceived in my expectations because those whom I thought I had subdued have gone away free, to my discomfiture." To which the pope is said to have replied with a scowling look, "Brother, what is that to you? You have freed your soul; we have done them a favour. 'Is thine eye evil because I am good?'"[1] When the bishop, sighing, said to himself, "Oh money! money! What power you have, especially in the Roman curia!" he was overheard by the pope, who replied in exasperation, "You English are the most miserable of men! Every one of you preys on and impoverishes his neighbour. How many monks, your subjects, your flock, both countrymen and domestics, occupied with prayers and hospitality, have you tried tyrannically and greedily to rob of their goods, to enrich others, even perhaps foreigners?" The bishop withdrew confused, to the hostile exclamations of everyone, and got on with some other business so that he did not appear to have achieved nothing.

1.   Matthew 20:15.

Many English nobles sell their estates to prepare for the journey to Jerusalem

Also in the same year Roger de Montalt, one of the higher ranking English barons, having taken the cross, made over his share in the woods and other revenues at Coventry to the prior and convent of that place in fee farm, in return for a large sum of money, so that he could procure necessaries for the journey; he also sold a good deal and irrevocably [alienated] much else. Other nobles, both on this and the other side of the sea, did the same. Besides this same Roger a great many of the English nobility took the sign of the cross at this time, to assist and follow the king of the French in the cause of the cross. Among them were prelates as well as knights, namely the bishops of

Worcester and Hereford [Walter Cantilupe and Peter d'Aigueblanche], the earls of Leicester and Hereford [Simon de Montfort and Humphrey de Bohun], Geoffrey de Lucy, Robert de Quincy and many more, whom it would take too long to enumerate. Innumerable, too, were those who, fearing the mousetraps of the Roman curia, would neither publicly take the sign of the cross nor wear it on their shoulders, but secretly and firmly vowed and proposed to go to the Holy Land devoutly and in strength.

The Parmans are pressed by F., whose power is on the increase

In these same days Frederick's influence in stirring up animosity against the Roman curia increased so much that William of Holland and his legate Peter Capoccio were driven out, and many powerful people submitted to him and gave him their allegiance. The Parmans and Reggians too, as well as the Bolognese and other rebels against him, were so pressed by him that they dared not show themselves far from their cities, fearing Frederician snares. Because of this the merchants of those cities, who usually abounded in riches, now that the markets and ports were closed and travel along the road blocked, felt the pinch and began to favour peace with Frederick and to detest the papal rebellion against him. Many people, indeed, were impressed by Frederick's constant patience and humility and the satisfaction which he was said to have devoutly offered to the Church. For he wanted, and humbly asked leave, to campaign for the Church in the Holy Land against the enemies of Christ for the rest of his life, or at least until he could, both by force of arms and by prudence, restore to the Christians whatever had at any time been Christian, on condition that his son Henry, nephew of the lord king of the English, whom he loved more than any of his other sons, should be recognised as his successor in the Empire. He also offered to restore much confiscated church property and make good many losses. To which the lord pope constantly replied that he could in no way so easily restore to his former status the person whom the general Council of Lyons had condemned and deposed. It was positively affirmed by some that the lord pope thirsted above all after the destruction of [Frederick] whom he called the great dragon, and that, once he was trampled under foot and crushed, he would overthrow and at his pleasure[1] despoil of their property and prelates the kings of the French and the English, as well as the other Christian kings, all of whom he called kinglets and little serpents who would more easily be terrified by the example of the said F. These speeches, together with outrageous deeds which bore powerful testimony to [the pope's] words, caused offence in the minds of many and at the same time justified the said F., so that his cause began to rally day by day.

1.   The words "at his pleasure", erased in B, have been supplied from C.

The treasure extorted from England by Archbishop Boniface of Canterbury is reckoned up

At the same time too, the bishops of the province of Canterbury assembled at Oxford to calculate if the money collected in their bishoprics for the archbishop of Canterbury amounted to what had been granted him. They knew this from the collectors appointed in each diocese, but the archbishop [appointed] many more in order that every sort of expense might be reckoned for his benefit. The bishops granted what he asked for against their will for they realised that the lord pope was favourable to him in everything.

The lord king seeks the pardon of the citizens of London

On the Sunday next before the feast of Saints Perpetua and Felicitas [6 March] all the citizens of London, with their families down to twelve-year-old boys, were summoned by command of the lord king to appear before him in the large palace which is called the great hall, at Westminster; and it and the whole of its courtyard were filled with crowds of people. When they were assembled, the lord king humbly and as if with rising tears entreated each and every one of the citizens cordially in heart and voice to forgive him his anger and every sort of rancour and malevolence towards them. As he publicly confessed, he had often and his officials more often, done them all kinds of injury by injuriously confiscating, occupying or retaining their property and by frequently violating their privileges; for this he asked them to be pleased to pardon him. The citizens, realizing that anything else would be inappropriate, agreed to everything the lord king demanded, but absolutely nothing that had been taken away was restored to them.

The lord king assumes the cross and many nobles with him

On the same day the lord king took the cross from the hand of

Archbishop B. of Canterbury. And afterwards the same archbishop signed other nobles with the cross, among them Ralph FitzNicholas, the lord king's seneschal, William of Valence, the uterine brother of the lord king, Paulinus Peiure, a special councillor of the same lord king, and many other magnates and courtiers. The abbot of St. Edmunds too, Edmund by name, was signed with the cross in defiance of every vow, to the derision of all and the prejudice of the holy order, thus setting a pernicious example to the monks.[1] Also [signed with the cross were] John Mansel, Philip Lovel and many others whom it would take too long to mention. Adverse interpreters dared to assert that the king took the cross for no other reason than to extort money forcibly on this occasion from his nobles, who had refused it on a previous occasion when he asked for it, on the pretext of the conquest of the Holy Land and the advancement of the cause of the cross. But discreet and more rational people deferred to the judgement and proof of his subsequent actions. For it is appropriate for a good mind to assume the best in doubtful matters until the contrary is proved; and who apart from God knows the thoughts of mortals? The seed bed of this doubt was supplied by the pernicious example of the king of the French, who had scraped from his kingdom an infinite amount of money, though little to his profit at the hands of an avenging God, in order to prosecute his pilgrimage. But the narrative that follows will show what fruit he gathered from this.

1. This sentence, beginning "The abbot", is in the margin of B.

The unanimous resolution of the crusaders

In the same year, on the fifth of the ides of May [27 April], the more important among the English crusaders gathered at Bermondsey in London to discuss arrangements for their expedition, for they declared that they would not put it off on the king's account. Indeed they judged it shameful to put off the salvation of their souls or defer their service for the heavenly king to that of any earthly king. So they fixed a date, namely the feast of the nativity of the blessed John the Baptist [24 June]. The number of knights with their followers assembled there was reckoned at five hundred, their attendants and the people attached to them formed a countless multitude. For everyone in the kingdom of England, and many from the kingdom of France, who had got ready before the lord king of the English took the cross, were waiting for so famous an expedition. But the lord king, busily prying, had found out about these proceedings and, by means of gifts of money and promises of more, quickly obtained letters from the Roman curia on the authority of which he could suspend their expedition until he, as the principal leader, could set out overseas in force and in his own person; in this way he would travel more appropriately and in greater safety. The crusaders replied to this that it would be proper and safe for those who had taken the cross before the lord king had done so, and who had fitted themselves out with horses, weapons and travelling necessaries by pledging their lands, had sold many things and taken leave of their friends, to set out first and proceed in advance of their king; thus provisions would be found in greater abundance. Seeing this, the foreigners would say, "If so many and such great men proceed in such magnificence in advance of the king of the English, how many are we to imagine accompanying and following him when he comes?" Thus the king's repute would grow among neighbours and fear of him among enemies. But the threatening letters of the lord pope and the imperious entreaties of the lord king changed their whole plan, so that they remained. Although this was not praiseworthy at the time, it turned out afterwards to their advantage. But they did not go to the aid of the French king in time, as they had eagerly desired, and so the business of the crusade languished here and there, alas unhappily curtailed.

The Gascon rebels against the lord king are subdued by the earl of Leicester

In the same year Gascony was so far subdued by Simon de Montfort, earl of Leicester, that Gaston de Béarn, who was the most powerful or at least one of the most powerful of the enemies of the lord king of England, was captured and humiliated and, at the earl's command, came to England to his lord king, whom he had offended, who was then at Clarendon, humbly to beg the king's pardon for his life, limbs and holdings, placing himself altogether on the king's mercy, not judgement. On doing this, he met with undeserved clemency in the king, for royal power is overcome and diverted from revenge when it sees that is has conquered rebels; as Ovid says, "It is enough for the magnanimous lion to have brought the body to the ground; the struggle is finished when the enemy lies prostrate."[1] So the lord king took into his hands through Earl S. certain castles of this Gaston and his accomplices, namely Fronsac, Aigremont and many others. After his humiliation, though it was feigned, Gaston was received into the king's favour to such an extent, by intercession of the queen whose relative he claimed to be, that he was restored to the possession of his lands, though bound by the strictest conditions. The aforesaid earl, trying in every way to imitate his distinguished father and to follow in his footsteps or go beyond them, so subdued the insolence of the other rebels against the lord king at Bordeaux and throughout Gascony that he put to flight, disinherited and banished William de Solars, Rustein, and other proud and recalcitrant men; and he consigned many to the gallows.

Note that when the king was in Gascony and thought that he could leave freely, the Gascons and especially the people of Bordeaux, seeing him in a critical position, extorted from him before he could depart a grant of forty thousand marks, and cheated him into giving them an oath and a charter in pledge of it. So, immediately after his arrival in England, the king squeezed this money out of the prelates; thus impoverishing England after he had lost Poitou. He hated the Gascons so much thereafter that he sold his treasure to get his revenge on them.[2]

1. Slightly misquoted from *Tristia* 3.5:33.
2. This paragraph is in the margin at the foot of the page in B.

The French attack the Saracens, urged on by great hunger

On the Monday before Ash Wednesday the army of the French suddenly sallied forth with great violence from their quarters at Damietta and, attacking the Saracens who were besieging them, killed many of them. After the victory, the French returned with their booty to the city, unharmed and joyful. The next day, hoping to meet with similar good fortune in battle, they got the worst of the encounter, the enemy having been reinforced in the meantime. They lost ten times as much as the spoil they had congratulated themselves on the day before; indeed they returned covered in blood, wounded and maimed, and reduced in number. After this the Saracens began to rejoice in their hearts and to carry their heads high vis-a-vis the Christians, and they everywhere blockaded the roads through the surrounding country. So the sultan, now in better hopes, having collected galleys from Alexandria and other coastal places, indeed from wherever possible, ordered a close watch to be kept on all routes by sea or along the coast and on all places whence the French might expect relief, and above all he made a special effort to see that no provisions could be brought to them.

The sultan of Babylon offers much to the French to keep them quiet

At length, after discussions and conferences on each side, the sultan intimated to the king of the French that, after the cessation of fighting, he would be well advised to abandon Damietta together with its supplies, which they commonly call garnitures, before their fame dwindled, and the whole region of Jerusalem together with the Christian slaves would be amicably returned to the king. Nor should the king, according to him, aspire to anything more than the return of the Holy Land to the Christians. Many of the crusaders approved of this plan, namely the lesser ranks and ordinary people, who were in need, and some of the magnates, declaring that if they did not accept these peace terms in all modesty, the pride of the magnates would harm the entire army. The king, considering this, would have been inclined to accept, had he not been flatly opposed by the arrogance of the count of Artois, who still demanded Alexandria as well. But the sultan was in no way willing to cede Alexandria to the Christians, for it was the noblest city of Egypt and the resort of all the merchants both from the East and the South; nor, he said, would the Alexandrians or the Egyptians suffer it.

The French become hateful to God because of their pride so that many died from hunger

The condition of the French, besieged on all sides, began to deteriorate in no small way, for they, people who are clean and fastidious in food and drink, had to eat dirty and detestable food, nor could Frederick or any Christian from neighbouring lands help them. To sum up in brief, they were so hard pressed that they were forced to eat their horses in Lent, though these were precious and absolutely necessary to them, which was a wretched thing to see. And what was more serious, a dispute and hatred arose between the magnates and the people because the magnates had wantonly refused the reasonable peace terms which had been offered. Moreover the Saracen princes, detesting the impudence of the Christians, allied more closely together and pressed the Christians harder, so that many Christians, in this time of affliction, secretly left the fortifications and the city, joined the crowds of Saracens on reasonable conditions, and effectively opposed our people. The Saracens received them gladly and, because they were suffering from hunger, allowed them sufficient daily rations. Although some of these Christians persisted in their own faith out of the tolerance of the

Saracens others became apostates and subscribed to their filthiness and confirmed this by doing them homage. These were abundantly enriched with wives and castles, and raised to many honours; they did mortal injury to the Christians by revealing their secret plans to their enemies [the Saracens].

Many of the French go over to the sultan as apostates

When it became clear to the sultan through these apostates that the Christians were suffering from a shortage of all sorts of food, he ironically sent word to the king of the French to ask why he had brought by ship, to a part of the East unknown to him, hoes, forks, carts, ploughs, and other agricultural implements. If he did not take the trouble to use them, they would be consumed by rust. But if he became his friend he would very easily find sufficient for him and his army during his stay there in wheat, wine, oil and meat. The king, not without profound grief, put up with all these provocations of his enemy and prudently concealed his heavy heart behind a calm countenance.

The death of the sultan

Soon afterwards, this same sultan died, poisoned, it was said, by his own servants, because he was loathed both by his own people and by all the neighbouring princes. For he was proud and greedy and unjust to all. When they heard this, the Christians were extremely pleased though they ought rather to have grieved, for many of the Saracens only feigned allegiance to this sultan while pursuing him with secret hatred. Soon afterwards, another was substituted for him, who enjoyed the support of the entire East. This man attacked the Christians powerfully and with great perseverance, and more vehemently than his predecessor, and positively refused to grant the peace terms already offered, which almost all the Christians had wanted and asked for. The condition of the Christians began to deteriorate not a little from then on, and their fame became worthless in the view of everyone in the East.

Faith begins to waver

Many people, who were not strengthened by a firm faith, now began to give way to desperation and blasphemy as well as hunger. And alas! the faith of many began to waver and they said to one another, "Why has Christ, for whom and with whom we have up to now been fighting, abandoned us? Nowadays we are frequently defeated and put to confusion and our enemies, rather Christ's enemies, triumphantly glory in our blood and booty taken from us. First at the city of Damietta, when surrounded by the waters of the Nile, we were forced to give up that city, won at the cost of so much blood. Again, not far from Antioch, the distinguished knights of the Temple, their standard- bearer decapitated, were defeated in confusion. Again, a few years later we were defeated by the Saracens at Gaza after having been redeemed by the Englishman Earl Richard. Afterwards, almost the entire Christian community in the Holy Land was cut to pieces by the Khorasmians, who polluted and destroyed all the places that are called holy. Now indeed, what is worse than everything, our most Christian king, who was miraculously raised from the dead, is exposed to the most ignominious danger along with the entire French nobility. The lord has become like an enemy to us and he who is often called the Lord of Hosts is now, alas, despised by his enemies for having been repeatedly defeated. What benefit to us is our devotion, the prayers of the monks, the alms of our friends? Is not the law of Mahomet better than the law of Christ?" And thus delirious words resounded from the tottering faith and the Lenten days seemed more a time of punishment than penance.

The condition of ecclesiastical liberty deteriorates because of the bishop of Lincoln's violence

In the same year it happened that the bishop of Lincoln deprived a certain cleric accused of incontinence, called Ranulph, beneficed in his bishopric, of his benefice, and, having deprived him, he excommunicated him because, when condemned, he refused to abandon his incontinence. When he had remained under sentence of excommunication for more than forty days, the bishop notified the sheriff of Rutland, in whose jurisdiction the said cleric was living, that he should arrest him and hold him as contumacious. But the sheriff, because he was a good friend of the said Ranulph, put off doing this, or refused, for he was no friend of the bishop. As Seneca says, he who delays for a long time refuses for a long time. The bishop therefore, realizing the sheriff's hostility, solemnly excommunicated him, and the sheriff, angry and ashamed, went on the spot to the king with a serious complaint about this. When the king and his courtiers heard this they were all perturbed and the king, who was extremely annoyed, replied with a great oath, "If any of my people incur a penalty at the hands of this bishop or anyone else they should complain to me. It seems that he holds me in contempt." So, having sent solemn messengers to the Roman curia, with the help of money, the king was quickly able to obtain the following letter, to the prejudice of eccleciastical liberty.

Papal letters

Innocent bishop etc to his beloved sons the abbot and convent of Westminster at London, greetings etc. We have freely assented to the wishes of our most beloved son in Christ his highness the illustrious king of England that we should show ourselves favourable to him in the business which he rightly requires from us. Since therefore, as has been stated to us on his behalf, some pontiffs and other prelates of his kingdom, to the said king's prejudice and inconvenience, compel the bailiffs of his kingdom to appear before them at their pleasure to litigate in matters pertaining to the royal jurisdiction and pronounce sentences of excommunication against them if they do not do so we, inclining to his entreaties, by the authority of these our apostolic letters have decided strictly to forbid any archbishop, bishop or other prelate of that kingdom to compel the royal bailiffs to appear before them on matters which belong to the royal jurisdiction or to pronounce any sentences against them on account of this. Wherefore we command you by these apostolic letters, at your discretion, not to permit the aforesaid king to be improperly molested by anyone in this matter, against the tenor of our prohibition, evil doers etc. Given at Lyons, the seventh of the ides of March [9 March], in the seventh year of our pontificate [1250].[1]

The lord king did this, not without the disapproval of experienced persons, because a complaint about it had been made to the lord pope.

1.   This letter is also in the *Book of additamenta*, BL Cotton MS. Nero D i, f.94.

Earl R. arrives on his way back

On the Monday next before Rogation week [25 April], Earl Richard arrived on his return from the Roman curia and, when he came to

London, he was received with honour and reverence lest he be treated with less honour than he had been overseas. For the queen, Lady Blanche, had treated him with every possible respect and had opened the heart of the whole of France to him, and everybody knew, from the account of the said earl and his people, how many and what great honours had been done him by the pope when he arrived at Lyons.

The honour done to him by the lord pope

As [Earl Richard] approached the city [of Lyons] almost all the cardinals and the clerics of the Roman curia went to meet him, so that one solitary cardinal and as few clerics remained with the lord pope. What with his own people and others going to meet him, there was such a press of men and horses, such a tumult and so great a crowd of his own splendidly equipped retinue and packhorses, that the citizens, together with everyone who had come to the curia on business from elsewhere, were astonished at the arrival of so great a prince. As he entered the building the pope got up and, walking towards him, received him with an embrace, complimenting and welcoming him respectfully. With a cheerful countenance he invited him to dine with him that day. The earl gladly agreed and was placed at table at the lord pope's side, with Earl Richard of Gloucester not far off. They feasted courteously and joyfully, as is the custom of the French and English, entertaining themselves with eating and drinking and friendly conversation. Afterwards they held many prolonged and secret conferences together. Everyone witnessing these proceedings was amazed, especially by the unusual hospitality of the pope. After making his devotions at Pontigny to St. Edmund the Confessor he returned happily to England, as has been said, at the end of April.

Various opinions on the cause of Earl Richard's crossing

Various opinions and conclusions arose concerning the purpose of these intimate and prolonged discussions, many affirming that the lord pope wanted [Earl Richard] to help check the insolence of the Greeks and bring them under the authority of Rome, knowing that he was eager and ambitious and was rolling in money which the lord pope hoped to use for this purpose. Others however claimed that the lord pope was indubitably doing his best to gain the favour of the said earl so that he would be well received when he came [to England], which he wished to do.

A *purchase*

At the abbey of Saint-Denis on his way back [Earl Richard] gave the abbot [William III] of that place satisfaction for the purchase price of a certain priory in England belonging to the church of Saint-Denis, called Deerhurst, not far from Gloucester, where some monks were living. To this church belonged eight fine vills, and the church was worth about three hundred marks yearly, with a park and all appurtenances, always returning one mark for thirty shillings at the bench.[1] He had obtained the ratification of this sale in the Roman curia, so that after he had returned to England, having expelled the monks and razed the buildings, he took possession of the priory. Nor, after this, was he afraid of any neighbour, religious especially, but arranged everything as he wanted, secure under papal protection. Thus the condition of the Church began to deteriorate. He proposed to build a castle there to guard the crossing of the River Severn.

1. The words from "with" to "bench" are in the margin of B.

Concerning the arm of St. Edmund the Confessor

In this same year too the monks of Pontigny, either because they were fed up with the frequency of pilgrims, especially Englishmen, for others were not given permission, who flocked to the tomb of St. Edmund in crowds, or urged by cupidity, with rash presumption horrible to relate cut off the saint's right arm. But this did not drive away the numerous people of both sexes who came in crowds to view and venerate the body, so the monks were deservedly frustrated in their purpose. Moreover, through what seems to have been a defect of faith, whatever part of the saint's body, which however the Lord had preserved entire, they presumed, whether from distrust, faint-heartedness or, saving the respect due to their order, lack of faith, to embalm, turned to a most repulsive colour.

A *disgrace*

So the disgrace of the monks of Pontigny, indeed of the entire Cistercian order, mounted, and many regretted that so venerable a body should rest in a Cistercian church, considering how reverently the bodies of the saints were looked after in the churches of the order of

Black monks. What rash presumption! What God conserved entire and uncorrupted, man dared to mutilate. So when the pious king of the French was a pilgrim and part of the body was offered to him, he replied, "It would not be pleasing to God if something he has conserved entire was mutilated for me". Again, what lack of faith! What the Lord conserved uncorrupt and beautiful, these monks embalmed, in an attempt to protect the body better with such anointing. But the colour of flesh was changed into that of earth and the Lord, rightly angered, began less often to work the miracles there which formerly were frequent. The venerable religion of the Cistercians, therefore, was esteemed less by the magnates, prelates and clerics and, saving the respect due to the order, this is believed to have happened as a melancholy portent for the whole of Christianity.

The bounty of the lord king's table is reduced

At this same time the lord king, shamelessly departing from his father's footsteps, ordered the expenses of his court and the customary pleasures of hospitality to be cut back, even so as to incur the reproach of inexcusable avarice. He also ordered the usual gifts in alms and the number of candles in the church to be reduced. However, it was praiseworthy that he carefully freed himself from the debts by which he was bound to many merchants.

The Jews are mercilessly impoverished

In these same days the lord king became dry with the thirst of avarice so that, laying aside all mercy, he ordered so much money to be extorted from the Jews that they appeared to be altogether and irremediably impoverished. For he demanded whatever they had in their chests. However, though miserable, they deserved no commiseration, for they were proved to have been often guilty of forgery, both of money and of seals. And if we are silent about their other crimes, we have decided to include one of them in this book, in order that their wickedness may be better known to more people.

The unheard of crime of a certain Jew

There was a certain quite rich Jew, Abraham by name but not in faith, who lived and had property at Berkhamstead and Wallingford. He was friendly with Earl Richard for some improper reason or other. He had a beautiful and faithful wife called Floria. In order to dishonour Christ the more, this Jew bought a nicely carved and painted statue of the blessed Virgin, as usual nursing her son at her bosom. This image the Jew set up in his latrine and, what is thoroughly dishonourable and ignominious to mention, as it were in blasphemy of the blessed Virgin, he inflicted a most filthy and unmentionable thing on it, daily and nightly, and ordered his wife to do the same. Noticing this after some days, by reason of her sex, she felt sorry and, going there secretly, washed the dirt from the face of the disgracefully defiled statue. When the Jew her husband found out the truth of this, he impiously and secretly suffocated his wife. However, these crimes were discovered and the Jew, clearly proved guilty, although there were other grounds for putting him to death, was thrust into the foulest dungeon in the Tower of London. In a bid to be freed, he promised most positively that he would prove all the Jews in England to be the basest traitors. Thereupon he was gravely accused by almost all the English Jews, who tried to put him to death, but Earl Richard spoke up for him. So the Jews, accusing him of clipping coins and other serious crimes, offered the earl a thousand marks to stop protecting him, which however the earl refused because the Jew was said to be his. This Jew Abraham then paid the king seven hundred marks so that, with the help of the earl, he could be freed from the life imprisonment to which he had been condemned.[1]

1.   The passage from "Thereupon" to the end of the paragraph is in the margin in B.

Justices are sent to investigate the Jews' money

At this same time the lord king sent justices of the Jews through the whole of England to investigate all their money both in debts and in possessions, and with them a certain most wicked and merciless Jew to accuse all the others corruptly and in violation of the truth. He reproached without fail Christians who were grieving over and bewailing the sufferings of the Jews and called the royal bailiffs lukewarm and effeminate. Gnashing his teeth in fury at each one of the Jews, he claimed with a great oath that they could give the king more than double what they had given, although he was lying in his teeth. This man, to do more effective harm to the Jews, revealed all their secrets to the Christian justices of the king.

Concerning a certain Armenian who died at St. Ives

And at the same time certain Armenian brethren, fugitives from the Tartar invasions, arrived as pilgrims in England. When they came to St. Ives one of them was taken ill and unfortunately died in that town. He was reverently buried next to St. Ivo's spring, the water of which is said to have great virtue. These brethren were of most honest life and amazing abstinence, being always in prayer, with rugged, honest faces and beards. The one who died was their leader and master, George by name, and he is thought to have been a most holy man and a bishop; he now began to perform miracles.

Financial help is sent to the hard pressed king of the French

During this same period no small amount of money was sent to the aid of the king of the French, who was in difficult straits. He was staying in a tented camp set up around Damietta, surrounded with trenches, in need, and destitute of all kinds of provisions. Ceaselessly, by day and by night, he had to put up with attacks from the innumerable Saracens in the hills around, even though a vigilant watch was kept throughout the night. In the city, to defend it, he posted five hundred knights with a large body of infantry, who remained there with the legate [Eudes de Château-Roux] and several bishops, as well as the queen and other noble ladies. As much money had been sent to him in gold and silver coin, namely talents and sterlings and approved coin of Cologne, and not the base coins of Paris and Tours, as could be loaded onto eleven long waggons, each drawn by four of the most powerful horses, together with some packhorses, and transported to the sea, where it could be taken aboard some Genoese ships to be conveyed, with no small supply of provisions, to the needy king. Each waggon carried two large casks, bound with iron and prepared for this purpose, filled with the aforesaid treasure, all of which had been extorted over a three-year period from the goods of the Church. The narrative that follows will plainly show what was achieved with it.

Some English magnates return from overseas

During Rogation week Earl Richard, the earl of Gloucester, and also Earl S[imon] of Leicester,[1] and other magnates, returned from overseas. Moreover the bishop of London [Fulk Basset] and some other prelates who, as has been said, had crossed over, returned safely to England, but two bishops remained abroad, namely those of Winchester and London. The bishop of Winchester stayed in the kingdom of the French with a small household to reduce expenses. The bishop of Lincoln remained at the Roman curia to make arrangements with the pope for a preconceived plan. Concerning the cause of Earl Richard's journey, it was the opinion of some, not without reason, that the lord pope had summoned him with a view to promoting him into the empire of Romania, which he knew abounded in wealth. In the opinion of others, which subsequent events showed to be probably correct, it was to hinder the crusaders from setting sail. Others however thought it more likely, and this was soon afterwards proved to be the case, that he went to arrange for the purchase of Deerhurst with its appurtenances from the abbot of Saint-Denis, and to obtain supplies for the crusaders' journey.[2] It is believed and asserted that the reason why the lord pope welcomed him so warmly was because the pope, who very much wanted to come to England, hoped to be received favourably and respectfully [there] by him, and also because he hoped that the earl would influence his brother the lord king and the magnates of the country, especially those belonging to the royal council, into inviting him to visit England. But these things are touched on above.

1.   The words "Also Earl S. of Leicester" are in the margin of B.
2.   The words from "and" to "journey" are in the margin of B.

Concerning the false rumours which excited many credulous people

At this same time, either as a vain consolation for the Christians or to encourage the crusaders who were putting off their pilgrimage, dubious letters[1] containing the most welcome reports were sent from the Holy Land, drawn up by genuine and reliable people, namely the bishop of Marseilles [Benedict of Alignano] and some of the Templars, which excited those hearing them with false good news. This was that Cairo and Babylon were captured and Alexandria had been left desolate by the fleeing Saracens. Like the scorpion, these rumours hurt their credulous hearers more in the end than they had at first soothed them with their blandishments. From then onwards we regarded such letters, even if they were true, with more suspicion and dislike.

1.   See BL Cotton MS. Nero D i f.99 = Luard 1882:167 and above p. 193.

Concerning the advowson of the church of Wengrave

In the same year in Rogation week, after a dispute had arisen between the abbot of St. Albans and John de Wedone over the advowson of the church of Wengrave then vacant, a settlement was made between them. In the presence of the justices of the lord king Roger de Thurkeby and Robert de Brus and others of their colleagues, the said J. recognised that the right to the said church was in the gift of the abbot. But J. had obtained the following writ of summons against the abbot.

> The king to the sheriff of Buckingham, greetings. Order the abbot of St. Albans duly and without delay to allow John de Wedone to present a suitable person to the church of Wengrave, which is said to be vacant, and which belongs in his gift, but concerning which a complaint has been made that the abbot is unjustly opposing him. And, unless he gives you security that he will prosecute his claim, summon the aforesaid abbot by means of good summoners to appear before our justices at Westminster on the morrow of our Lord's Ascension [5 May] etc.

But what use was this or any similar case to the church of St. Alban? The Romans or the royal agents, each vying with the other, forcibly carried away all the vacant churches.

Concerning Archbishop Boniface of Canterbury's plan to make a visitation

During the same days Boniface, archbishop of Canterbury, encouraged by the bishop of Lincoln's example, who had obtained authority to visit his canons at Lincoln,[1] tried to make a visitation of the bishops, abbots, clergy and people in his province. He began with a most rigorous and merciless visitation in the chapter of his monks at Canterbury, so that they said among themselves, "It is our own fault that we suffer this, because we have sinned against his predecessor the blessed Edmund, whom we thought austere and strict; we are putting up with what we truly deserve, having chosen a foreigner, illiterate, unknown and inexperienced, more suited to and experienced in warlike than spiritual affairs. What predecessors he had, martyrs, genuine teachers, holy confessors of God! Alas! Why did we obey the earthly king in this outrageous election rather than the heavenly!" From there the archbishop came to the abbey of Faversham, the pusillanimous monks of which, because of his tyranny, did not dare oppose his visitation. Then he came with great impetuosity, pomp and state to Rochester Priory, where he extorted more than thirty marks from that poor house. From this it seems that he exercised this office of visitation more for greed of financial gain than for the reform of the order or the improvement of behaviour, for he was ignorant both of the order and its customs, and devoid of learning.

---

1.   Here a leaf has been removed from B and some lines at the beginning of the next leaf have been rewritten over an erasure. The missing material on the archbishop's visitation, which follows, has been recovered from C.

How impetuously Archbishop Boniface behaved at London

On the fourth of the ides of May, namely the day of St. Pancratius and his companions [12 May], the aforesaid archbishop of Canterbury B. came to London to visit the bishop and chapter and the monks of that city. He established his household without permission from anyone, neither the owner nor the custodian, in a splendid house belonging to the bishop of Chichester which is not far from the lay brothers' houses; not staying at his own house in Lambeth. He got his marshals to obtain his provisions violently and fraudulently with threats and shouts, from the king's market, to the harm of the tradesmen there. He invited few or no guests to his table.

The bishop of London is visited

The next day he visited Bishop Fulk. If anyone were to particularise the impudence of the said archbishop at his place, both in eatables and in drinks, as well as in horseshoes, namely in shoeing a hundred horses, it would offend the ears and minds of the hearers, or rather break their hearts.

The chapter of St. Paul's resists

Going to the chapter of St. Paul's in London, he came to that church in great pomp in order to visit the canons. They were unwilling to admit him, resisting spiritedly, and firmly appealed to the supreme pontiff. When the archbishop heard this, extremely annoyed and threatening, he precipitately and in a spirit of anger and fury excommunicated the dean [Henry of Cornhill], and some other dignitaries of the church, after some statements which anyone who wants to hear should look for in the *Book of additamenta*.[1]

1. BL Cotton MS. Nero D i, f.98 = Luard 1882:188–92.

The church of St. Bartholomew resists

And on the following day, still swollen and inflamed with yesterday's anger, and, according to the testimony of people who saw, wearing a coat of mail under his vestments, he came to the priory of St. Bartholomew to visit the canons there. As he arrived and entered the church, because the prior was away at the time, the subprior came to meet him accompanied by the convent in procession with solemnity and reverence both in the lighting of numerous candles and in the ringing of bells. They were in costly choir copes, the most precious of which was worn by the senior one of them at that time, namely the aforesaid subprior. The archbishop did not care much for the honour thus done him; he said he had come there to visit the canons. Now all the canons were in the centre of the church, that is in the choir, with the archbishop himself and the greater part of his retinue, pressed together in a disorderly manner. One of the canons replied to him on behalf of all, saying that they had an experienced and diligent bishop whose task it was to visit them when this was necessary, nor would they, or ought they to, be visited by anyone else, lest he should seem to be held in contempt. On hearing this, the archbishop, flying into a more furious rage than he ought or was proper, rushed at the subprior, forgetting his station and the holiness of his predecessors, and impiously struck that holy man, a priest and a monk, with his fist, as he stood in the middle of the church, truculently repeating the blows now on the aged breast, now on the venerable face, now on his grey-haired head and yelling "This is how English traitors should be dealt with!" And, raving horribly with unrepeatable oaths, he vehemently demanded that his sword be brought to him.

As the tumult increased and the canons tried to rescue their subprior from the hands of so violent an aggressor, the archbishop tore off the precious cope that the subprior was wearing and broke away the clasp, which is commonly called a morse, which was decorated with gold and silver and gems, and it was smashed and lost underfoot in the crowd.

That splendid cope, too, trampled on and torn, was irreparably damaged. Nor was the archiepiscopal fury averted even now, for, like a madman, pushing and forcing back that holy man with a violent onslaught, he so crushed his senile body against a pier which divided two of the stalls and was made for a podium, that he shattered his bones to the marrow and caused internal injuries. When the others saw the archbishop's lack of restraint, they managed to rescue the half-dead man from the jaws of death, after pushing the aggressor back. As he was thrown back and his vestments fell aside, his coat of mail was plainly visible to many, who were horrified to see the archbishop in armour, and because of this not a few maintained that he had come there, not on a visitation or to correct errors, but rather to provoke a fight. Meanwhile, his officials, who were impetuous Provençals like himself, truculently assaulted the remaining canons, who were unprepared, unarmed and unwarlike, and, together with the archbishop himself, following his command and example, they ill-treated very many of them, by hitting, wounding, throwing to the ground and trampling.[1] As a result of this, the canons came with feet disfigured by blood and bruises, badly hurt, unshaven and wounded, to the bishop of the city and tearfully lodged a serious complaint about this detestable affair. To which the bishop replied, "The lord king is at Westminster; go and describe this to him, so that at the least he may be disturbed by such a violent and manifest breaking of his peace in his principal city."

1.   Near the beginning of this sentence Matthew Paris has written in the margin of B "Worse follows" and, with reference to the beginning of the next paragraph "The compassion of the citizens".

Complaints made to the king

So four of these canons, the rest being unable because of the pain of their wounds, went to Westminster in order to gain access to the king, in view of a crowd of very sympathetic people who detested such a preposterous deed. They showed everyone the marks of the blows, namely their bruises, swellings and torn clothes. The fifth, namely the aforesaid subprior, was in no way strong enough to go to court, either on horseback or on foot, but was carried groaning to the infirmary, where he was put to bed; he passed the rest of his days in a state of weakness. But the king, though they waited a long time at the door of his chamber, would neither see nor consider the complaints of the aforesaid canons. So they returned in great confusion to their polluted church, which the said archbishop had profaned with the blood of priests and monks. Meanwhile the entire city was convulsed with excitement and the citizens proposed to ring the communal bell as if rebellion had broken out and to cut the said archbishop in pieces whatever the consequences. As he hurried to his house at Lambeth, insults and reproaches resounded and crowds of people rushed about searching for him, shouting, "Where is that ruffian, that impious and blood-stained aggressor, not a gainer of souls but an extorter of money, who was promoted neither by God, nor by a legitimate free election, but was intruded illicitly by the king, illiterate and married as he was, and whose foul infamy has now polluted the whole city"? Soon after, having travelled secretly along the Thames, he made a serious complaint about this to the king, justifying himself as a defendant and vigorously accusing the other party; then he complained even more energetically to the queen. The king, who was in great fear of a rebellion, had it proclaimed in the city by public crier that nobody was to interfere in this dispute on pain of life and limb.

Thus disdained both by the canons of St. Bartholomew's and at Holy Trinity, which firmly appealed against his actions, the archbishop proceeded on his way and, encouraged by the king's favour, solemnly renewed, in the chapel of Lambeth, the sentence he had pronounced against the canons of St. Paul's, including also the bishop of London in it, together with the aforesaid canons, as a supporter. The canons, having suffered harm and injury on all sides, tearfully entrusted their cause to St. Bartholomew, whom they served perpetually night and day, praying, since man either would or could not, that God, the Lord of vengeance, would deign to punish such great offences.

The archbishop turns back after coming to Harrow

The archbishop, still fuming with anger, proceeded the next day to a manor of his called Harrow, about seven miles distant from the monastery of St. Albans, in order to make a visitation there, and at that place he renewed the aforesaid sentence. But when he was told by his friends and clerics, discreet and learned men, about the noble privileges conceded to that church by the apostolic see, he dissembled and refrained, and, having returned, got ready to cross overseas in order to prepare traps for innocent people at the Roman curia, where he was very influential and where he was more used to staying than, like a good shepherd, looking after his own flock. However, the dean of St. Paul's in London, a good man, aged and of great experience, Master Robert Barton, and Master William of Lichfield, discreet and learned men, canons of that same church, with the proctors of their bishop and of the aforesaid canons, also went to the papal curia to lodge a complaint about all this with the supreme pontiff, having been sufficiently instructed to prove their point, and strengthened by the testimony of many people.

The bishop of London wrote to the abbot of St. Albans

No wonder that the bishop of London, not a little upset by these troubles, greatly feared papal avarice on one side, the dubious friendship of the king towards his natural subjects on the other, and yet again the Savoyard nobles, whom he dared not offend. Hoping to have the advice and help of the abbot and convent of St. Albans in these straits, he wrote to him as follows.

To the venerable men and most beloved friends in Christ J. by God's grace abbot of St. Albans and the convent of that place, and to all others subject to that house, F. by divine permission bishop of London, greetings and the continued increase of sincere love in the Lord. Fame, which with its much wandering step is gliding through the land, threatens to upset the balance of public opinion as it disseminates in innumerable places news of a new danger. The long lasting peace of our diocese has been impugned by our father the venerable archbishop, and we believe we have adopted measures of just defence as fighters for the rights of you and of one and all in the province sent ahead in the arena of fortune, and we predict that the war now imposed on us will be more violently imposed on you unless we can recover breath with the solace of your advice and the help of the Almighty. For this same lord, as you perhaps know, making a visitation of all the clergy and people of our diocese and demanding procuration, met with opposition, though it was polite, and refusal, firstly by the members of our chapter, then by the two priories in the city. He fulminated sentences of excommunication in the first place against them for not admitting him to make the visitation and in the second place against our person because we ordered some of our people not to admit him to the prejudice of our church. This in spite of our legitimate appeals expressed in just, true and reasonable form. Nor is he disquieting us with this disturbance alone, for it is said that he has published the sentences originating in this way in his diocese and elsewhere. So, having now sent proctors to the curia, we have discussed this affair with some of our co-bishops and they boldly declare that they will defend their rights and liberties. Wherefore we have thought it right to beg you in your affection, considering the grounds for this request and your own honour and security, not to let your probity become lukewarm nor your courage cool, but, putting your faith in Him who guards the oppressed from the injuries of the unjust, to stretch out towards us the hand of your salutary counsel. May your community ever flourish in the lord.

The decretals which the archbishop used as a pretext for his plan are fully transcribed in the *Book of additamenta*, together with the objections of the parties.[1]

1. BL Cotton MS. Nero D 1, f.98 = 1882:188–91. Here ends the missing section of the text of B.

Concerning a very general chapter of the brothers Preachers

During the same days, namely around the feast of the nativity of St. John the Baptist [24 June], by a general summons the brothers of the order of Preachers were assembled from all the countries of Christendom, even from the territory of Jerusalem, in their house at Holborn in London, to discuss generally their position and function. And because they had no means of their own, the magnates and prelates generously found provisions for them, especially those who lived in the city of London and neighbouring places, such as the abbots of Waltham and St. Albans and the like. This chapter was held in Whit week and the Holy Spirit, which was sent at that time to the disciples, was invoked. There were about four hundred brothers present. On the first day the king came to their chapter to seek the help of their prayers. He supplied them with food on this same day and took his meals with them in their honour. Afterwards, the queen sent food to them, then the bishop of London sent food, then Lord John Mansel, then other prelates such as the abbot of Westminster and others, whom they had entreated by letter to alleviate the wants of the needy out of the abundance of their riches.

Concerning a great disturbance among
the citizens of London

About the same time the city of London was not a little agitated because the lord king exacted certain liberties from the citizens for the benefit of the abbot of Westminster, to their substantial loss and in infringement of their privileges. The mayor of the city [Roger FitzRoger] with the entire commune unanimously opposed, in so far as they could, the wishes or rather the violence and raving, of the king; but the king behaved harshly and inexorably towards them. So the citizens, in a state of great excitement, went to Earl Richard, the earl of Leicester, and other magnates of the kingdom, grieving and complaining, to explain how the king was not ashamed to violate their charters granted by his predecessors, perhaps "turned aside like a deceitful bow",[1] by the example of the pope. The aforesaid magnates, extremely disturbed by this, fearing that the king might attempt something similar against them, remonstrated severely with him, adding threats and, having remonstrated with him, reproved him, and even more severely contradicted the abbot, whom they believed to be the author and originator of this wrong, adding insults and imprecations which it would not be right to recite here out of respect for the order. And so the discretion of the magnates happily recalled the king from his planned aggression.

1. Psalm 78:57.

The king draws up and concedes new charters contrary
to the old charters of his predecessors,
and in derogation of his good faith

During the same days, the lord king, moved by a similar idea, contrary to the charters of his predecessors, including those who reigned before the conquest of England, in derogation of his good faith and of his first oath, produced a charter for the same abbot of Westminster to the manifest loss and injury of the church of St. Albans, in respect namely to the extremely ancient town of Aldenham, a fact from which it took its name. For *Ald* means 'ancient'; from which it appears that the aforesaid town was given in very ancient times to Alban, the protomartyr of the English, even though all the charters are silent on the matter. Moreover the aforesaid lord king granted and conceded by charter to a certain knight, a tenant-in-chief of the church of St. Albans, who however was neither of noble ancestry nor born of knights, Geoffrey [of Childwick] by name, because he had married the sister of the royal clerk, John Mansel, freedom of warren in the lands of St. Albans and in the neighbourhood of that town, contrary to the ancient liberties of that church and the charters obtained from pious kings of old and continuously enjoyed, and also contrary to a charter of the present king H.III. Nor was the said Geoffrey Rufus ashamed to kick against his lady the church which had educated and advanced him, so that he was stained with the mark of paternal, but not maternal, treachery; indeed he most unjustly and shamelessly impugned the mother who had borne him as well as the church which had enriched him and his forefathers. The above-mentioned special clerk of the lord king, whose wealth attained to episcopal heights, and whose sister, as was mentioned, the aforesaid Rufus had married, encouraged him in this. She was called Claricia, thus far childless, the daughter of a country priest, who exalted herself in her pride above her station, to everyone's amusement; her husband is believed to have been infatuated by her suggestions. However, I do not think he should be excused because of this, but rather accused, according to the Lord's words fulminated against the first man Adam, "Because thou hast hearkened" more "unto the voice of thy wife" than to me "cursed is the ground for thy sake."[1] When the writer of this book,[2] namely Brother Matthew Paris, undaunted, reproached the king over this affair, the king said, "surely the pope does likewise, clearly subjoining in his letters the words 'Notwithstanding any privilege or indulgence' "? However, speaking with more moderation, he added, "Well, well, we will think about it". But the memory of these words and promises died away with their sound.

1. Genesis 3:17.
2. The scribe of the fair copy C has changed B's *scriptor* to *confector* and omitted *Parisiensis*.

The custody of the royal seal is commited to Master William of Kilkenny, a discreet, modest and learned man

In the course of the same time the lord king, acting on good advice, committed the custody of his seal, which is acknowledged to be, as it were, the key of the kingdom, to Master William of Kilkenny, a modest, loyal and learned man, expert and circumspect in canon and civil law.

The king of the French directs his reins and standards towards the East

Also at this same time, that is after the king of the French had left the fortifications of Damietta, having posted a watchful garrison in the city, namely the duke of Burgundy [Hugh III] and a great many other magnates and knights, a numerous body of infantry together with the legate and some bishops and clerics, as well as the queen and other noble ladies with their households, because "It is no less a virtue to keep what you have than to gain it,"[1] the king with his army directed his journey and standards towards the East. Lord William Longespee followed with the people who had joined him, that is Robert de Vere and other Englishmen, whom it would take a long time to enumerate, together with the knights and sergeants he had retained with him.

1. Slightly misquoted from Ovid *Art. amat.* 2:13. The rest of this sentence is in the margin in B.

Note the envy and pride of the French

The French, because of their innate pride, scorned this W. and his people, deriding and detesting them, though the most pious king of the French had particularly forbidden this, saying, "What fury is this, Frenchmen, that excites you? Why are you persecuting this man who has come from remote parts to the help of me and you, and who is fighting loyally as a pilgrim for God and for you?" However, the king could not placate the feelings of the French, either by arguments or by entreaties, to make them cease disliking and annoying the English. As the poet has it, "Every proud man is impatient of a partner."[1]

The origin of this envy and hatred was as follows. This same W., by a fortunate and fortuitous chance, not by force, had taken a certain very strong tower not far from Alexandria, full of ladies, that is the wives of some noble Saracens. The French were caught completely unawares by this; because of it, his renown, and fear of him, flew even to distant parts of the East. And, since he had acquired much wealth both here and every- where because of the fortunes of war, and had enriched his household and increased his honours, which the French, in spite of their numbers and power, had not done, they enviously slandered him and pursued him with hatred. Nor could they speak with him in a friendly manner.

1. Lucan *Phars*. 1:93–4.

Concerning the departure of Wiliam Longespee from the army

Again, it happened that this same W. had learnt, from the secret report of the wary spies he had sent out, that some very well supplied eastern merchants were most imprudently on their way with a small escort to a certain fair near Alexandria where they confidently hoped to make a profit. He hurried there secretly by night, taking with him all his military strength, and with a sudden assault, like lightning, rushed on them unawares. The merchants having been slaughtered on the spot and their escorts completely dispersed or else taken prisoner, he took over for himself the whole of that company, which common people call a caravan. With them they found camels, mules and asses laden with silks, pigments, spices, and gold and silver, besides several waggons with their oxen, and provisions necessary for both beasts of burden and men, of which they were much in need. And although in this conflict the same W. killed and captured many of the enemy, he lost only one knight and eight sergeants killed. Others however he brought back wounded, to be restored with the help of medicine. So the happy and wealthy victor returned to the army. But the French, who had remained inactive and in need, urged at once by the stimulus of envy and avarice, met him on his arrival like an enemy and forcibly, as is the custom of bold robbers, seized all his gains, attributing to him as a sufficient offence that he had rashly dared, against the royal edict and the ordinances of the army leaders, to separate himself most proudly and foolishly and contrary to military discipline, from the company of the whole army. When W. heard this he promised to give them satisfaction for everything, namely by distributing all the food throughout the entire destitute army. But the French rebuffed this and, laying claim to everything, not without abuse, seized the whole lot for themselves.

A complaint

On this, William, saddened to the point of bitterness by so great a wrong, made a very serious complaint to the king, adding that his brother the count of Artois was the captain of this misconduct and violent robbery. The king indeed, who was extremely pious in character and looks, replied in a low voice, "William, William, he who ignores nothing knows all about this. I am sorry about the injury and loss inflicted on you. I greatly fear that pride, with other sins, will cause our downfall. You know how serious a thing it would be for me to upset my magnates in any way among these dangers in which I am placed." As he was talking, the count of Artois came up, flushed and excited like a madman, and, raising his voice inordinately without any salutation to the king or those sitting around, angrily exclaimed, "What does he want, my lord king? Surely you don't presume to defend this Englishman and oppose your Frenchmen? This man, in contempt of you and the whole army, led only by his own inclination, of his own accord carried off booty clandestinely by night contrary to our decrees, so that his fame alone and not that of the king and his Frenchmen is now spreading through the East. He has dimmed all our names and titles." The most Christian king averted his face when he heard this and, looking at William, said in a soft voice, "Now do you understand, my friend? A quarrel, which God forbid, can arise so easily in the army. Such things, and even worse things, must needs be tolerated in such a time of crisis." To which William replied, "Therefore you are no king, since you cannot bring your people to justice nor punish offenders, although I promise, if I have done wrong, to make amends in everything." and, cut to the heart, he added, "Besides, I will not serve such a king; I will not serve such a lord." And he angrily departed, to the great sorrow of the king.

Arriving at Acre, [William Longespee] stayed there with his companions in arms for some days, publicly complaining to all the inhabitants there of the injuries done to him. This made everyone, especially the prelates, sympathetic, and critical of the French. People of understanding who were experienced in military affairs unhesitatingly predicted that this would be a sad presage of future events and that the anger of the most high would be seriously provoked by such sins. The count of Artois is alleged to have said about this with a laugh, "Now the army of fine Frenchmen is well rid of the people with tails", which gave offence to many hearers. From then on William resolved to stay at Acre with the citizens, Templars and Hospitallers, to await the arrival of the crusading magnates of England and to inform them of the pride and offences of the French. They would urge them to try, with the advice of discreet and modest men, to attack the enemies of Christ in force without the French.

The English magnates who had taken the cross are forbidden to cross over

At this same time, namely on the celebrated day of the blessed

Augustine [26 May], all the magnates of England who had taken the cross, whose names have been mentioned above with their followers, and whose firm plan was, as already mentioned, to set out on their journey to Jerusalem on the feast of St. John [24 June], had sold or mortgaged their lands or got them involved in the snares of the Jews or Cahorsins, said farewell to their friends, and were ready and prepared to go. But the lord king, like a hurt or offended child which is wont to run complaining to its mother, had sent urgently to the pope entreating him to hold up this expedition, intimating to him that certain noble magnates of his kingdom who had taken the cross firmly proposed to set out for Jerusalem against his wishes and prohibition. Nor did they think it right to wait for the king himself their lord who had also taken the cross and was proposing to set out on the same journey, but indeed preferred to follow his capital enemy the king of the French, who, they said, had prepared the way and entry into the lands of the East for them, rather than him. So the pope in his letters, like the king in his words of command, under penalty of excommunication strictly forbade any of them to cross over against the king's will, no matter what danger or crisis threatened the king of the French.

The custodians of all the ports are instructed to see that none of the crusading magnates crosses over

Moreover the lord king immediately sent word to the castellans of Dover and to the custodians of the other ports, that no magnate who had taken the cross should be allowed to cross over. It was alleged against this that the king had acted unwisely, because if so many and such people set out in advance of him, – there were about five hundred mounted combatants, besides their innumerable followers – the community of the whole of Christendom, astonished, would say, "How great a king this is, and how formidable, who sends such a force in advance of himself! How many are we to imagine will accompany him!" And so all paganism would tremble. But what is the point of this discussion? Things turned out well for these crusaders, though this was because of the obstacle of the prohibition. For if they had crossed over then, they would undoubtedly not, sad to say, have arrived at an opportune and seasonable time to come to the aid of the lord king of the French, as they so ardently desired. This will be fully explained in what follows, because things that happened all at once can by no means be narrated all at once.

An inestimable sum of money is extorted from the Jews and the magnates of the land by the devices of Geoffrey of Langley

Meanwhile the lord king never stopped scraping up money on all sides, mainly from the Jews, but also in the second place from his own Christian natural subjects. He went so far that from one single Jew, by name Aaron, who was born in York and continued to live in that city, he extorted 14,000 marks and 10,000 in gold for the use of the queen. This had to be paid within a short period, lest he languish in gaol, because he had been convicted, it was said, of forging a certain charter. After he had paid all this, it was ascertained that this same Aaron had paid the king 30,000 silver marks and the queen 200 gold marks, after the king had returned from overseas, as Brother Matthew, the writer[1] of this page, was assured by this same Jew A. on his faith and legal testimony. However, although they were miserable, none of them was worthy of commiseration, for they were proved to be, and condemned and reproved as, corrupters and forgers of the royal coinage and of seals and charters.[2]

1. The scribe of C has here altered B's *scriptori* to *compositori*.
2. This is repeated from above, p. 214.

Concerning Geoffrey of Langley

At about the same time a certain knight, a bailiff of the lord king, an inquisitor into offences committed in the king's forests, called Geoffrey of Langley, travelling through many parts of England, extorted an infinite sum of money, especially from the nobles in northern parts, so astutely, so boldly and so forcibly, that the amount of treasure collected either caused astonishment to, or exceeded the estimation of, those who heard of it. This immoderate oppression with which the king afflicted the northerners, seemed to have originated from an old hatred. The said G. was surrounded by a copious retinue and company, and since the justices were their enemies, if any of the aforesaid nobles, excusing themselves, dared to mutter, he ordered him to be arrested on the spot and consigned to the royal prison. Nor could he expiate the crime in any reasonable way. Indeed for one little animal, a fawn or a hare, although straying in an out of the way place, he ruinously impoverished a most noble person, sparing neither blood nor fortune.

Compared to this man, Robert Passelew was considered extremely pious; indeed all his predecessors were thought just and were spoken well of, in comparison with him. This G., promoted a short time before to the office of marshal in the lord king's household, to carry the staff for the grand marshal, had to the best of his power reduced the generosity and customary hospitality of the royal table and, thus flattering the lord king, he pleased him and undeservedly gained the royal favour. Afterwards the said Robert, supposing this G. to be suitable and loyal, appointed him to be his own colleague in the office of justice of the forests of the lord king. But G., stealing a march on his patron, afterwards basely supplanted him and ignominiously dismissed the bailiffs that the same R. had appointed, nor did he shrink from impoverishing them. Thus he harmed the said R. no little by shaming him. But who feels sorry for the enchanter struck by a serpent? On this account the said R., shunning the snares of the court and courtiers and having been ordained a priest, as is mentioned above,[1] fled to enjoy the benefits of a better life.

1.   Above, p. 191

Archbishop B. of Canterbury crosses over

At the same time, too, the archbishop of Canterbury B., realising that the dean of St. Paul's, together with some of the canons of that church and the protectors of those he had injured [had set out for the curia], on the advice of some legists, armed with royal letters and protection, and trusting to the influence of his relatives, crossed over in great pomp and splendour to go to the Roman curia so as to become more powerful in his tyranny by means of papal authority.

Robert de Lexinton died

In the same year on the fourth of the kalends of June [24 May], died Robert de Lexinton, a cleric, who had been a justice for a long time and had acquired a famous name and abundant possessions. However, a few years before his death, struck by paralysis, he resigned the said office so that, like the blessed apostle Matthew, he was called from collecting taxes to a better life. He ended his declining days laudably with generous almsgiving and devout prayers.

How joyful but vain rumours of the capture of Cairo and destruction of Alexandria spread around

At this same time most welcome but unfounded rumours of the conquest of Cairo and Babylon and the destruction of Alexandria spread around and soothed all the Westerners with vain encouragement. It was ascertained that their cause and origin, which require a lengthy but fruitless narrative, because "Through a bad end the whole series deserves shame,"[1] were as follows.

1. Geoffrey de Vinshauf *Nova poetria*, 67.

The story of how the Christians almost achieved a vast lordship

When the sultan of Babylon was informed in the previous year of the arrival of the most famous king of the French with his army, he entrusted the defence of Damietta to one of his princes in whom he had great confidence, and the defence of Cairo and Babylon to that prince's brother. But after the unexpected capture of Damietta [by the Christians], the said sultan, having assembled all his principal leaders, gravely accused the prince to whose guardianship he had entrusted Damietta, and under whose care it had been lost, in front of everyone, alleging against him that he had not only treacherously, negligently and in a cowardly manner lost his principal city, which was agreed to be impregnable, but had handed it over to the public enemy so that the Christian enemies of all the Saracens had an open entrance into Egypt and all the lands of the East, the hope of conquering everything quickly and definitively, potently and patently, and an extremely well defended place of refuge, to the confusion of the whole of paganism. To this the accused prince replied as follows.

"Most potent lord, I your faithful and devoted servant, having sent my spies to the island of Cyprus when the king of the French was wintering there, learned from them that when he left there he would make for Alexandria and attack it. So I quickly sent all my men there from Damietta, to the powerful aid of our friends and your subjects the Alexandrians, so that, having captured the said king, I could present him to you with his entire fleet. But fortune was unfriendly to us, and the wind changed in his favour and brought our enemies against us when we were unprepared. And so, as you know, although we resisted to the best of our powers, he occupied the coast, and, on the following day, the fortune of war favouring him, he laid siege to Damietta, which he found entirely destitute of defenders. He arrived on the spot with so vast a fleet that the sea seemed to be covered. Considering the situation realistically, we, lacking the captains and arms of the city, consulted our and your safety, and, having brained and strangled the Christian prisoners we had, withdrew secretly by night until, after recalling the forces we had sent to Alexandria, we could attack the Christians more powerfully. But some Christian prisoners, when they saw their fellow-Christians approaching and us slaughtering their companions, began to resist us, attacked us ferociously, and killed some of our people. These men, moreover, after our departure, led the advancing French along unknown paths, and brought them into the innermost parts of the city. As we left, we started a fire burning, lest our enemies glory in our possessions, but the slaves extinguished it as quickly as they could. When we were forced to retreat we execrated the law of Mahomet in our grief and, cursing him, wished to die rather than to live."

When the sultan heard this he flared up into violent rage, for he was extremely proud and merciless, and, although in some people's opinion the said prince could have adequately cleared himself, yet the sultan inveighed more fiercely against him and ordered him to be hanged on the gallows as a traitor and blasphemer.

His brother, namely the guardian of Cairo, whose heart had for a long time been inclined towards the Christian faith, "but secretly, for fear of the" pagans[1], when he heard of this, secretly had some of the prisoners he held confined, namely Templars, Hospitallers and some Frenchmen recently taken in battle at Gaza, summoned, and said to them, "I have a private secret which ought to be revealed confidentially to you and, if you promise with conscientious regard to your faith and law to keep it concealed and assist me in a determined manner, I will reveal it to you." When in response to this proposition the prisoners had pledged themselves to keep faith irrevocably in everything on their word and oath, he took up his narrative as follows.

"The sultan of Babylon thus far, but now no longer, my lord, whom I have served loyally for a long time through many perils, has recently done me an intolerable injury, shameful and serious, for he has hanged my brother, whom I loved more than a brother, indeed more than the whole of my family, on a gibbet, accusing him of surrendering Damietta, voluntarily and out of cowardice to the French, although reasons backed by evidence could not be found to support him in any way. Indeed it is agreed, as you perhaps know, that this criminal accusation of his was completely false. You know how courageously and loyally he fought to prevent the French from occupying the shore, so much so that we lost there, besides many friends and kinsmen, our Rok, the greatest amongst us and second after the sultan, who had killed many Christians in the past and had triumphed over your people at Gaza. This is why, seeking revenge for such tyranny, I am surrendering to the most pious king of the French that impregnable castle in which all the hopes of paganism are placed, namely Cairo with Babylon together with the sultan's entire treasure there. Also, I give and concede myself and everything of mine to Jesus Christ and my lord the king of the French, demanding the sacrament of baptism. For what the said sultan has now done to my brother, he would indubitably do to me, even though I am innocent, if I fell into his hands. Take care, therefore, to go at once after being released from your imprisonment, with the utmost haste, to this king of the French and tell him all this faithfully; and, so that he can be further assured of my good faith, let him bring his entire army, which we consider invincible, here with him in battle order. When this reaches the ears of the sultan he will send all his forces out to oppose him as he approaches. But you will have no reason to be afraid, for you will have the aforesaid castle together with Babylon at hand, open to you as a place of refuge, and, to the sudden confusion of all the pagans you will have my guidance, advice and help in everything."

These prisoners therefore, now to their great joy freed as a first proof of the truth of his word, at once went secretly to the king and, because those who brought this message were well known and reliable, they were deservedly believed in everything. The king, hearing it, prohibited its disclosure to anyone until his plan was drawn up definitively. Sorrowful that, through the absence of William Longespee and his people, who had suffered an outrageous injury, his army was in large degree mutilated and discredited, he sent hurriedly to him asking him to come, to receive every satisfaction for the injuries done him; and he added at the end of the message "and to hear a welcome report which will be followed by the long-desired event and hoped-for joy, which we wish and desire to share with you".

This message spread through the inhabitants of that country, having been divulged among the citizens of Acre. At the mandate of so great a prince, especially because of the final addition, William came to the king with all his followers. After learning of the aforesaid guardian's message from the king's account, he was so pleased that he abandoned all bitterness and rancour towards those who had offended him. It was because of this that some investigators into secret affairs and eager reporters of good news, as if they were already in possession of what was promised, sent vain letters to their friends whom they wanted to cheer up stating that Cairo and Babylon having been captured, Alexandria was left open to the Christians. Thus arose the rumours together with the said letters.[2]

1. John 19:38.
2. The letters are in BL Cotton MS. Nero D 1, f.99 = Luard 1882:167–7. A marginal note in B referring to this paragraph runs as follows: "Note whence the vain rumours which soothed many people's ears".

To remove the Christians the sultan offers many fortresses for the benefit of peace

The king therefore, excited with good hopes, having posted the duke of Burgundy and many of his loyal followers as a secure garrison in the city of Damietta, directed his reins and standards towards Cairo with his entire army drawn up according to military discipline. On the way he killed some Saracens placed in ambush to prevent provisions being brought to Damietta. Meanwhile the sultan was told that the French had left the fortifications of Damietta rejoicing and unafraid and with banners displayed, and that they entertained the confident hope of conquering everything. Thereupon, fearing French attacks, he sent some noble messengers from his entourage offering the entire Holy Land to the Christians, namely the whole of the kingdom of Jerusalem and more, besides an infinite treasure in gold and silver and other desirable things, on condition, however, that the king handed back Damietta together with all the prisoners he was holding captive. All Christian slaves would similarly be released, to be received by the French king, and there would be joint and peaceful trade and communication in both their territories. Thus they could enjoy the benefits of peace and friendly intercourse. And it was said and affirmed as a fact, that the sultan and many of the chief Saracens were inclined to relinquish the law of Mahomet, which it was agreed was most deplorable, and faithfully to adhere to the law of Christianity, which was considered excellent, so long as they could peacefully retain their lands and possessions. But these peace terms were flatly rejected by the legate, acting on papal orders, which had instructed him to this effect if the Saracens by any chance offered them.

The sultan is warned of treachery

While the useless delay over these affairs was being prolonged, some of the above-mentioned Saracens from the hilly country who were placed in ambush with some shepherds feeding their flocks in the valleys, to intercept provisions, learned from some exceptionally astute spies of the treachery of the aforesaid guardian of Cairo. They therefore mounted their swiftest horses and made all speed to the sultan, announcing explicitly to him the cause of the Christians' arrival and of their audacity and confidence. He immediately sent some experienced soldiers to Cairo with all haste and they seized the guardian and held him prisoner until they had proofs of the truth; the first of which was that they found the prison empty of captives. So the guardian's guilt was proved, and the sultan at once strengthened Cairo and Babylon with the best garrisons his troops could supply, saying "Now at last I hope that Jesus Christ, the Lord and God of the Christians, lover of modesty and humility, will confound them because of their pride." Thereafter the sultan, becoming more composed and steadfast, was unwilling to concede to the Christians what he had first offered them, though they humbly requested him and, minded to fight, he strove confidently to resist or rather to triumph over them. So he had an infinite number of troops summoned from the East, both people who cared for the common good, and those who longed to enrich themselves with abundance of silver and gold, and he caused it to be publicly proclaimed by herald that anyone who presented him with a Christian's head would receive ten talents over and above his usual and agreed wage, anyone bringing a right hand, five, and for a foot, two talents, as a reward.

The lord Frederick's affairs prosper, for he conquers the Parmans

In this same year the lord Frederick, taking seriously the hardened insolence of the Italians, resolutely began to draw up plans against them, above all the people of Parma and Bologna; the Parmans for the murder of Thaddeus [of Suessa] and others loyal to Frederick and for the destruction of the fortress he had called Victoria, and the Bolognese for the capture and imprisonment of his son Enzio and his people and the Cremonans. The Parmans, because of the long peace which they said Frederick had allowed them to enjoy, were travelling about unharmed and perfectly safe, at first in the area adjacent to their city, afterwards indeed carrying their goods more distantly to market, transacting their affairs undisturbed and returning peacefully. One day, however, when some of the more influential citizens, taking this as evidence of a secure peace, had gone out of the city unarmed and nonchalant on foot to inspect their gardens and the fortresses built in its neighbourhood for its defence, without hindrance from Frederick's followers waiting in ambush, these suddenly rushed out from their hiding places armed to the teeth and closed off access to the city to the unprotected citizens. They took all those incautious citizens, who were numerous and distinguished, like little birds in a net and, approaching the city and passing through the first guards at the gates, were about to occupy everything at will, but the people who had remained in the city, raising a dreadful cry, quickly placed chains, barricades and beams across the streets in their path. They also rolled empty casks along the pavements which, making a horrible din, put the terrified horses to flight. But when they were informed of the capture of their fellow-citizens, who were the captains of the whole city and its most prominent people, they humbly requested terms of peace and many of them, leaving it, having offered no little money, gave their right hands to Frederick and submitted to his will. Others however, to whom the very strong towers offered confidence in resistance, took up positions in them and hurled javelins and boulders, preferring to undergo any danger there rather than the judgement of Frederick. Hearing of this, the Bolognese, having sent messengers to the said F., sought peace with prayer and humility; but F. put off listening to them. At this same time, having sent reliable messengers to Avignon and Arles, very renowned cities not far from Lyons, he received the oaths of allegiance of their citizens. When all this reached the papal ears, he was extremely sorry to have laid out so much treasure to no purpose on the above-mentioned affairs.

Reiner of Viterbo died

To add to the sorrows of the Roman curia, the lord Reiner of Viterbo, cardinal and chamberlain, went the way of all flesh. He was a man of illustrious family and rich in possessions, a tireless persecutor and defamer of Frederick. On his death, the Romans intimated to the lord pope with threats that, as he was their pastor and bishop, he should come to Rome without delay.

Master Berard de Nimpha collects no little money from the crusaders for the benefit of Earl Richard

At about the same time Berard de Nimpha, a cleric armed with papal documents, collected [money] in a most dishonest way for Earl Richard's benefit, so that it appeared to be rapine rather than justice. The manner of this unmannerly robbery, lest it offend the ears and minds of many, is more fully set down in the *Book of additamenta*.[1]

1. BL Cotton MS. Nero D 1, f.90 = Luard 1882:134–8.

A gloomy message

On St. Kenelm's day, namely the kalends of August [1 August], as Earl Richard was sitting in the Exchequer at London, a certain speedy but sorrowful messenger came to him, bearer of the most shocking letters and reports, the tenor of which was as follows.

The most Christian king of the French, having held a general council, encouraged by the reports of a certain guardian of Cairo, of whom mention has been made above, moved camp from Damietta towards Cairo, forcibly slaughtering those who forcibly barred his way. And since the fortunes of war favoured him in everything, a fierce battle was engaged in and, after a most severe and dreadful conflict had raged hither and thither for a long time, the Christians triumphed gloriously over the Saracens. Then, about the Sunday after Easter [3 April], many crossed a certain large river flowing from the Nile, called the Tafnis, by means of flat boats placed together and a secret ford which a certain convert, formerly a Saracen, had shown the king.

The king's brother, namely Robert, count of Artois, taking with him many nobles, one of whom was William Longespee, crossed over to the opposite shore unknown to the king his brother. His intention was alone to triumph and carry off the honour, instead of everyone, so that the victory would be ascribed to him alone, for he was extremely proud and arrogant and was filled with vainglory. Coming upon some Saracens, they put them to the sword and Robert, advancing boldly but incautiously, resolved to make a violent attack on a certain village ahead of them called Mansor and, having killed everyone they found there, to demolish it. Forcing his way in, but almost overcome by stones, he withdrew in confusion, having however killed many of the inhabitants. They then held council together over what to do, and Count Robert, hopeful that the outcome would happily correspond to the beginning, persuaded and encouraged them to advance, and he said to the master of the knights of the Temple [William de Sounac], who was then with him, in the presence of William Longespee, "Let us follow up the enemy who are near at hand and are said to be fleeing while things are going well for us, while we see that our people are full of ardour and thirsting for the enemy's blood, and while the enemies of the faith are despairing for their safety. Thus by crushing them all we shall the sooner bring our war to a blessed conclusion. Let us act confidently, because one third of the French army is following us, and, if anything unlucky – which God forbid! – should happen to us, the unconquerable army of my brother and lord the king will come to our aid at a nod."

To this the master of the knights of the Temple, a discreet and wary man skilled and experienced in military affairs, replied, "My lord and noble count, we can commend well enough your efforts, your innate generosity and your bravery freely devoted to the honour of the Lord and his universal Church, which we know about and have often experienced. However, we would like and we advise and entreat you advantageously to restrain this fervour with the bridle of modesty and discretion so that we can recover breath a little after this triumph and honour which the Lord has given us. For after the heat and labour of battle we are tired, wounded, hungry and thirsty; and if we are consoled by the honour and glory of our victory, no honour or joy can revive our wounded and exhausted horses. We shall be better advised to return so that, united with the army of our lord the king, we may be strengthened both in advice and aid, and recuperate ourselves and our horses with a little rest. When our enemies see this they will praise and fear us all the more for our moderation and good sense. Having taken fuller council with our own people when we are all united together, for this undertaking, we shall rise again stronger, more confident because strengthened by our collected forces. For now the clamour of the fugitives, carried on the swiftest horses, will arouse the sultan and our other enemies, confident in their strength and numbers, and forewarn and encourage them because of our small numbers and because of the division of our army which they have long hoped for. Thus, informed of all this, they will attack us more boldly and confidently, this time sending out their forces against us to our destruction and ruin. For they know that, if they are crushed now, they will be completely disinherited and, with their wives and children, irreparably reduced to nothing."

The defiance of the count of Artois

When the count of Artois heard this he was highly indignant and, excited and flushed with anger and pride, replied, "See the time- honoured treachery of the Temple! The ancient sedition of the Hospitallers! What deceit hidden for a long time, now appears openly in our midst! This is what we predicted long ago in a prophecy which has now come true. The whole country of the East would have been conquered long ago had it not been for the Templars and Hospitallers and others who call themselves religious, who have hindered us, the laymen, with their deceit. Look how the capture of the sultan and the complete confusion of paganism lies open to us, as well as the permanent exaltation of the law of our Christians, all of which this Templar here is doing his best to prevent with his fictitious and fallacious arguments. For the Templars and Hospitallers and their associates, who are fattened by ample revenues, are afraid that, if the country is subjected to Christian laws, their supremacy will come to an end. It is because of this that they mix various poisons for the faithful coming here fitted out for the cause of the cross, and kill them in different treacherous ways with the help of the Saracens. Surely Frederick, who has experienced their deceits, is a most reliable witness of this?"

The shocked reply of the master of the Temple

To these satirical and stinging words the aforesaid master of the knights [of the Temple] and his brothers, and the master of the Hospital likewise with his confraternity, cut to the quick, replied with one voice, "Why noble count, should we have taken the habit of a monk? Surely not to overthrow the Church of Christ and thus lose our souls through intend-ing treachery? Far be that from us, and indeed from every Christian." And the irate master of the Temple, said angrily to his standard-bearer in a loud voice, "Unfurl and raise our banner and we shall advance to battle to experience together today the uncertain fortunes of war and the chance of death. We would have been insuperable had we remained inseparable, but unfortunately we are divided, like sand without lime, so that we are unfit for the spiritual edifice and, lacking the cement of mutual affection, we shall forthwith become like ruined walls."

The moderate reply of William Longespee

On hearing this, William Longespee, who greatly feared the schism

now engendered in the army, wishing to calm the impetuous enthusiasm of the count of Artois and mitigate the anger of the master of the
Temple, replied thus, "According to the Lord's word,[1] desolation
follows from such a schism and division. Let us therefore, most noble
count, listen to this sincere and saintly man. He has for a long time
been an inhabitant of this country and, taught by manifold experience,
he knows the strength and the craftiness of the Saracens. No wonder
that we, newcomers, young men and foreigners, are ignorant of the
dangers of the East. As far distant as the East is from the West, so far
different are the Westerners from Orientals." And, turning to the
master of the Temple, he spoke to him calmly and with soothing
words, hoping to lessen his agitation. But the count of Artois,
snatching the words from his mouth, shouting as the French do and
swearing indecently, gave tongue to the following invective in the
hearing of many. "How cowardly these timid people with tails are!
How blessed, how clean, this army would be if purged of tails and
tailed people!" The shamed William, provoked and upset by these
insulting words, replied: "Count Robert, I shall assuredly advance
unafraid of any danger of impending death. We shall be today, I fancy,
where you will not dare to touch my horse's tail." And, putting on their
helmets and unfurling their banners they resumed their advance against
their enemies, who covered a spacious plain, and the hills and valleys
on all sides. Count R., wishing to ascribe everything to himself in the
event of a Christian triumph, disdained to notify his brother the lord
king of the French of the possible danger.

1.   Matthew 12:25.

How the sultan encouraged his people

The sultan, however, informed of all this by the swiftest scouts, eagerly
encouraged all of his numerous multitude, which had been assembled
in an extraordinarily short time, to do battle, with these words. "This is
what I have for a long time hoped for. The Christians are divided so
that one brother no longer supports another. Furthermore even these
people, who constitute scarcely one third of the total, are at variance
among themselves. They are ours for booty and plunder. Even today,
squabbling among themselves, they have been basely reproaching one
another. The king of the French, far off, is wholly unaware of what
they are doing or about to do. These men, emaciated by hunger, worn
out by battle and the labours of the march, bruised by the stones

hurled at them in Mansor, few in number and in every way weakened, must first be crushed so that we can then more easily conquer the others, whom we have cut off from every kind of provision."

This plan, heard by all the Saracens, was approved by them all, and so the sultan with his innumerable forces furiously charged the Christian army and engaged it in fierce combat. Within a short time the Christians began to be surrounded by the multitude of Saracens, like an island surrounded by the sea, and the Saracens stationed themselves between the Christians and a river they had crossed so that not one of them could escape. Seeing this, the count of Artois regretted that he had not taken the advice of older and wiser men, "But the soldier once helmeted is too late to regret having to fight."[1] When Count R. saw W. Longespee surrounded on all sides by a dense mass of enemies and bearing the brunt of the whole battle he called out most imprudently and impudently, "William, God is fighting against us; we cannot resist any longer. Consult your safety by fleeing, and escape alive while your horse can still carry you, lest you begin to want to when you are no longer able to." To which William briefly replied, in so far as such a tumult permitted, "God forbid that a son of my father should flee from any Saracen. I would rather die happily than live unhappily."

Count Robert of Artois, therefore, seeing himself now hedged in on all sides by the enemy and with hardly any possibility of escape, turned round and hurriedly took to flight. Carried by a very swift horse towards the river, which was either the Nile or the Tafnis which flows into it, he entered the water armed, hoping to swim across, for he knew his horse was extremely strong. But he could not do it, because he was encumbered with iron and much other equipment. So he perished by drowning, miserable, but commiserated by no one, proud but a fugitive, humiliated not of his own accord but unwillingly, mourned by no one's tears for, though born of the noble blood of kings, he set a pernicious example to others. As the poet says, "The more distinguished the criminal the greater is the offence considered."[2] The count being thus drowned, all the Frenchmen in the battle began to despair and withdrew into scattered groups. Seeing this, William, against whom all the Saracens had charged, realised that it was a matter of life and death. He manfully sustained the attacks of them all, and, mutilating the bodies of many, sent their souls to Tartarus. At length the feet were cut off his exhausted horse but he still severed the heads, hands or feet of some of his assailants.

1. Juvenal *Sat.*, 1:169.
2. Juvenal *Sat.*, 8:140.

Concerning the death of William Longespee

Finally, after enduring many blows and wounds and having lost blood, he was overwhelmed by stones as he began to fail, and he breathed out his soul, manifestly to be crowned as a martyr. With him perished his standard-bearer, Robert de Vere, a distinguished knight, and a great many Englishmen who had followed his standard from the beginning.

A vision of William in a dream

On the night before this battle a vision appeared to his most noble mother the lady countess [of Salisbury] and abbess of Lacock, Ela by name, in which a certain knight, fitted out in full armour, was received into the opened heavens. Recognising the device on the shield, she asked in amazement who this was ascending to be received with such glory by the angels, whose arms she recognised. A clearly articulated voice replied, "William, your son." She noted which night that was, and afterwards the meaning of the vision became apparent.

Robert count of Artois being drowned and William Longespee killed, the Saracens, certain of victory, pitiably put the surrounded and helpless Christians to the sword. Out of all that splendid and famous body of knights, only two Templars and a Hospitaller escaped, and one lesser person who swam the river with nothing on and announced this eternally deplorable event to the king of the French and the rest of the army. Others who escaped were so exhausted and wounded and out of breath that they were unable to cross the river but awaited the darkness of night concealed in the sedge. Nor did the anger, or rather the fury, of the Lord allow anyone of note to escape.

The king of the French encourages his people

When this came to the ears of the most pious king of the French, heaving a deep sigh and touched to the heart with grief, he could not restrain his copious tears and, with clasped hands and eyes raised to heaven, he said, between sobs, "As it pleased God, so has it happened. Blessed be the name of the Lord." And, summoning the French leaders, he addressed them as follows: "Friends and loyal followers and most steadfast comrades-in-arms, who have shared my labours and perils, what is to be done in this lamentable crisis? If we appear to accept what has happened and withdraw, our enemies will exult as if they had won a victory over us all. They will glory more in our retreat than in the slaughter of our brothers and they will be more encouraged to attack and pursue us, especially as they can move faster than us. Thus they will more quickly wipe us all from the face of the earth, to the confusion of Christianity, the universal Church will be more seriously confounded, and France will be blackened with indelible opprobrium. Having called on God, who seems gravely offended by our sins, let us unanimously and with confidence attack our enemies, who are stained with the blood of our brothers; and let us with a condign vengeance demand the blood of our friends which was shed by the hands of our enemies. For who could any longer tolerate such an injury to Christ with equanimity?"

The king's ill-fated advance to battle

Everyone is armed and animated as one man by the king's commands; and while each one remembers the death of a friend or kinsman, groans and sighs are multiplied, sobs break out with tears, "rivers of water run down their eyes,"[1] and thus they are consumed more by grief than hunger. Those who appear to be the stronger advance, preceded by the oriflamme, and follow the tracks of their brothers who, as has been said, had been killed, sending the weaker ones, who entirely lacked arms and victuals, in small boats down the river to Damietta, so that at least they could recover breath there in the shelter of the city. The sultan, informed of this, ordered some small boats to be hastily transported there on ox-drawn carts, so that, besides those he already had there to cut off provisions, he would have a larger fleet of boats to exterminate the wretched Christians. These boats, filled with Saracens, opposed the Christians as they sailed down the river, whereupon a most bloody naval battle was fought, and massed projectiles flew like hail. At length, after a protracted and horrible struggle in which Greek fire was thrown, the enemies of Christ, through some obscure decision of God, triumphed at their pleasure over the Christians, who were worn out by grief and hunger. Because the Saracen fleet which had come from Damietta and which had been posted to stop provisions being taken there by river was in the way, anyone who wished to take flight was prevented. Not a single Christian escaped, not even to tell the Christians remaining in Damietta what had happened, for they all perished woefully, either drowned, burnt, or pierced with weapons or killed in some way. One person, however, following in the rear, far behind the leaders, managed to escape and return, not by advancing to the city, though the Saracens pursued this fugitive and inflicted five large wounds on him. His name was Alexander Giffard and he was English by birth, the son of a noble lady who was staying with the queen of England.

1.   Misquoted from Psalm 119:136.

The great despair of the French

The French, informed of these events, were more and more consumed with grief, nor could the king console them, so that despair depressed the minds of them all. The sultan however, hearing of the Christians' misfortunes on all sides, was aroused to joy and greater audacity. When he heard of the hostile advance of the king of the French and his army he was amazed at the audacity of this handful of famished men in daring to provoke such a vast army, namely the whole of the East, to battle, after such misfortunes. So, having convoked his principal men, he encouraged them, saying, "Most noble men of the East, who have now triumphantly and splendidly defeated almost half the French army and who are now rejoicing in the spoils, the weapons and the horses of the slain, oppose this approaching rabble, which is consumed by grief and hunger and should be quickly crushed, boldly. Put all who oppose you implacably to the sword so that not one of them can escape or elude your victorious hands. What rash insanity incites them to attack us in the hopes of disinheriting us, who have inhabited this most noble country since the flood? Surely they do not want us to believe in their Christ against our will? Who can be converted or believe, unwillingly? The Christians have some small pretext for wanting the land they call Holy; but what has Egypt got to do with them? Surely they are unworthy to hold sway over the land which is watered and made fruitful by the river sent from Paradise? Beardless and shorn, more imbecile than bellicose, more like hermaphrodites or even women, than men, what do they presume?" On this they all got ready for battle as if bursting into flames, and confidently advanced to attack our people.

The confused French are shamefully defeated

As our Christians advanced, they came to the place where their French brothers had miserably died and found the headless bodies of the slain, mutilated, with hands and feet cut off. For the Saracens, to obtain the rewards offered by the sultan, had rushed eagerly to cut off the heads and limbs of the dead bodies, leaving the rest to be devoured by the beasts and birds of prey. When the French saw this, giving way to doleful cries, they tore their hair and clothes and wetted their weapons and shields with tears so that their grief could have evoked the compassion even of their enemies. Meanwhile, the enemy troops appeared near at hand and a lamentable conflict at once broke out. But what could they do, few in number, with emaciated horses, worn out by hunger and want, grief and misfortune, against so many thousands of thousands? The French succumb; they are overthrown and destroyed; they are eager to give themselves up to the army. What more? The defeated French army is dispersed, while few of the enemy are killed.

In this unfortunate battle only one of the distinguished Saracens is known to have fallen, namely Melkadin the son of Rok, and even if as many had fallen on the opposing side as we had on ours, their army would scarcely have seemed smaller. We had 2,300 excellent mounted men and 15,000 other combatants, almost all of whom were either killed or captured at the enemy's pleasure. Adding grief to grief, the king, together with a very few others, namely Charles, count of Provence, Alphonse count of Poitou, and some others who were defending him with a few magnates, who remained at his side, was taken prisoner, to the eternal disgrace of the French and to the confusion of the whole of Christianity and the Church universal. Nor has it been found, in the contents of any histories, that the king of the French was ever taken prisoner, especially by infidels, or completely conquered, except this one. If he alone at least had been preserved in safety and honour, even though everyone else had died, the Christians would have had some means of recovering breath and avoiding disgrace. This is why in the psalm David prays especially that the king's person be saved, when he says "Lord save the king,"[1] because the safety of the entire army depends on that. In the force which Robert, count of Artois, the king's brother, took with him with rash daring almost 1,000 knights perished, and 7,200 other combatants. Of the Templars no more than three knights escaped; of the Hospitallers, four, and a fifth died from loss of blood from his wounds before he reached Acre. From the house of the Teutonic Knights three escaped, half-dead. Besides the Templars and the other distinguished men above-mentioned, in this same deadly battle there died Ralph de Cuscy, an excellent and famous knight, Hugh count of Flanders, a powerful and illustrious man, Hugh de Brun, count of La Marche, whose father died at Damietta a short time before, and also [Matthew de Montmorenci], count of Ponthieu, a pilgrim. And to conclude in a few words, the entire nobility of France perished there massacred. Gauthier de Châtillon too, a vigorous and invincible knight, was captured and, taken to the caliph, was presented to him as a token of victory; it is his custom never to allow any Christian brought to his goal to go free. William Longespee was also killed, after he had steeped his sword in the blood of many of his enemies, with Robert de Vere and many other distinguished knights and sergeants. This man, though he could have been persuaded to escape, was unwilling, lest he should have seemed unworthy to be associated with the other martyrs.

1.   Psalm 20:9.

Those who were left to guard Damietta and the fleet

The duke of Burgundy, who commanded the knights and people remaining there, and Olivier de Termes, a distinguished warrior and fighter who commanded the crossbowmen and mercenaries, were left to guard Damietta. Also in the city were the legate Eudes, the bishops of Amiens [Gerard de Couchy] and Soissons [Guy de Château Porcien], with many other prelates and clerics; also the queen of France and with her many noble ladies and women. Some distinguished knights had been posted to guard the fleet, which was numerous, indeed a nobler or larger one had never before been seen, together with some Pisans, Genoese, Flemish, Poitevins and Provençals, loyal to the king of France.

It should be noted that, on the same day on which the king of the French was taken prisoner, Earl Richard was dining with the pope and, just as the sultan of Babylon took the king prisoner, so the pope tried to take in the earl and carefully incline him to his will.[1]

1.   This paragraph is in the margin of B and is not in C.

The king of the French is asked about the restitution of Damietta and his ransom

When the king was taken and held prisoner, the Saracens, just as they had previously done when they captured Robert the king's brother, decapitated the bodies of the slain and cut off their hands and feet as a sign of complete vengeance, as the sultan had decreed, as well as in the hopes of the above-mentioned reward. But the greater the injuries suffered by the holy martyrs of God, the greater rewards they will doubtless obtain. The sultan planned to take the king as a captive to the more distant regions of the East, as a spectacle and object of ridicule for every infidel, to be scoffed at by all the Saracens, and to win praise for himself. He would present the very distinguished Christian to the caliph in Mahomet's honour, so that the downfall of this most noble person would inspire in them the hope of confounding the others. But, because they longed so much for Damietta, the plan was changed lest by chance the king should die of grief. Indeed, he would not eat or drink anything for two days after his capture, and he wanted to die. If he had died, the besieged could have sustained the attacks of all the forces of the East unafraid for a year at least, both by sea and land; meanwhile Christian assistance would have relieved them. For Damietta was very well fortified with walls, earthworks and towers, and at sea the fleet was unconquerable. Pondering this, the more eminent and wiser of the Saracens consulted the king at once over the restitution of Damietta and the ransom of his own person, namely for the sum of a hundred thousand pounds of gold. To this the king replied with a crestfallen look and deferential voice, "The Almighty knows that I came here from France not to acquire lands or wealth, but rather to win over your endangered souls to God. Nor did I undertake the burden of this perilous expedition in fulfilment of my vow on my account, but on yours. For I possess sufficiently numerous, temperate and healthy lands, though I am unworthy and a sinner, but I pity your souls, which will surely perish. The confusion I have suffered in every kind of way because Christ is offended with me should be sufficient for you. I can be put to death, money can be extorted from me till I am destitute, but never shall the city of Damietta, won by a divine miracle, be surrendered to you".

Note the Saracens' ruse, which was however detected

While the Saracens were discussing this, one of the most cunning said, "Why are we hesitating? We can get hold both of Damietta and the money we are asking for, whether or not this captive kinglet is willing." On the advice of this man, therefore, a strong and numerous force of Saracens was mustered, about the same size as or larger than the Christian army was estimated to have been. Fraudulently taking over the armour, shields and banners of the slaughtered Christians, they set out forthwith for Damietta in this disguise so that they would be received as if they were Frenchmen and, having been let into the city, they could immediately massacre everyone they found. As they approached the city the Christian guards watched them from the ramparts of the town and towers and at first they thought they were Christians happily bringing back booty and spoils. But, the nearer they approached the more unlike Frenchmen they seemed. For they came hurriedly, crowded in disordered groups, with irregularly slanted shields, behaving more like Saracens than Frenchmen. And when they reached the edge of the fortification and the gates of the city they showed themselves more clearly to be Saracens because of their dark features, beards and barbarous language. They boldly demanded entrance to the city, for all the ways into the city and the forts were carefully and vigilently guarded.

The grief of the Christians in Damietta once they realise the truth

When the city's guards saw the Saracens fitted out in the spoils of Christians and were thus informed of the defeat of the Christian army, the entire city was filled with their lugubrious lamentations. They altogether denied the enemy entrance to the city and forts, confidently maintaining that even if the whole Christian army with the king himself had perished they would for a long time readily endure a siege and the onslaught of all the Saracens of the East in the certain expectation of help. But when those watching from the higher towers saw the size and number of the advancing army, since their own forces were quite unequal to the enemy's, they were unwilling to sally forth to attack them, especially as they were nearly exhausted by grief and hunger. Who indeed could adequately describe their heavy hearts when they saw the enemies of Christ taking derisive pride in the armour, the banners and the painted devices which were familiar to them?

The Saracens return from their fraud disabused

The outwitted Saracens returned from their scheme and thenceforth began to deal more patiently with the king of the French. They therefore allowed him to be served with food and drink by his loyal followers, who had been made prisoner with him, as he had humbly requested, for he was afraid that he might be infected with poison according to Saracen custom. He was held by them for a month or more, during which time the king was frequently asked by the Saracens, with terrible threats, to give back Damietta; but he would on no account do this. They then demanded the payment of the sum of money in full or else he would be put to an ignominious death by means of protracted tortures, or he would be presented to the caliph, never to return and without hope of ransom, to the confusion of the Christian faith. The king therefore, placed in a difficult position, considering that he could in no way escape from their hands nor hold on to Damietta nor save it from reduction by a hostile siege, – for who could rescue it or that country by force of arms? – in the hope of somehow ameliorating his condition, replied as follows. "We Westerners do not abound in gold as you do in the East, nor do we use pounds in our reckonings. Therefore, alter the gold to silver and the pounds to marks and, after the restitution of prisoners on both sides, let me be taken to Acre under your safe-conduct, and let those remaining in Damietta, unharmed in their persons and with their arms, be taken by your people to a place of safety. Thus, though I say it with a heavy heart, I will surrender Damietta, if I can persuade those within to agree."

Since these terms, together with a ten-year truce, were acceptable to the sultan, the king sent four of his knights together with some Saracen leaders, with letters and secret tokens, to the legate and the duke and others, who were the leading men in the city, informing and persuading them that they must surrender Damietta to the Saracens on the prescribed terms. When the royal messengers arrived at the gates of the city in company with the above-mentioned Saracens and made known their instructions, the Christian magnates, indescribably sorrowful, were for a long time in doubt about what they should do. For they were very much afraid of the enemy's tricks, namely that, having surrendered Damietta, they would find that the king and his companions had been poisoned and that they would live for a short time [only]. For they were aware of this kind of Saracen treachery. But after they had ascertained from the king's messengers that the king had received neither food nor drink from any Saracen hands, the guards of the city, at the request of the legate, the queen, and other friends of the king who valued his life, having received security for the king's safe-conduct to Acre, and for their own and the sailors' release, handed over the keys of the city, alas! not without cruel grief. When the people heard of this, in the excess of grief and anger, they destroyed what remained of the victuals belonging to the king and others, against the terms agreed on, breaking open the casks of oil and wine and burning or throwing away the corn, barley and salted meats. They were overcome with grief at the thought that the enemies of the faith might fatten themselves on the stores that they had conserved throughout a long period of famine, and preferred that they should never fall into their hands.

The Christians in Damietta are beheaded

When the sultan, having sent the king under safe-conduct to Acre, took possession of the city of Damietta, he found it wholly destitute of every kind of provision, the containers in which the food was stored having been smashed. He therefore ordered the Christian common people whom he found there to be beheaded, for the nobles had escaped, and he regretted that he had allowed the leaders, who had agreed to the terms, to go free. Moreover, he ordered the Christian fleet found there to be burnt. Besides this the Christians who had left the city in groups, intercepted by the ambuscades of the Saracens sallying forth from the mountains and valleys, were slaughtered. Fortunately the prisoners had been handed back before this happened.

The Saracens rebel against the sultan

Meanwhile the Egyptians and people from the East, hearing that the said sultan, corrupted with money, had allowed such a great king and his brothers to go free, were extremely angry and, accusing him in a hostile manner, they attacked him. Nor was he able to excuse himself on the grounds that he had recovered Damietta, for the safety of all paganism, lest the port and access to the country there be open to other Christians. They either put him to flight or killed him. This rebellion of the Saracen people against the sultan was made more serious because, out of all the money he had received both before and after the capture of the king, he had not given the agreed pay to those who had served throughout the war and who had decapitated the conquered French according to his instructions. There also arose among the principal Eastern leaders a deadly dispute and struggle over which of them should glory in possessing such great booty, but, after they were certified of the release of the king, all their anger was directed against the sultan of Babylon.

In the city [of Damietta] therefore perished Olivier de Termes with all his troops, whom we call mercenaries, and many others whom it would take a long time to enumerate, but whose names are manifestly inscribed in the book of life. The cause of this great misfortune was evidently the pride of the count of Artois who in the first place insolently opposed the humility of the Saracens when they offered a great deal for the sake of peace, as has been mentioned above. Again, so that everything would be ascribed to him, taking one third of the army with him, he secretly withdrew from the royal army. In order that we may be fully informed of this we have inserted in this volume the following letter sent to Earl Richard.

A letter sent to Earl Richard

To his respected lord R. earl of Cornwall, his chancellor J. etc. Since at times the minds of great men are wont to be wearied and tested by the reports of various rumours until the truth is known, I have thought it right to intimate to you some lugubrious and lamentable reports concerning the French army in a true and definite form although they are not published, just as I received them orally from a former clerk of mine sent to the queen of France, who did not bring letters but only credible reports as follows.

After the Purification of the blessed Mary [2 February] the king set out for Cairo, and the duke of Burgundy, the magnates' wives, the queen and many women remained in Damietta. When he tried to cross the Nile the sultan of Babylon and many Saracens opposed him in force on the opposite bank. Tents were pitched on both sides and the king assembled small boats so that he and his army could cross over them, when tied together, as if on the firmest of bridges. On the first day of Lent [9 February], the sultan himself being absent, though he had left a great number of men in his camp by the river, the said count [of Artois] and the master of the Temple with all the brothers who were there, on the advice of a certain convert, a former Saracen, were carefully instructed how to cross the river. This convert was one of the count of Artois's people, a servant of his. Lord William Longespee with his people, and many others, followed them, so that they were thought to number one third of the whole army. They all crossed the Nile and, suddenly attacking the Saracens, fought them courageously so that a big battle took place. At length, after many had been killed, namely all the Saracens they found in the open country and in the tents, and after a great slaughter of both sexes, the Christians won a glorious victory.

The count and his people were not content with this, for the count wantonly wished to advance further, namely to a certain village called Mansor which was quite near them, although the

Templars opposed and advised them against this, giving as reasons, among others, the many inconveniences caused by exhaustion and injuries both to themselves and their horses. But neither the count nor his men would on any account return and, after some mutual reproaches, coming to the said village, they boldly assaulted the enemy. Seeing this, all the Saracens who were in that village and the neighbourhood took to flight with tremendous shrieking, wailing and grief. So much so that the sultan heard the clamour and learned the facts on the very same day, for it seems that he was not far away. The Christians, however, incautiously entered the aforesaid village and, shut in there, many of them were overwhelmed by stones thrown by people remaining in ambush on the ramparts. The army, dispersed and considerably diminished, scarcely made its way out, and already began to despair.

The sultan now came up with an immense army and engaged them in a most bloody combat, and at length, God permitting, all the Christians were killed, except one wretched person who scarcely managed to make his way back. No wonder the king was grief-stricken on hearing this; eagerly he prepared with all possible speed to cross over on the said boats and other vessels, saying, "Today France must necessarily muster all its valour and put all its strength to the test." Meanwhile many Christians were failing through hunger and thirst and their exhausted and hungry horses began to weaken; and, what was more serious, grief and the recollection of the slain made the hearts of all heavy with despondency. And now adversity followed adversity, for the sultan, from whom many of the Saracens were divided in soul and body by personal hatred on account of his pride and deviousness, died suddenly at this same time. The community of Saracens at once appointed someone in his place, reportedly his son, and they allied themselves with and swore to this man as their lord. For, seeing themselves threatened with general ruin, they all joined in one body and were much more strongly united against the Christians than before.

The newly-created sultan, following the advice of the older and wiser among his people, carefully investigated the doings and plans of the Christians, while the king sent many of the Frenchmen in his army who were exhausted by illness and hunger by ship down the Nile towards Damietta, so that at least they could recover breath there in safety. The sultan, forewarned of this, had a great many boats and armed men transported in ox-carts to bar their way. A very fierce naval battle was then fought on the river, and missiles were shot to and fro like hail. But the Saracens, hurling their Greek fire, which burned many of the Christian boats, killing the people in them, triumphed. The Christians were drowned, killed or burnt and so the angry Lord annihilated them all with the sword or by hunger. One person alone escaped, an Englishman by birth, to announce the doleful event to the king, who was like Job in his afflictions.[1]

At length, on the octave of Easter [3 April], the king with his army crossed a river which, flowing from the Nile, has been given another name, Tafnis. The sultan confronted him in hostile array and battle was joined with disastrous results; for the Christian army, weakened by the distress of so much suffering and grief, succumbed, and irreparable misfortune fell upon Christ's people. The king was taken prisoner with his surviving brothers and all the rest who were not killed. And so the Christian cithara, according to the hidden judgements of God turning to sorrow, instead of its former sweet sound emitted a shocking groan. The king and the others having been thus taken prisoner, the sultan spoke with him and his people about peace and, while they were negotiating, and were still not in agreement, for the king was grieving to the point of death, the sultan fraudulently sent a large body of troops to Damietta with the oriflamme and the French devices, in order the sooner with this ruse to conquer the city and the Christians, who would know nothing of it. But, forewarned of this deceit by their disorderly advance, the Christians closed the gates and, after a conference at which the duke [of Burgundy] and others in the city opposed their demands, maintaining that they had no fear for the safety of the city for two years or more, when the Lord would advantageously provide advice and collect help to come to their assistance, and that they would not be turned aside for the sake of the life of the king, they returned to the sultan cheated of their purpose. But the king made a truce on behalf of himself and his heirs, binding himself by means of hostages to the payment of one hundred thousand marks of silver and the surrender of Damietta, and the guardians of the city having been mollified by the entreaties of the queen and other friends of the king who wanted to save his life, Damietta, alas, was restored to the enemies of Christ, to the confusion of the universal Church.

In this unfortunate battle almost all the nobles of France died,

Count John of Dreux, the flower of France, had died in Cyprus as a sad presage of future misfortune.

1. See Job 1:19.

The news is announced to Lady Blanche and published in France

Afterwards, when these disasters came to the ears of Lady Blanche and the French magnates by means of some people returning from the East, they either could not or would not believe it, but ordered the bearers of the news to be hanged; we believe them to have been manifest martyrs. At length, when they heard the news repeated by others whom they dared not call pedlars of gew-gaws, and when they saw letters on all this with unambiguous credentials, the whole of France was plunged into grief and confusion and both ecclesiastics and knights were consumed with grief and refused to be consoled. For everywhere fathers and mothers mourned the loss of their children, bereaved children and orphans that of their fathers, kinsmen that of kinsmen, and friends that of friends. The beauty of women was changed, garlands of flowers were discarded, singing was interrupted, musical instruments forbidden, and every sort of enjoyment was converted to sorrow and lamentation. And what was worse, accusing the Lord of injustice, and hysterical in heaviness of heart and enormity of grief, people blurted out blasphemous words which seemed to savour of apostasy or heresy. And the faith of many began to waver. Moreover the splendid city of Venice and many Italian cities, inhabited by semi-Christians, would have lapsed into apostasy had they not been encouraged by the consolation of the bishops and holy religious men, who truthfully asserted that the slain were now reigning as martyrs in heaven, nor would they wish to return to the vale of darkness of this world in exchange for all its riches. And so the indignation of some, but not all, was with difficulty assuaged.

The king of Castile A. takes the cross

When the most victorious king of Castile Alfonso,[1] who had already had more than thirteen confrontations with the Saracens, heard the news, he felt sorry for the French in their sufferings and took the sign

of the cross, thinking it more worthy to subjugate the Holy Land to
Christ than any other country.

1. Matthew Paris is wrong here and in the heading: Ferdinand III was the king in
   question. Both heading and paragraph are in the margin in B; Alfonso did not
   succeed to the Castilian throne until 1252.

A complaint about the extortion of money

Such therefore, are the fruits produced by the rapines and slaughter
practised by the magnates on the all-suffering poor with the permission, or rather by the teaching, of the Roman church, in order to fill
their purses whenever they set out on a pilgrimage to fight for God. It
emerges as clear as daylight from the above how displeasing to God this
way of obtaining money is which derives from the oppression and
impoverishment of the poor.

An example of the infamous extortions
in the kingdom of the French

Although some of the extortions of money practised throughout the
kingdom of the French are unmentionable and worthy of eternal
silence, yet we have thought it right to insert one example on this page.
It is known that the lord king of the French, with the permission of the
Roman church, had defrauded the French church of a tenth for three
years, on condition that the pope could afterwards extort the same
amount from the same, in order to combat Frederick more effectively.
However, after the first three-year tenth had been collected, namely his
own, the king of the French, forewarned, countered the skill of this
manifold extortioner by flatly refusing to allow the pope to gather his
grapes and alleging, as the reason, that he could in no way allow the
church of his kingdom to be impoverished for a war against Christians.
He could indeed tolerate it with more equanimity for a war against
unbelievers, waged rather by a layman than a priest. Besides, if the
French church was preyed on for another three years ensuing, it would
suffer irreparable damage which the pope would not care about. He
extorted the above-mentioned money by means of some papal officials,
so that he could raise it the more effectually and so that he would know
with more certainty to what sum the papal share would amount, when
collected. Because of this the hearts of many became heavy with grief

and they cursed and prayed that the saying of Isaiah, or rather God, might be verified, who thus far has always "hated robbery for burnt-offering".[1]

Would that the lord king of the English and his brother Earl Richard and other crusading princes intent on obtaining filthy lucre would weigh these things in the scales of reason. For although the act of holy pilgrimage is agreed to be pious, yet travelling expenses acquired dishonourably defile the performance of the pious deed. This is thought to have been the cause of the above-described disaster, though doubtless there were others.

Of the extortionate deeds practised in France we think it right to record one, because it was most shameful. The above-mentioned papal exactor happened to meet a poor cleric coming from town carrying water in a small container, with a sprinkler, and some pieces of bread that he had been given for sprinkling some holy water. The Roman trickster said to him, "What is this benefice given you by the Church worth annually?" To whom the cleric, ignorant of the snares of the Romans, replied, "As I estimate, up to twenty shillings". And the Roman, declaring himself, said, "This, therefore yields twenty-four pence per annum to the use of the fisc, namely two shillings". And he choked the wretched door-to-door beggar with the words "Pay the king what you owe him." To pay this small sum and to prolong his half-starved and wretched existence the poor man was forced to give lessons for a long period, having sold his books in the parvis.

1. Isaiah 61:8.

Concerning the magnanimity of Countess Ela, abbess of Lacock

When the aforesaid disaster came to the ears of the pope he was extremely sorry, and so was the entire community of the Roman curia. Bulls were suspended for some days, and the pope's disgrace increased and was broadcast in no small degree. Among the complaints of the French this sort of talk was heard: "Alas! Alas! How much evil has the pope's pride brought upon us, which so wantonly opposed the humbled Frederick, and would not accept due satisfaction from him, but rather provoked him to bitterness of spirit. Truly [the sultan] benignly offered to hand back to us whatever possessions the Christians had at any time held in the Holy Land. Alas! How much noble and generous Christian blood is being shed to no purpose in the Holy Land, in Germany, and in Italy! And what is more damaging, faith is tottering and the Holy Land is open to danger, the

Christian religion is waning, and pagan superstition is on the increase. Under how unlucky a star must [the pope] have been born, since so many disasters have occurred in his time in the Church of our Lord Jesus Christ, whose vicar he declares himself to be!

When news of this great calamity reached the ears of the abbess and countess [of Salisbury] Ela, who, not at all effeminately, ruled the convent of religious ladies at Lacock, and who was the mother of the magnanimous William Longespee, she, remembering the glorious vision she had seen of her son at the time when, as mentioned above, he had died a manifest martyr, enthusiastically clasped her hands, knelt down and held forth as follows in praise of God, which was highly pleasing to Christ. "My Lord Jesus Christ, I give thee thanks that you have wished such a son to be procreated from my body, unworthy sinner that I am, whom you have deigned to adorn with the crown of such manifest martyrdom. I certainly hope that, with his help, I shall speedily be promoted to the heights of the heavenly kingdom". When those who brought these reports, who had for a long time kept silent through fear, saw and heard this, praising the more than womanly steadfastness of this woman, they wondered at her matronly and maternal piety which did not express itself in words of querulous lament but rather exulted cheerfully in spiritual joy.

Concerning the deaths of some nobles

In the course of this woeful year some very illustrious men died, earls and marquises, bishops and knights, in the above-described pilgrimage, some at sea, some on islands, and some drowned. One was the bishop of Noyon [Peter Charlot]. His name and the names of the others are manifestly inscribed in the book of everlasting life. In the same year around the feast of St. Margaret [20 July] died Robert de Muschamp, a man of great repute in the northern parts of England. In the same days died Henry Hastings, an excellent knight and rich baron.

The Saracens prepare to besiege Acre

During these same days the Saracens, seeing that the fortunes of war were prospering in their hands, both because of the booty, horses, arms, ballistas and other engines, ships and provisions, which their defeated enemies had enjoyed in abundance, as well as because of the boldness they now experienced, the recent defeat of the Christians and the abandonment of the truces, made preparations to lay siege to Acre.

They very much regretted that they had allowed the king of the French and his surviving brothers either to be ransomed or to depart after they had been ransomed, even if the money had been doubled. The blame for this they heaped on the sultan of Babylon, detesting his greed, and they firmly believed that they would recover what they had lost, and again ensnare the king and his brothers.

The king of the French sends his brothers back to France

Considering all this, the pious king of the French, after he had paid the aforesaid sum of money in full, which he had obtained as a loan from the Templars, Hospitallers, Genoese and Pisans, and recovered the hostages, wisely sent his two surviving brothers, namely Alphonse, count of Poitou, and Charles, count of Provence, secretly and suddenly in a sound ship back to the West. With God's guidance and protection they reached the kingdom of France safe and sound. But the king remained sad and inglorious in Acre, swearing with the utmost heaviness of heart that he would never return to sweet France in such disgrace. For who without sobs and tears can describe his sobs and tears as, with his third brother dead, namely R., and himself defeated, he entrusted the other two, also inglorious, to Neptune's billows? These counts, together with the duke of Burgundy, who was with them, went at once to the pope as the king had instructed them, arguing effectively, rather than weakly requesting, that speedy aid should be sent to the king, who was in such danger and was fighting for the honour of the universal Church, and that, recalling the humiliated Frederick, who alone among all Christians could relieve them in such perils, to the peace of the Church, he should persuade him quickly to organise adequate help for the king, now almost desperate. Otherwise, the said duke and counts would remove the lord pope from his seat at Lyons as obstinate in his hatred and caring nothing for the honour of the Christian faith. And if the bishop-elect of Lyons [Philip of Savoy] and his brother the archbishop of Canterbury, whom he relied on, defended him, all France, led by the aforesaid magnates, would rise against them.

Concerning an unusual flood and rough sea

In the course of this same time, namely in the month of October, the moon being in its first quarter, on the first day of the month the new moon appeared swollen and reddish in presage of future storms, as the experimental writings of the philosopher and poet say: "A reddish new moon usually portends winds, unless extreme heat or cold prevents this; an inflated one, rain, but a pale bright one means fair weather." Daily in the first week of the waxing moon the air began to be much disturbed by dense mist and violent winds. The winds began to tear off the branches and the leaves which were then withering on the trees and carry them a great distance through the air. And what was more damaging, the rough sea, rising above its usual level and the tide flowing twice in succession without any ebb, made such a horrible roaring noise that it resounded in places remote from it, to the amazement of the hearers, even old ones. No one living now could remember seeing this before. In the darkness of night the sea seemed to burn as if set on fire and waves joined with waves as if in battle, so that the dexterity of the sailors could not come to the aid of their doomed ships. Even large and strongly-built vessels foundered and sank. And if we remain silent concerning others, at one single port, namely Hartburn, besides small and medium-sized boats, three fine ones were swallowed by rough seas. At an eastern port called Winchelsea, apart from sheds for salt-making, fishermen's buildings, bridges and mills, more than three hundred houses and several churches were destroyed in that place by the violent rise of the sea. Holland in England and Holland overseas, with Flanders and other low-lying places near the sea, suffered irreparable damage. Rivers flowing into the sea were forced back and overflowed, so that meadows, mills, and the neighbouring houses were destroyed, and the corn not yet stored in the barns was swept away from the flooded fields. So the anger of God was made clearly apparent to mortals both at sea and on the land and the punishment of sinners seemed imminent, as the prophecy of Habakkuk says: "Was the lord displeased against the rivers? Was thine anger against the rivers? Was thy wrath against the sea?"[1] And what wonder? For from the Roman curia, which is supposed to be the fount of all justice, unmentionable enormities emanated, one of which, though unfit to be described, we have thought it right to insert on this page.

1. Habakkuk 3:8.

A certain detestable exaction from Binham Priory

Although the prior of Binham had plenary rights over the church of Westley [Waterless], to be had for his own use, both by the collation of the patron and through the confirmation of two bishops and their chapters, as well as by grant of three pontiffs of the Roman church, namely Lucius, Eugenius and Gregory IX, a certain Genoese, illegitimate and illiterate, has obtained the following letter from the lord pope, against justice and piety.

Innocent bishop etc. to his well-loved son Master Berard de Nimpha, our secretary staying in England, greetings and apostolic benediction. Our well-loved son and chamberlain N. formerly gave the church of Westley in the diocese of Ely to Reiner de Solerio, provost of Ypres, who recently went the way of all flesh. This church belonged to the presentation of our well-loved sons the prior and convent of Binham of the order of St. Benedict; the said provost held this living in England during his lifetime. We have thought fit to bestow it, on our authority, on our well-loved son and clerk Herrigettus, son of the noble Perrino de Malachena de Volta, citizen of Genoa, declaring null and void anything that may be attempted contrary to his collation. We, ratifying whatever has been done in this matter by our aforesaid chamberlain, order you by these apostolic letters to arrange for the induction of the proctor of the said H., or any other person you like in his name, into possession of the said church and to protect him once he has been inducted, removing from it anyone trying to detain it, postponing any appeal, and restraining any opponents with ecclesiastical censure; notwithstanding the indulgence by which the English are assured that when an Italian cleric dies or resigns his benefice another Italian may not obtain possession of it at once, and notwithstanding any other indulgences which ought to have been mentioned in these presents or by means of which this collation or assignation could be impeded or delayed; notwithstanding, too, the constitution "Concerning two days' journey" promulgated by the general council.[1]

Given at Lyons, the third of the kalends of May [29 April], in the seventh year of our pontificate [1250].

1. Article 37 of the Constitutions of the Fourth Lateran Council, 1215, prohibits the obtaining of papal letters which would have the effect of compelling a litigant to travel more than two days' journey out of his diocese for judgement; see Mansi 1778: col. 1023.

How the archbishop of Canterbury undermined the resolve of some complainers

During these days too the archbishop of Canterbury, who had a guilty conscience because of the gross offence he had perpetrated in London, mainly in St. Bartholomew's church, as has been mentioned above, secretly sent messengers with threats and blandishments from the king, the queen and himself, and managed to suppress the complaints of the canons.

Concerning the death of William [Raleigh] bishop of Winchester

In the same year around the feast of St. Matthew [21 September] Bishop W. of Winchester died at Tours. In order to save expenses, he had stayed there about eleven months with a reduced household, for his bishopric was saddled with inestimable debts to the pope, which had been growing since the time the lord king, by persecuting him, drove him out of England. As has been mentioned above, the lord pope, after being richly remunerated, opened the bosom of consolation to him. So, having made his peace with the pope and got round the king, he cut back the normal expenses of his table and the number of his household personnel in order the sooner to collect the money agreed on to release his church from debt. When he was on the point of death and saw the viaticum of salvation being brought to him, he said, as the priest came through the door carrying the eucharist, "Wait my friend, it is proper that I, as a traitor to and disparager of my God, should go to meet him". Then, carried by his attendants before the body of Christ, he received the viaticum of salvation with tears and contrition. And so he breathed out his contrite soul in fear of God.

How much trouble the king took to replace him with his brother

When the lord king heard this, with dry tears and some brief and quite cheerful laments, he immediately did all he could to substitute in his place his brother Aethelmar, though he was insufficient as regards holy orders, age and knowledge. He therefore at once sent to Winchester two of his special clerks, whom he knew to be extremely clever at all kinds of persuasion, with his letters, to incline the minds of all the monks of the cathedral church, to whom the right of election belonged, with all kinds of blandishments, threats and promises, to postulate this Aethelmar as their bishop and pastor of their souls. The clerks sent for this purpose were John Mansel and Peter Chaceporc. They did their utmost to carry the king's wishes into effect, and weakened the resolve of many of the monks so that they postulated the said A. as their bishop. I say 'postulated' because he was in every way insufficient and unsuitable for the episcopal dignity. After about fifteen days, during which time the said clerks daily used their best endeavours to win over those members of the convent who seemed to be more inclined to the will of their terrestrial king, having laid aside fear of the celestial one, the king himself came to Winchester and, going straight to St. Swithin's church, that is the cathedral, entered the chapter just like a bishop or a prior and, taking the seat of the presiding prelate, began the following speech on the theme "Righteousness and peace have kissed each other".[1]

The speech of the king, in the form of a sermon, in the chapter at Winchester

To me and other kings, and to princes and to our justiciars, whose job it is, with the help of justice, to rule peoples, belongs the vigour of judgement and of justice. To you, however, who are men of peace and students of religion, belong peace and tranquility. Today, because, as I hear, you have happily shown yourselves favourable to my petition, which is just as well for you, "Righteousness and peace have kissed each other". When you were opposing me in the postulation of your late bishop William Raleigh, who was unacceptable to me, I was severe with you. Now, however, I have become well-disposed and most friendly towards you, and, remembering your kindness, shall be a most grateful bestower of favours in return. Now it is agreed that ruin was first introduced into the world by a woman, and the remedy also found by a woman. Likewise in the present case, in order that I might satisfy my wife the queen when she wanted to promote her uncle William, elect of Valence, to this bishopric, I disquieted you with my entreaties and in disquieting you I harmed you. Now, however, that I definitely wish to promote my uterine brother who, because of a woman, namely our mother Queen Isabella, is indubitably related to me by blood as a brother, I will be reconciled to you. I will effectively support you and your church, and I will embrace you with the arms of friendship. Besides, you ought to weigh in the scales of reason the by no means unimportant fact that I was born in this city and baptized in this church; because of this you are bound to me with ties of greater affection, nor ought you in any way to oppose my wishes, but rather support me promptly in everything. Another reason for your grateful assent is that my brother A., if he is postulated, will we hope for a long time illuminate this church, like the sun, with the rays of his regal generosity, which distinguishes him on his mother's side, his illustrious blood, which prevails on his father's side, and his very likeable kindness and youth, with which he pleases both God and man. So, go in peace and, having discussed the matter, return soon without any hint of opposition and, according to our pious proposition concerning which you have led me to be hopeful, happily and publicly in front of me and all nominate my brother A. by common assent your elect or postulant.

At the end of the speech he added that, if he found these monks opposed to his persuasions, he would forthwith ruin them all. As the poet says, "The man in power begs with a drawn sword".[2]

1. Psalm 85:10.
2. See Luard 1874:xxxii.

How the Winchester monks are forced to postulate Aethelmar as their bishop

The hard-pressed monks withdrew to confer attentively about this and, recalling to mind the serious troubles they had formerly endured because of William, elect of Valence, and the more serious ones over the postulation of their recently deceased bishop William, reflected as follows.

Look at these armed entreaties of our lord the king! It would be a serious and most formidable matter to oppose them, and dangerous to our church. The pope is complying with the king in everything and, because he is in a difficult position, he is afraid of and avoids offending princes. So, if we were to elect or postulate some suitable person other than his brother, the king would be provoked to anger, or rather fury. Even if we agreed on St. Peter if he were alive, he would annul our proceedings and persecute us. Thus we should have the king as a powerful enemy here and the pope, who is easily corruptible, there; and, crushed as if between two mill stones, our confusion and irreparable ruin would be imminent. Besides, after we had postulated Bishop William of Norwich for promotion to be our bishop and put our necks under his yoke, against the wishes of the king, who consistently opposed this and persecuted us for it, the same W., having obtained full power, although he was a native and expert in the laws of the land, and someone we hoped would be in every respect pleasing to God and beneficial to us, mercilessly persecuted and irreparably damaged us, forgetful of the favours he had received and the innumerable injuries we had put up with for his sake. For we were imprisoned, dragged about, and flogged. We were starved, wounded and fettered like thieves. Who can we rely on? In whom can we place our hopes? Who is there to save us? We are afraid that Scylla is imminent on one side and Charybdis on the other. If we do this, our death-warrant is signed; if not, we shall still not escape the king's clutches. Besides all this, what deservedly ought to scare us is that, if we promote the said A. to the bishopric, he will always be a bishop-elect, not a bishop, which has never happened to this church before, and it would be better if it never did happen. Also, he may well get permission from the pope to retain, as bishop-elect, the innumerable revenues he now possesses. What indeed can someone with money to spend not obtain and possess nowadays in the Roman curia? If this happens he will be second to none in England in wealth and power except possibly the king. Then he will be able, if he wants — unless as we hope he does not take after his father or the Poitevins — to take the whole of England to Poitou, or like an all-powerful door-keeper of the kingdom, bring Poitou to England; thus he will delete the memory of the English from the face of the earth.

At last, after the many difficulties which entangled them, seeing that they had fallen on evil days, and that no refuge lay open to them in the bosom of our father the pope who usually supports people who flee to him "turned aside like a deceitful bow",[1] they were forced to incline to the king's wishes.

1. Psalm 78:57.

They consent

With common accord therefore, but not unanimous at heart, the Winchester monks, overcome by the king's importunity and despairing of help from the pope, postulated Aethelmar, the uterine brother of the king, as their bishop and spiritual pastor of their souls. Born in Poitou, his father was Hugh de Brun, count of La Marche, and his mother that count's wife Isabella, former queen of England. Although he abounded in innumerable annual revenues, sufficient for an archbishopric, he was inadequate in age, knowledge and holy orders. And so in the king's presence they solemnly and publicly nominated A. as their bishop-elect or postulant, on condition that such a person could be promoted to the episcopal dignity by means of a dispensation of the lord pope.

In pursuit of his wishes the happy king sends solemn messengers to Rome

The king therefore, demonstrating his joy in looks, gestures and elated voice, ordered his clerk Robert de Sothindon, who was skilled in rhetoric, to compose a most elegant and effective letter for despatch to the lord pope, in which he was to mingle urgent entreaties, terrible threats and numerous promises. Then the lord king sent solemn and eloquent messengers to the Roman curia, who well knew how to bend both pope and cardinals to their purpose, to discuss this arduous affair, which the king had so much at heart, with the pope and to do their best with entreaties and bribes to persuade him to agree.

A plaintive pronouncement

Alas! Why should the languor of the world be any further prolonged? Where have peace and justice, from which the king took the text for his speech and sermon, been exiled to? Where is free election, the peace of the Church, which the king at his original coronation swore inviolably to maintain? Now alas! the natural subjects of the kingdom, holy, educated and religious men, are despised, and foreigners are intruded, unworthy of any honour, totally ignorant of letters and of the English language, altogether useless for confessions and preaching, neither well-disciplined nor well-behaved, extorters of money and disdainers of souls. Once upon a time holy men, religious and learned, were dragged, through the collaboration and revelations of the Holy Spirit, even against their will, to the bishop's thrones which, legally or illegally, courtiers, officials or barbarians now occupy. All the religious houses to which the right of episcopal election belongs are being destroyed because of this. Patronage is now a burden not an honour, harmful not beneficial. All the churches, both episcopal and conventual, when, on becoming vacant, they fall into the king's hands, which ought without fail to defend and protect them, lie open to pillage and robbery. Oh pope! father of fathers, who do you allow Christian regions to be polluted in such a way? Deservedly therefore, deservedly, were you forced to exile yourself as a fugitive and other Cain expelled from your proper city and see. Your Frederickite enemies are prospering; you fly from your pursuers and "they that pursue you"[1] are swift and powerful. On all sides your bull fulminates against your subjects, but it has become worthless against your opponents. On all sides prelates are suspended from the collation to benefices and provisions are ordered to be made for unworthy and unknown persons and barbarians, who, seeking the milk from the sheep of the Lord's fold, shear and scrape their fleeces, and flay and eviscerate them. Nor can privileges granted by pious fathers be of any help to anyone. Among other nations and regions England, where, as the world knows, the Christian faith flourishes more, is the more basely trampled on and despoiled by the overbearing pope of its goods and the fruits of its labours. Though he plunders everyone, no one plunders him. For where is any Englishman known to have revenues round about Rome, Italy, Genoa or in other kingdoms? Yet people from there are carrying off everything in England. Oh God, Lord of vengeance! When will you sharpen your sword like lightning to steep it in the blood of such people? Certainly our sins have brought such hardships deservedly upon us.

1. Isaiah 30:16.

The bishop of Rochester died. Master Laurence of St. Martin is elected

At the same time of the year, namely about the feast of St. Michael [29 September], the bishop of Rochester [Richard Wendene] died and the Rochester monks elected in his place Master Laurence of St. Martin, a clerk and special councillor of the lord king, lest, if by chance they had elected someone else, the king would have opposed the election.

The bishop of Lincoln returns from the Roman curia

At about the same feast, namely of St. Michael, Bishop Robert of Lincoln, after he had been at the Roman curia for some time at the cost of much useless expenditure and had been unsuccessful in bringing his purpose into effect, returned sad and empty-handed to England. He had, however, harassed and in no small way harmed many religious people who had to defend themselves against his aggression. When he had returned to his bishopric, seeing cause for the confusion of the universal Church approaching near at hand and instructed by the example of Bishop Nicholas of Durham, he turned his back on worldly affairs, in which he had often been entangled to no advantage, so that he could devote himself more freely to contemplation, prayer and study. Proposing to say farewell to this perishable world and to resign his bishopric, he entrusted the care of the administration of his office to his official, Master Robert de Marisco. But, fearing royal rapine, which usually impoverished vacant churches and then intruded unworthy persons into them, he put off his secret intention, delaying while he waited anxiously, not knowing what to do in such a crisis in the affairs of the world.

The bishops of England provide for themselves against the archbishop of Canterbury

Meanwhile the bishops of England, learning from the report of the said bishop, recently back from the Roman curia, and from others, their proctors and spies, whom they had sent there, that the archbishop of Canterbury was making preparations to ensnare them harmfully, collected money to lavish in payments at the Roman curia, which, like "a reed shaken with the wind",[1] was habitually bent first one way and then the other according to the money proffered. So they took two pence per mark from every beneficed person; for what the aforesaid exactor demanded was a great deal, namely visitation and procuration taxes from all the clergy and people in his province, which was large. This troubled everyone the more because it was clear that the said archbishop, morally and intellectually lacking, was undoubtedly intent on this visitation not for the benefit of religion or the reformation of morals, but for the sake of filthy lucre, now a habit with him.

1. Matthew 11:7.

Concerning an earthquake in the Chilterns

In the same year, actually on St. Lucy's day [13 December] about the third hour, an earthquake occurred at St. Albans and neighbouring parts, which are called Ciltria, where from time immemorial no such event had been seen or heard of. For the land there is solid and chalky, not at all cavernous, watery or near the sea, so that such an occurrence was unusual and unnatural and the more to be wondered at. This earthquake, if it had been as damaging as it was unusual and astonishing, would have severely shaken every building. Accompanying the movement and tremor there was a terrifying noise like thunder underground, and during the earthquake a remarkable thing happened; the pigeons, jackdaws, sparrows and other birds, which were perching quietly on the houses or the branches of trees, as if terrified by a sparrowhawk swooping over, suddenly took wing like missiles and flew to and fro in confusion, coming and going away, to the fear and horror of spectators. But after this earthquake with its noise had subsided, they returned to their usual nests, which the earthquake had disturbed. This earthquake struck horror into the hearts of all, more, I think, than amazement or fear, and is believed to have been indicative of future events.

Thus, in this year unusual and dreadful disturbances were experienced, both by land and sea, which imminently threatened the end of the world. As the gospel menaces, "there shall be earthquakes in divers places."[1]

1. Matthew 24:7. The heading and paragraph which follow have been erased in B and are taken from the margin of C.

The archbishop prudently curbed the frightful clamour of the canons of St. Bartholomew's

The archbishop of Canterbury, realising that the sulphureous stench of infamy and scandal arising from the outrageous deed he had perpetrated at London in the church of the canons of St. Bartholomew had infected the whole extent of the kingdom, carefully sent messengers to suppress their complaints with blandishments and promises, mixed with threats. They therefore, both because they were poor, and because the archbishop was powerful enough to justify himself even though he was clearly blameworthy, held their peace and, possessing their souls in patience,[1] commended their cause to God and the blessed Bartholomew.

1. Compare Luke 21:19.

The lord pope wants to sojourn at Bordeaux

At this same time, having sent solemn messengers, the lord pope asked the lord king of England to allow him at least to stay for a time in his city of Bordeaux in Gascony. For the brothers of the lord king of France had spoken peremptorily to him, requesting him on behalf of the said king and themselves to make peace with Frederick, who had been humiliated and had humbly offered satisfaction to the Church, if he valued the honour of the universal Church. The said brothers of the king, namely the counts of Poitou and Provence, put it to the pope that the whole of the above-described misfortune was due to papal avarice. For he the pope, corrupted by money, had prevented the crusaders from going to the help of the king, and he had absolved from their vows of pilgrimage those who had taken the cross a short time before at the hands of the Preachers and Minors he had sent. Moreover, he sold the crusaders to Earl Richard and other magnates, just as the Jews of old used to sell sheep and doves in the Temple, whom, we read in the gospel, God punished by angrily expelling. The pope showed himself to be obdurate and inexorable in the face of these persuasions, so that he and the said counts parted from one another with harsh and contentious words. The counts hastened to England to persuade the lord king of the English, if he wished to honour Christ, to make all speed, according to his vow, to come to the help of the French king, who desired and expected his presence.

The king of England's perplexity

The king of England was placed in a position of some difficulty. If he closed the roads against the pope, the pope would be offended and would certainly not promote his brother A. If he opened the bosom of protection to him he would provoke Frederick to anger, and he had of necessity to pass through his territories when he went on crusade. Nor would this please the French. Moreover, what very much frightened the more prudent of the English was that, if the pope was allowed to reside in Bordeaux, he would in a short time sail to England and injure, and it was feared, defile, that country with his presence. For those who believed the country was being corrupted by the usuries of his Cahorsins feared that it would be polluted all the more by his curia, if he was present, which God forbid! Hence the royal council over this was more readily deferred.

Papal letters sent to the abbots of St. Albans and Waltham and the archdeacon of St. Albans

During the same days, namely in Advent, the lord pope let the abbots of St. Albans and Waltham and the archdeacon of St. Albans know that the sentence promulgated by Archbishop B. of Canterbury against Henry, dean of London, Peter the archdeacon, Robert the precentor of London, Master William of Lichfield, William Leafete and other canons of London, because of an offence of their chapter, was wholly null and void. Nonetheless the said archbishop persisted in the Roman curia in his demand for visitation taxes and procurations from those visited, and that all the more urgently and confidently, because the bishop of Lincoln, who was known to be a lesser man than he, had obtained a few years previously from the pope permission to visit his own canons of the church of Lincoln, though they were extremely reluctant and uselessly expended a great deal of money in their defence. The letters on this, that is the letters of annulment, are fully transcribed in the *Book of additamenta*.[1]

---

1. BL Cotton MS. Nero D 1, f101 = Luard 1882:197–200. The heading and paragraph which follow are in the margin of B; below is the imperial shield, inverted. Frederick's will was copied out in the 1251 annal of the *Chronica majora* (Luard 1880:216–7) as well as into the *Book of additamenta*, BL Cotton MS. Nero D 1, f.102b.

Concerning the death of Frederick

About the same time died Frederick, the greatest of the princes of the earth, wonder of the world and admirable innovator, absolved from the sentence in which he was entangled, having assumed, it is said, the habit of the Cistercians, and amazingly contrite and humbled. He died on St. Lucy's day [13 December], so it seems that the earthquake on that day did not happen without significance or purpose. With his death, French hopes for the succour of their king were extinguished. He composed a noble will, by which he made good the losses he had caused to the Church. His death was kept secret for some days lest his enemies should exult the sooner, but it was made publicly known on St. Stepehen's day [26 December] and announced to the people. His most excellent will is copied into the *Book of additamenta* at this sign. . . .

*At the end of this year twenty-five half-centuries
have been completed since the time of grace.
The singular events of this half century*

This year having been completed, there have now elapsed since the time
of grace twenty-five half-centuries, which is one thousand two hundred
and fifty years. It should also be noted, and not considered trivial, that in
none of these half-centuries, namely the first twenty-four, have so many
singular and unusual novelties occurred, as in this last one, namely the
twenty-fifth, which has now elapsed. There are some, indeed many,
writers and careful investigators of histories who say that in all the other
half-centuries not so many prodigies and amazing novelties were seen as
in this one now ended. Greater events than these are now expected with
fear.

Note the wonderful events

In this half-century the Tartars, leaving their settlements, ravaged many
Christian and infidel regions of the East with deadly destruction. The
emir Murmelin, a most powerful ruler of the Africans and Spanish, was
defeated and took to flight and his whole army dispersed. When Master
Oliver was preaching in parts of Germany the crucified Christ appeared
manifestly to everyone in the sky. The Greek church withdrew from
subjection to the Roman church because of its various enormities, most
notably its usury, simony, sales of justice and other intolerable evils.
Damietta, a most celebrated town in Egypt, was twice taken and twice
lost, with much effusion of blood, both Christian and Saracen.

England lay under interdict for about seven years and the kingdom of
England suffered civil war for almost the same length of time. It became
tributary. The king of the English, John, in fulfilment of certain
prophecies,[1] when he died possessed no land in peace, so he was called
'the exile'. Judgement by ordeal with water and fire was forbidden. One
person was allowed to enjoy the proceeds of several bishoprics and to
retain the revenues he was already receiving. Saints Thomas the Martyr
in England and Edmund the Confessor in France, were translated. St.
Elizabeth, daughter of the king of Hungary, flourished in Germany.[2]
People were forbidden and afterwards, against a cash payment, allowed
to have several churches, and bastards were legitimized.

Louis, eldest son and legitimate heir of the king of the French was
elected lord and virtual king of England; soon afterwards, because he
broke his faith, he withdrew ingloriously. The Roman emperor Otto,

persecuted by Pope Innocent III, suffered pitiful ruin, conquered in battle, excommunicated and deposed. The brethren of the Temple, the Hospital, the Teutonic Knights of St. Mary and St. Lazarus were twice captured, killed and dispersed; and the holy city of Jerusalem with its holy churches and places consecrated by the presence of Christ, was twice destroyed. On the last occasion it was wretchedly razed to the ground by the Khorasmians and more wretchedly exterminated by the sultan of Babylon.

An eclipse of the sun occurred twice in three years; and another remarkable portent appeared in the sky, as is clearly described in this book, in the year of grace 1233.[3] Earthquakes occurred several times in England and also in the Chilterns. In the region of Savoy five villages with their churches, houses and inhabitants were overwhelmed by the mountain masses. There was an unusual and damaging rise of the sea, such as was never seen before. One night an infinite number of stars were seen to fall from the sky, so that at one and the same time ten or twelve could be seen flying, some in the east, some in the west, in the south, in the north, and in the middle of the firmament. If these had been the real stars, not a single one would have been left in the sky. No apparent reason for this can be found in the *Book of meteors*; but Christ's menace was threatening mankind, "And there shall be signs in the sun."[4]

A general council was held twice, at Rome and at Lyons; in the second, Frederick, emperor of the Romans, was deposed. At sea not far from Genoa Cardinal Otto was captured, one-time legate in England, with a great many archbishops, bishops, abbots, prelates and Genoese; he was taken prisoner, many were drowned.

Wales, having lost its prince Llywelyn and his two sons, who succumbed to a premature death, inclined towards the laws of England and the rule of its king. Gascony also was recalcitrant, but was subdued by Earl Simon of Leicester. King Henry III crossed the sea twice with an army to win back his overseas rights with armed force, especially Normandy, which his father had forfeited by judgement of the twelve peers of France as the murderer of his nephew Arthur, and twice returned inglorious, poor, and confused. A great part of Spain, with very many of its fine cities, namely Cordoba, Seville, Peñiscola and many others, and certain islands, namely Majorca and Minorca, and many coastal places, was conquered by the most victorious king [Ferdinand III] of Castile and surrendered to Christianity. In the north a great part of Frisia, and Russia to the extent of a twelve-day journey, was conquered by Waldemar [II] king of Denmark, so that seven bishoprics there were acquired for Christ.

The pope, like an exile expelled from the city, or as a fugitive, or someone in hiding, stayed at Anagni and Perugia, persecuted by the emperor F., who accused him of trying to seize the Empire while he was fighting for God in the Holy Land. The Templars, too, on the pretext of papal hatred [for Frederick], tried to hand him over to the sultan of Babylon. After Pope Gregory's death the papal seat was vacant for a year and nine months; three apostolic men sat on it in the space of two years. And one of the cardinals, more distinguished than them all, English by birth, namely Master Robert de Sumercote, whom the others feared would be elected pope, died, it is said suffocated because of envy, in the palace called Regia Solis, while the election was being discussed. At length Cardinal Senebald was elected as Innocent IV and, following his predecessor's footsteps, he excommunicated the emperor. Fleeing from place to place to avoid persecution, at last he came to Lyons where he held a general council and deposed the emperor F. Then, having shamelessly extorted a huge sum of money from the prelates of the Church, he tried to promote the landgrave of Thuringia, and afterwards William count of Holland, to the imperial throne; but the one died, the other was defeated, and he made no progress in his plan.

The usurers called Cahorsins, who went under the name of Christians, found a place of refuge and peace in England. First tolerated, and then afterwards openly protected by the pope, they unblushingly called themselves merchants or money-changers of the pope. Prelates were suspended from the collation to benefices until the pope's avarice on behalf of his unworthy barbarians, who never appeared in England and never troubled about the care of souls, was satisfied.

Brothers of many orders swarmed, now Preachers, now Minors, now Cruciferi, now Carmelites. In Germany an innumerable multitude of continent women sprang up, who wanted to call themselves Beguines; so many that a thousand or more lived in Cologne alone. The Preachers indeed and the Minors at first led a life of poverty and the utmost sanctity, devoting themselves wholly to preaching, hearing confessions, divine services in church, reading and study. Embracing poverty voluntarily for God, they abandoned many revenues, keeping nothing for themselves for the morrow by way of victuals. But within a few years were stocking up carefully and erecting extremely fine buildings. Moreover, though against their will, the pope made them his tax-collectors and many-sided extortioners of money. So the time seemed to have returned which Benedict, full of the spirit of all the saints, mentions at the beginning of his rule where he treats of the families of different sorts of monk. Nor did the order either of St. Benedict or of the blessed Augustine deteriorate from the beginning of their establishment for such a length of time as now. St. Edmund archbishop of Canterbury, uncorrupted in body at Pontigny, also St. Robert the hermit at Knaresborough, St. Roger bishop of London, too, and many others in England, as well as St. Elizabeth the daughter of the king of hungary and the prophetess St. Hildegard in Germany, shone forth with remarkable miracles. The church of Westminster was rebuilt and a gold shrine of most precious workmanship was made by King Henry III for the relics of St. Edward. Some of the blood of Christ and the impression of his footstep were brought to England and deposited at Westminster as a gift from the same King Henry. The heresies of the Albigensians, the Jovinianists, and of many Italians, which had sprouted forth, were destroyed. Haakon was anointed and crowned king of Norway.

The Cistercian monks, following in the footsteps of the order of Black monks, having obtained a papal dispensation and constructed suitable buildings in Paris and elsewhere where the community of scholars flourished, took up studies lest they should be held in contempt by the Preachers and Minors. The noble see and church of Canterbury, made illustrious by the holiness of so many saintly archbishops in the past, was occupied by a totally unqualified person intruded by the king. Encouraged by the example of the bishop of Lincoln, who obtained the right of visiting his canons in spite of their opposition, he extorted the first year's revenue of vacant churches throughout his province for seven years and persecuted numerous persons.

In this last year of this forty [sic] years the Saracens triumphed at their will; the entire Christian army, alas! comprising the nobility of all France and the knights of the Temple, the Hospital, the Teutonic knights of St. Mary and the knights of St. Lazarus, was slaughtered in Egypt. There, the pious king of the French Louis was captured with his two brothers the counts of Poitou and Provence. William Longespee too, with many English nobles, was killed there and the king's brother Robert, count of Artois, fled from the battle and was drowned. The pope and the entire Roman curia, because crusaders were sold, absolved from their vows for a cash payment, and delayed in all kinds of ways, daily lost favour with both clergy and people. The whole of Christianity was troubled and the universal Church endangered by the wars which arose from the hatred and discord between the pope and Frederick. The king of England H.III took the cross with many of the country's nobles, and many Christian kings, princes, magnates and prelates took the cross. The only abbot to do so was the abbot of St. Edmunds [Edmund de Walpole]. Forgetting that, with the cowl, he had undertaken perpetually to carry the cross of Christ, he assumed the ostensible sign of the cross to the derision of many, in the king's presence and together with him, which savoured of manifest flattery.

In this most lethal year there departed to Christ an infinite number of nobles who, leaving their native country, their wives and children, their relatives and friends, fought loyally for Christ. They are established as martyrs and their names, which cannot be written in this volume because of their great number, are inscribed in indelible characters in the book of life, with the crown of martyrdom for their merits. Moreover Frederick, the wonder of the world, died on St. Lucy's day, in Apulia.[5] These remarkable events and novelties, the like of which have neither been seen nor heard of nor found in writings by any of our forefathers in past times, all happened during this last period of forty [sic] years.

Here end the chronicles of Brother Matthew Paris, monk of St. Albans, which he has committed to writing for the benefit of posterity, for the love of God and in honour of the blessed Alban, protomartyr of the English, lest the memory of present-day events be destroyed by age or oblivion.[6]

From the incarnation of the Lord twenty-five half-centuries have elapsed. Nor does it seem that Easter has fallen on its own day, namely the sixth of the kalends of April [27 March], in any jubilee year, namely the fiftieth, except in this last year.

1. From here to "against a cash payment" the text is rewritten on an attached slip of parchment. The passage originally continued from this point as follows: ". . . died having no land. It was indeed predicted by one person that he would die in exile, by another that, from the following Ascension day next after this was said, he would no longer be king."
2. This sentence is in the margin of B and is not in C.
3. Luard 1876:242.
4. Luke 21:25.
5. This sentence is written over an erasure. See Vaughan 1958b: 60–1.
6. Six lines in verse follow, which I have omitted; their tenor is repeated in the paragraph next following.

Here end the marvels of the twenty-fifth half-century

> Matthew's chronicle here ends
> And the jubilee year sends
> Repose down from the skies.
> May repose to him be given
> Here on earth and up in heaven
> When he there shall rise.[1]

It is thought to be not without significance that in this last year all the elements suffered unusual and improper degradation. Fire, because in the night of this last Christmas it broke out terribly, against the usual course of nature. Air, because unnatural thunder and storms disturbed it for a long time, with dense clouds in the bishopric of Norwich and fog in neighbouring parts far and wide. Nor for a long time had such terrible thunder been heard, nor such lightning been seen, even in summer. The sea, because it over-reached its normal limits and devastated neighbouring places. The earth, because in England, indeed even in Ciltria, which is chalky and compact, it shook violently.

> Matthew, here your toils are o'er
> Stop your pen and toil no more.
> Seek not what the future brings
> Another age has other things.[2]

1. Here and at the end I have left Matthew Paris's verses in the English version of Giles 1853: 411.
2. Matthew Paris afterwards changed his mind and continued his great work until his death nine years later.

Index

L367746

DATE DUE

DEC 8 1993			
NOV 24 199			
MAY 2 5 2007			
GAYLORD			PRINTED IN U.S.A.